W9-BNG-481

the
sono
BAKING COMPANY
C O O K B O O K

the sono
BAKING COMPANY
COOKBOOK

The Best Sweet and Savory Recipes for Every Occasion

JOHN BARRICELLI

HOST OF PBS'S "EVERYDAY BAKING FROM EVERYDAY FOOD"

CLARKSON POTTER/PUBLISHERS
NEW YORK

Published in the United States by
CLARKSON POTTER/PUBLISHERS,
an imprint of the
CROWN PUBLISHING GROUP,
a division of
RANDOM HOUSE, INC.,
New York.
www.crownpublishing.com
www.clarksonpotter.com

CLARKSON POTTER is a
trademark and POTTER with
colophon is a registered trademark
of RANDOM HOUSE, INC.

Library of Congress Cataloging-in-
Publication Data is available on request.

ISBN 978-0-307-44945-0

Printed in China

DESIGN BY JENNIFER K. BEAL DAVIS

10 9 8 7 6 5 4 3 2 1

First Edition

To all the children of the world who
go through life without parents . . .
life is tough enough. . . . I miss you,
Mom and Dad.

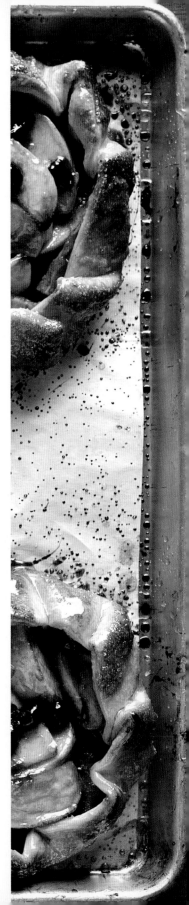

Contents

[*Acknowledgments*]

There are many people I wish to thank for their help with this book and with my career. I would, first and foremost, like to thank Martha Stewart, who introduced me to the world of media. You were kind and patient as my skills and talents evolved at Martha Stewart Omnimedia.

My agent, Coleen O'Shea, found me a publisher with class. Pamela Cannon brought my techniques and recipes to the page and my Brooklyn accent to life. A big thank-you to Stephanie Lyness for her endless efforts to test and retest the many recipes in this book. A big thank-you to the entire team at Clarkson Potter, especially Pam Krauss, Emily Takoudes, Peggy Paul, Doris Cooper, Lauren Shakely, and Jennifer K. Beal Davis. To Ben Fink for the beautiful photographs he created and to Frances Palmer Pottery and Juliska for enhancing these photographs with their wonderful ceramicware and glassware. To Rick Steffann, who was my first chef at the River Café. Rick, you taught me when, how, and why we do things the way we do in the kitchen. I am forever grateful to you. To all the people at Martha Stewart Television who help put *Everyday Food* and *Everyday Baking* together. To Jeffrey Hamelman, for teaching me how to make excellent bread and for his professional guidance. To all my instructors at the Culinary Institute of America, thank you for creating a foundation to build upon. To my cousin Richard, who listened to me when I said, "I want to be in the restaurant biz" at the tender age of sixteen. To my cousin Louis for his support and help with Cousin John's Café in Brooklyn, New York. To my seven brothers, thank you for the practice in discipline you gave me through regular physical interventions on behalf of our father, Joseph. Thank you to my aunts Connie, Mildred, and Ducky (what a name) for the upbringing you provided, in the absence of my mother, Mary Ann, whom I miss more than I realize or will ever admit. To my grandparents Julia and Anthony Barricelli, who taught me how to eat and to appreciate good food. I would also like to thank my many cousins, nieces, and nephews to whom I owe a great many apologies for working all the time, causing me to miss many family events and holidays. To all my friends, too many to mention here, I think of you frequently, even if I don't get to see you as often as I'd like. A huge thank-you to my wife, Veronica, for her patience during this project, even while giving birth to our son Peter! To my children Nikolai, Nola, Peter, and Sophia—I hope you grow to understand that my absence in your lives was due to my crazy bakery work hours. I promise to make it to more events. Most important, I want to personally thank each and every one of our bakery, farmer's market, and Website customers. And last but certainly not least, I want to express my thanks and gratitude to the staff at SoNo Baking Company and Café for all of their hard work, especially Ed, Val, Fran, Lesli, Bruno, Juan, and Issy. I have the best staff in the world.

Like many chefs and bakers, John Barricelli is passionate—passionate about his craft, passionate about his skills, passionate about his businesses, and passionate about his life. In fact, in the many years that I have known this friendly and talented man his passions have grown more pronounced and his skills more honed. He continues to learn and to perfect, and the success of his beautiful bakery/café and wholesale bakery business in South Norwalk, Connecticut, has been a very excellent confirmation that his customers are happy and his followers content.

I met John when he was the pastry chef at the Elms Inn in Ridgefield, Connecticut. We photographed a lovely Thanksgiving feast that John prepared for our magazine, and his food graced the cover. Everything he prepared—including many desserts—was tasty, pretty, and well-conceived. It was at that early date that I even had the pleasure of tasting some of John's ice creams, and it was then that he gave me his "secret" of always adding a pinch of salt to ice creams to enhance the flavors. When we were searching for a chef and kitchen manager for our early television productions, we lured John away from the restaurant world and he helped me create one of the best television "prep" kitchens. He managed, he cooked, and he baked.

Coming from a line of Italian bakers and cooks—both amateur and professional, John had a large repertoire of really tasty recipes that translated well to our style of family and entertaining cooking. Generous and forthright, and with a really fine set of cooking skills, John became an invaluable member of our staff and contributed not only to television but also to our magazines and ultimately to our weekly cooking series, *Everyday Food* and *Everyday Baking*. During these years John continued to think about the further development of his recipes and about his future dreams for a real bakery that would allow him to follow in his family's footsteps as an entrepreneurial chef and baker. He took courses when he could—master baking classes at King Arthur, where he learned more about the chemistry of baking—and practiced his newfound knowledge while developing new breads and rolls and pastries.

After eight years of working for media, his dream was realized in 2005 when he opened the SoNo Baking Company in a very large and beautiful space in one of South Norwalk's old brick factory buildings. We all knew it would thrive as a business, and it has. The breads and cakes and pastries are all mouthwateringly good, and the refrigerated cases filled with goodies as you enter the café draw in the crowds, who are always pleased with what they try. I especially love John's breads, and I have tried almost all of them. I know John uses only the best ingredients—he talks about that all the time—but even the best ingredients need the gentle handling of a great baker to turn out as they do in John's kitchens.

I have met many talented chefs and bakers over the year, and I can tell quickly if they actually have what it takes to withstand the rigors of running an establishment while at the same time producing really fine products. That John does have those talents is obvious, but that he also has the ability to teach via the printed page and demonstrate "how to" via television makes him even more appealing.

All of us will learn when we use this book and try the many recipes in it. This book will make us heroes as we serve a glistening plum tart or a crusty loaf of bread or a sublime lemon mousse or a hot, puffy popover. And we will improve our skills as we read and experiment because John's careful techniques do tend to make all of us better bakers and better cooks.

Thank you, John, for sharing with us so many of your ideas, your recipes, and your obvious love of really good food.

Introduction

I t's 3:00 a.m. Most of the houses are dark along the highway. Connecticut is sleeping, but for me, as for most bakers, the day has just begun.

The SoNo Baking Company and Café is tucked away on South Water Street, in South Norwalk, Connecticut, on the bank of the Norwalk River and Norwalk Harbor, forty miles northeast of New York City. Each morning, as I open the door, I hear the hum of the bakery—the whir of the giant mixers, the steam from the deck oven, the cream being whipped. The mixers are filled with vats of croissant dough that will be used for *pain au chocolat,* lunchtime ham and cheese croissants, and monkey bread. The air is warm as the deck oven heats up. The smaller, more delicate breads such as brioche will go in first. Next up will be the baguettes, ciabattas, multigrains, and rye breads. The imported Italian deck oven offers blasts of steam, which help provide the breads with crusty exteriors and moist, chewy interiors. I watch as my bakers skillfully wield the ten-foot-long wooden and metal peels (long-handled, flat-surfaced tools) to move the cakes and breads in and out of the oven. Next, I check in with the pastry chefs, who are making ganache, cookies, tarts, cupcakes, and roulades. I then head toward the office to check the daily orders. By 6:30 a.m. the entire staff has arrived: three sales clerks, two chefs, three pastry chefs, and three bakers. At 7:00 a.m. we open for business.

The bakery gets all types of customers—parents with young children, businesspeople grabbing a box of danishes for a morning meeting, locals wanting to read the paper over coffee and granola, high-school kids looking for a treat after school. We seat thirty people inside at tables and at counter stools that look into our open kitchen, and we also seat sixteen people outside. When it gets packed we sometimes seat customers in the kitchen, which can be the best seat in the house.

Our breads and seasonal desserts are inspired by traditional favorites from Italy, France, Germany, Austria, Switzerland, and of course America. They range in style from classics such as the SoNo Chocolate Ganache Cake (page 169) and Sour Cream Coffee Cake (page 54) to more modern confections like Raspberry Coconut Trifle (page 151) and Chocolate Bavarian Torte (page 173). Our baked goods have a

rustic but refined quality to them. All of our items are made fresh each day. We adhere to a high standard of excellence for all of our offerings, which ultimately results in the best-tasting breads and desserts.

The SoNo Baking Company and Café is the realization of a thirty-year dream for me. Little did I know when I first set foot in this former ceramics warehouse that I would be able to convert it into a 4,000-square-foot kitchen, retail, and dining space that would turn out hundreds of loaves of bread and dozens of varieties of desserts and savory bites each day.

I spend up to fourteen hours a day at the bakery, baking and selling our goods, and on the road dealing with accounts, deliveries, and setting up for farmers' markets. For me baking is both a business and a never-ending passion, a constant quest to learn and improve upon what I already know from my restaurant experience and education.

I've been cooking and baking for most of my life. When I was nine years old, I started helping my father prepare meals for my seven brothers in our small Valley Stream, Long Island, kitchen. Meatloaf and mac-n-cheese were my staples. I became the family's primary chef at age seventeen, after my father died. Throughout my childhood, weekends were spent visiting my grandparents Julia and Anthony, in Williamsburg, Brooklyn, where we would eat all kinds of homemade Italian specialties, including antipasto of Italian cheeses and cured meats, steak pizzaiola, spaghetti and meatballs, Great-Aunt Ida's baked chicken, sausage and peppers, and dozens of other delicacies. My grandmother would send us home with a cooler full of sandwiches for the car ride, just in case we were still hungry.

My grandmother, her two sisters, Ida and Anna, and her daughter, Connie, took their cooking seriously. They were responsible for teaching me how to make a good meatball, the perfect *pasta e fagioli* soup, and the best chicken cutlet. They made sure that before I learned how to bake, I learned how to cook.

While I enjoy cooking, I owe much of my interest in baking to my great-grandfather Giuseppe Barricelli, whom I never had the opportunity to meet, but whose recipes have been handed down to me by my grandfather. Giuseppe owned a turn-of-the-century *panetteria* in Williamsburg, Brooklyn, where he made Neapolitan focaccia-style pizzas and desserts. The building, with its brick oven, originally a coal-fired oven under the sidewalk steps, is still there. Many of the

ABOVE: A sampling of the handwritten cookbooks I've kept over the years, including an Italian one from my great-grandfather's *panetteria* and one from my time at the Helmsley Palace.

desserts I have made during my nearly thirty-year career have been inspired by his earlier creations.

This interest in food led me to the Culinary Institute of America (C.I.A.) after graduating from high school. At that time, in order to get accepted to the school you had to have restaurant experience, which I did not yet have. I quickly got an apprenticeship at Brooklyn's famous River Café, working for Executive Chef Rick Steffann, and from there attended the C.I.A. It was here that I first truly learned about professional cooking. At the time there was no specific pastry program, so I learned mostly about savory cooking along with the basics of pastry. I quickly realized that the skills and kitchen know-how taught in a traditional culinary program can help broaden and improve pastry technique.

At my C.I.A. graduation luncheon my professors recommended me for an opening in the pastry department at the Helmsley Palace Hotel in New York. I spent my time finishing cookies, making ice creams and sorbets, and kneading bread doughs. All of this detail work and basics helped provide me with an understanding of the science behind pastry and baking. After six months I was running the pastry department.

BELOW: My children, Sophia, Nola, and Peter, enjoying Saturday morning treats.

I then went on to study at the Wilton School of Cake Decorating in Chicago, and worked as a pastry chef in a number of different restaurants and hotels, including the award-winning Le Bernardin. In 1985 and 1986, I opened two of my own bakeries, Encore Patisserie in Manhattan and Cousin John's Café in Brooklyn. After ten years, I moved to Connecticut and started working as the executive pastry chef at the historic Elms Restaurant and Tavern in Ridgefield, where I worked alongside Executive Chef Brendan Walsh. In 1997, I met Martha Stewart. After trying my desserts and ice creams, Martha, who has referred to me as "a baker of great distinction whose cakes are as scrumptious as they are gorgeous," recruited me to run the staff commissary for Martha Stewart Living Productions at her television studio in Westport, Connecticut. While working there I developed and tested recipes for the *Martha Stewart Living* daily television show and magazine, collaborating with guest chefs and eventually becoming an on-air television personality, assisting Martha with baking techniques and recipes.

In 2003, I became a co-host of Martha Stewart Omnimedia magazine's *Everyday Food* television show, where I demonstrated everything from appetizers to entrees to dessert. I left to become the sole host of PBS's *Everyday Baking*.

While my professional experience has been varied, from a basement kitchen pastry chef to an in-front-of-the-camera television host, my philosophy has always remained the same. If you start with the best possible ingredients, techniques, and equipment, you can't help but produce the best possible results. This is the artisanal philosophy behind both the SoNo Baking Company and Café and this cookbook.

What also sets the recipes in this book apart are the tried-and-true techniques I have developed for making SoNo Brownies (page 86), the best you will ever taste, or Meringues (page 72), the lightest possible. Here I share the important techniques and tips *behind* the recipes that help to guarantee success. You will find all of these ideas, which I call "Technique Tips," peppered throughout the book. They are small tricks that I've picked up throughout my career that help ensure the best possible finished products, easy cleanup, and alternative uses for equipment. I also show you how to evaluate your own creations by learning what dough is supposed to *feel* like, what batter is supposed to *look* like, and what bread baking in the oven is supposed to *smell* like. I know the best approaches to getting perfect results and will teach you commonsense practices that will ultimately make for better baking.

The SoNo Baking Company Cookbook contains nearly 150 delicious recipes that have all been tested in home kitchens and written with the home cook and baker in mind. They are organized into eight chapters ranging from breakfast breads to cakes to pies to savory tarts. The book offers a wide range of recipes, from simple Strawberry Thumbprint Corn Muffins (page 28) for the novice baker to more involved and detailed recipes such as Hazelnut Chocolate Spirals (page 50) for those who are looking to take on a challenge. Most of the baked goods can be enjoyed the day they are made. There are also definitive Glossaries and Sources sections for ingredients and equipment, plus a Baker's Pantry section filled with thoughts on must-have items.

In the pages that follow I hope you will find not only the best classic recipes but also the techniques and the little bit of magic that will help transform any bread, dessert, or savory selection you are inspired to bake.

Baker's Pantry

Whether you are an occasional baker or a three-times-a-week baker, having an array of commonly used ingredients will make the process much easier, allowing you to spend more time in the kitchen and less time at the grocery store. Remember to buy small quantities of these ingredients, enough to last six months, because even dry goods can lose their potency or take on moisture, changing the end result of your baked goods. Also remember to store these items away from light and heat sources. To find out more about each of the ingredients listed below, look for details in the Ingredients Glossary (page 265). A typical Baker's Pantry should contain the following items:

- All-purpose flour (unbleached and unbromated)
- Baking powder and baking soda
- Chocolate (good-quality semisweet, bittersweet, unsweetened, and white chocolate)
- Nuts (almonds and hazelnuts are called for most frequently in this book; walnuts, pecans, and macadamia nuts are also used in baking)
- Old-fashioned rolled oats (never instant)
- Salt (I prefer coarse salt, as in kosher salt)
- Shredded coconut (both sweetened and unsweetened)
- Sugar: granulated, brown (both light and dark), confectioners', and sanding sugars (both regular and coarse)
- Vanilla extract (never imitation vanilla "flavored" extract) and vanilla beans
- Vegetable cooking spray

In addition to the items above, try to keep the following dairy items stocked in your refrigerator:

• Buttermilk

• Eggs (size large)

• Heavy cream

• Unsalted butter (can be frozen as well)

• Whole milk

A Note About Storage

At SoNo Baking Company, everything is made fresh and sold the same day. While I prefer for baked items to be produced and eaten this way, that's not always a reality, especially for home bakers, who may need to make them in advance or may be faced with leftovers.

When it comes to storage, there are a few general rules to keep in mind. First, be wary of the refrigerator. While the right place for storing custard-based desserts, refrigerators are full of moisture and trapped humidity, which can quickly break down a flaky pie crust, a crisp cookie, or a crusty loaf of bread. Be sure to keep only those baked goods that contain pastry cream, custard, or whipped cream in the refrigerator. Examples include Coconut Cream Tart (page 128), Crème Brûlée Tartlets (page 132), Lemon Mousse (page 155), Chocolate Pudding Icebox Cake (page 158), and Strawberry Shortcake (page 189). Store these items away from strong-smelling foods (garlic, onion, etc.) in the refrigerator, as they may take on unwanted odors. All other items—including muffins, scones, pastries, fruit pies and tarts (without pastry cream, such as Mile-high Apple Pie, page 102, and Maple Pecan Tart, page 127), cobblers and crisps, cakes (without pastry cream or whipped cream, such as SoNo Chocolate Ganache Cake, page 169, and Apple Spice Cake, page 187), and breads— can be stored at room temperature (away from direct sunlight and heat sources).

Also, when it comes to storage, I almost never use plastic wrap, or on the rare occasions that I do, I never let it touch the baked good, as it can impart an artificial plastic taste. I never use aluminum foil, as it doesn't fully seal, thus allowing air and moisture to seep into the item. Wax paper or parchment paper comes in handy to prevent air and moisture from entering a cake or pie that's been cut into and has a portion removed already. Cut out the required amount of wax or parchment paper and gently press it against the cut area of the cake to prevent the exposed areas from getting stale. I find that the best vessels to store baked goods in are sealed plastic containers (e.g., Tupperware) and domed cake stands/plates or cake savers.

Here are some general guidelines for storing baked goods:

Muffins, scones, and pastries Store in a sealed plastic container or covered cake stand for up to two days.

Breakfast cakes Store in a covered cake stand, covering the exposed cut surfaces with wax paper or parchment paper to prevent staleness, for up to four days.

Cookies Store stacked in a row, on their side (as opposed to stacked on top of each other) so less surface is exposed to the air, in a sealed plastic container for up to four days.

Bars Store cut bars or squares in layers, with wax paper or parchment paper in between layers, in a sealed plastic container for up to four days.

Pies and tarts Store refrigerated pies and tarts (see details above) in a covered cake stand for up to two days. Cover exposed cut surfaces with wax paper or parchment paper to prevent odors and moisture. Store room-temperature pies and tarts (see details above) in a covered cake stand for up to three days. Cover exposed cut surfaces with wax paper or parchment paper to prevent moisture.

Cobblers and crisps Cover loosely with plastic wrap, so that the wrap does not touch the top. Store at room temperature for up to three days.

Mousses and puddings Store ramekins in a sealed plastic container for up to three days.

Cakes Store refrigerated cakes (see details above) in a covered cake stand for up to three days. Cover exposed cut surfaces with wax paper or parchment paper to prevent odors and moisture. Be sure to let these cakes come to room temperature for 30 minutes before serving. Store nonrefrigerated cakes (see details above) in a covered cake stand for up to four days. Cover exposed cut surfaces with wax paper or parchment paper to prevent staleness.

Breads No need to cover breads with foil, wraps, or bags; instead, place the bread cut side down on the counter, preventing air from getting into it. Store for up to two days.

Lastly, I don't recommend freezing finished baked goods, as the quality, taste, and texture cannot compare to that of freshly baked items. I do, however, encourage you to freeze items in process, such as raw doughs (including Pâte Brisée, page 98, and Pâte Sucrée, page 99), cut (but not baked) scones, croissant dough (see page 231), and most cookie batters (scoop individual balls of cookie dough and let freeze on a baking sheet in a single layer; once frozen, place in a resealable plastic bag in the freezer for up to 1 month; no need to thaw before baking)—with the exception of egg-white-based cookies such as meringues and macaroons.

Muffins, Scones, Pastries, and Breakfast Cakes

Banana Streusel Muffins

Pumpkin Raisin Muffins

Strawberry Thumbprint Corn
Muffins

Blueberry Sour Cream Muffins

Zucchini, Carrot, and
Cranberry Muffins

Buttermilk Scones

Sour Cherry Chocolate Scones

Lemon Currant Scones

Cheddar Chive Scones

Tart Tropezienne

Apple Walnut Strudel

Cheese Danish

Danish Dough

Monkey Bread

Ginger Pear Danish

Raspberry Streusel Pinwheels

Hazelnut Chocolate Spirals

Sticky Buns

Sour Cream Coffee Cake

Blueberry Tea Cake

[*Chapter One*]

ll of the non-yeasted items in this chapter are considered quick breads. As the name suggests, they can be prepared and baked quickly, not requiring any time to rise, unlike yeasted breads, which need a few hours to properly rise and develop flavor.

If you are new to baking, know that the muffins in this chapter are absolutely failproof. They each require only a few steps and the most basic of ingredients. No matter what the season or occasion, you'll find plenty of muffins to choose from. The recipes can also easily be doubled or tripled to feed a crowd. After your first few successes following these recipes, try swapping different types of fruits and berries (for example, try cranberries instead of blueberries in Blueberry Sour Cream Muffins, page 30) or adding a cup of your favorite chopped nuts. These batters are versatile and can be made as muffins (regular, mini, or oversized, depending on your muffin pan) or anytime cakes, baked in a loaf pan or Bundt pan.

If you're looking for more of a baking challenge, try making some of the yeasted breakfast pastries in this chapter, such as Raspberry Streusel Pinwheels (page 48) or Cheese Danish (page 41). Their light, flaky insides and sweet, sticky outsides make a little extra time in the kitchen well worth the effort.

Finally, breakfast cakes such as the Sour Cream Coffee Cake (page 54) and Blueberry Tea Cake (page 57) are real standouts on a buffet table, and they can be served morning, noon, or night, for breakfast, tea, or dessert.

Most of these breakfast treats are best eaten warm or on the same day you bake them. The muffins and scones do, however, freeze well (freeze the muffins after baking and the scones after they are cut, but before they are baked) for up to one month. I suggest freezing in a double resealable freezer bag to help ensure freshness.

So, whether you're looking for something delicious to serve to visitors or the perfect dish to bring to a brunch at someone's home, this chapter is filled with a wide range of choices to help ensure big smiles on the faces of those lucky enough to sample them.

Banana Streusel Muffins

*These delicious, chewy muffins are the perfect tasty solution for overly
ripe bananas. The riper the banana (I like to use those that have turned
brown on the outside), the sweeter the muffin. Buttermilk is used to add
a tangy depth to the flavor and extra moistness to the muffin, although
sour cream and plain yogurt can provide this same taste and texture;
use whichever you have on hand. The streusel topping can be made in
advance and should be chilled until ready to use.*

MAKES 12 MUFFINS

Streusel Topping

- ½ cup all-purpose flour
- ½ cup light brown sugar
- ¼ teaspoon coarse salt
- ⅛ teaspoon ground cinnamon
- ¼ cup (½ stick) cold unsalted butter, cut into small cubes

Muffins

- 2 cups all-purpose flour
- 1 teaspoon baking powder
- 1 teaspoon baking soda
- ½ cup (1 stick) unsalted butter, at room temperature
- 1 cup granulated sugar
- 1½ teaspoons coarse salt
- 2 large eggs, at room temperature
- 2 teaspoons pure vanilla extract
- 3 very ripe bananas
- ½ cup buttermilk, sour cream, or whole-milk yogurt
- 1½ cups whole walnuts, chopped (optional)

1. To make the streusel topping: In a medium bowl, use a fork to stir together the flour, brown sugar, salt, and cinnamon. Add the cubes of butter, and using your fingertips, work it into the dry ingredients until pea-size crumbs form; set aside in the refrigerator.

2. Set the oven rack in the middle position. Preheat the oven to 375°F. Spray a standard 12-cup muffin pan with nonstick cooking spray, or generously butter with softened butter; set aside.

3. To make the muffins: In a medium bowl, whisk together the flour, baking powder, and baking soda; set aside.

4. In the bowl of a standing mixer fitted with the paddle attachment, beat the butter, sugar, and salt on medium-high speed until light and fluffy, 2 to 3 minutes, scraping down the sides of the bowl halfway through. Add the eggs one at a time, beating after each addition. Then add in and beat the vanilla and the bananas.

5. With the mixer on low speed, add the dry ingredients, beating until the flour is absorbed. Beat in the buttermilk. Fold in the walnuts, if using.

6. Use a 2-inch (¼ cup) ice cream scoop to divide the batter evenly among the prepared muffin cups. Sprinkle the streusel topping over the muffins, pressing some of the mixture into pea-size clumps with your fingertips, for added texture.

7. Bake, rotating the pan about two-thirds of the way through the baking time, until the tops of the muffins spring back when touched and a cake tester inserted in the center of a muffin comes out clean, 18 to 22 minutes.

8. Transfer the pan to a wire rack to cool for 10 minutes. Use a small offset spatula or a table knife to gently lift and turn the muffins on their sides in the muffin cups. Let cool completely in the pan.

Pumpkin Raisin Muffins

Cloves, nutmeg, ginger, and cinnamon make these muffins the perfect autumn breakfast treat, although they can certainly be enjoyed year-round. These moist quick breads are even better the next day, when the spices have had a chance to mellow. Try adding ½ cup chopped walnuts or ½ cup chocolate chips for even more flavor and texture. Extra unused pumpkin puree can be transferred to a resealable freezer bag and stored in the freezer for up to one month.

MAKES 12 MUFFINS

1½ cups all-purpose flour

1 teaspoon baking soda

1 teaspoon coarse salt

½ teaspoon ground cinnamon

½ teaspoon ground ginger, or ½ tablespoon grated fresh ginger

¼ teaspoon grated nutmeg

⅛ teaspoon ground cloves

1¼ cups sugar

½ cup canola oil

2 large eggs, at room temperature

½ (15-ounce) can pumpkin puree (about ⅞ cup)

¼ cup unsweetened applesauce

½ cup raisins

TECHNIQUE TIP: When a recipe calls for butter and eggs "at room temperature," it means full room temperature, not almost. Don't try to soften butter in the microwave; it changes the consistency. Instead, at least 4 hours ahead, set the butter and eggs on the kitchen counter. Note that dry ingredients should be at room temperature too.

1. Set the oven rack in the middle position. Preheat the oven to 375°F. Spray a standard 12-cup muffin pan with nonstick cooking spray, or generously butter with softened butter; set aside.

2. In a medium bowl, whisk together the flour, baking soda, salt, cinnamon, ginger, nutmeg, and cloves; set aside.

3. In a large bowl, whisk together the sugar, oil, eggs, pumpkin puree, and applesauce. Add the dry ingredients and fold with a rubber spatula until the flour has been absorbed. Fold in the raisins.

4. Use a 2-inch (¼ cup) ice cream scoop to divide the batter evenly among the prepared muffin cups.

5. Bake, rotating the pan about two-thirds of the way through the baking time, until the tops of the muffins spring back when touched and a cake tester inserted in the center of a muffin comes out clean, 20 to 25 minutes.

6. Transfer the pan to a wire rack to cool for 10 minutes. Use an offset spatula or table knife to gently lift and turn the muffins on their sides in the muffin cups. Let cool completely in the pan.

Strawberry Thumbprint Corn Muffins

The addition of preserves in the muffins makes these corn muffins a real standout from the typical corn muffin. At the bakery we use our own homemade strawberry preserves. We bake these muffins in a square shape, but they can also be made in a standard round muffin pan, as written and shown here.

1½ cups all-purpose flour
1 tablespoon baking powder
1 teaspoon baking soda
1 teaspoon coarse salt
¾ cup sugar
¾ cup coarse yellow cornmeal
3 large eggs, at room temperature
½ cup buttermilk
½ cup vegetable oil
½ cup sour cream
¾ cup strawberry preserves

- - - - - - - - - - - - - - - - - - -

TECHNIQUE TIP: For failproof standard-size muffins, use a ¼ cup (2-inch) ice cream scoop to transfer the batter from the bowl to the prepared muffin pan. This will prevent drips along the edge of the pan and will help with even distribution and portion consistency among the cups.

1. Set the oven rack in the middle position. Preheat the oven to 350°F. Spray a standard 12-cup muffin pan with nonstick cooking spray, or generously butter with softened butter; set aside.

2. In the bowl of a standing mixer fitted with the paddle attachment, mix the flour, baking powder, baking soda, salt, sugar, and cornmeal until combined.

3. With the mixer on low speed, add the eggs one at a time, beating after each addition. Add the buttermilk and oil. Mix until combined, scraping down the sides of the bowl halfway through. Add the sour cream and mix to combine.

4. Use a 2-inch (¼ cup) ice cream scoop to divide the batter evenly among the prepared muffin cups.

5. Bake, rotating the pan about two-thirds of the way through, until the muffins are golden brown and a cake tester inserted in the center of a muffin comes out clean, 15 to 18 minutes.

6. Transfer the muffin pan to a wire rack and allow to cool for 5 minutes. Using your thumb or the back of a teaspoon, press down in the middle of each muffin, creating an indentation deep enough to hold 1 tablespoon of preserves. Spoon or pipe (fill a pastry bag fitted with a large plain tip with the preserves and gently squeeze) 1 tablespoon of strawberry preserves into each indentation. Let cool for another 10 minutes. Use an offset spatula or table knife to gently lift the muffins and transfer to a wire rack. Serve warm.

Blueberry Sour Cream Muffins

These fruit-filled muffins offer both a crisp top and a tender, buttery inside infused with a hint of lemon. They were originally developed at Skylands, Martha Stewart's home in Seal Harbor, Maine. Martha brought home a scrap of a recipe and stuck it on the wall of the kitchen, asking me to use the fresh local berries on hand. I added vanilla extract, and lemon zest to build flavor. These muffins are topped with coarse sanding sugar (available at some supermarkets and most gourmet specialty stores or by mail order; see Sources), a shiny heatproof finishing sugar that keeps its coarse shape when baked, providing a crunchy texture to the muffin, cookie, or crust it's applied to. If fresh blueberries aren't available, frozen ones are an acceptable alternative (no need to thaw before baking). You can also use cranberries instead of blueberries.

MAKES 12 MUFFINS

2 cups plus 1 tablespoon all-purpose flour

1 teaspoon baking powder

½ teaspoon baking soda

1½ cups fresh or frozen (unthawed) blueberries

½ cup (1 stick) unsalted butter, at room temperature

1 cup granulated sugar

1 teaspoon coarse salt

2 large eggs, at room temperature

1½ teaspoons pure vanilla extract

Grated zest of 1 lemon

½ cup sour cream

Coarse sanding sugar, for finishing

TECHNIQUE TIP: The blueberries in this recipe and in the Blueberry Tea Cake recipe (page 57) are tossed with flour to keep them from sinking to the bottom. The thin flour coating allows the blueberries to "float" throughout the muffin or cake rather than all ending up along the bottom.

1. Set the oven rack in the middle position. Preheat the oven to 375°F. Spray a standard 12-cup muffin pan with nonstick cooking spray, or generously butter with softened butter; set aside.

2. In a medium bowl, whisk together the 2 cups of flour, the baking powder, and baking soda; set aside. Toss the blueberries in a sieve with the remaining 1 tablespoon flour; set aside.

3. In the bowl of a standing mixer fitted with the paddle attachment, beat the butter, sugar, and salt on medium-high speed until light and fluffy, 3 to 4 minutes, scraping down the sides of the bowl halfway through. Add the eggs one at a time, beating after each addition. Beat in the vanilla and lemon zest.

4. With the mixer on low speed, add the dry ingredients, beating just until the flour is absorbed. Add the sour cream, beating until combined. Gently fold in the blueberries with a rubber spatula.

5. Use a 2-inch (¼ cup) ice cream scoop to divide the batter evenly among the prepared muffin cups. Sprinkle with the sanding sugar.

6. Bake, rotating the pan about two-thirds of the way through the baking time, until the tops of the muffins spring back when touched and a cake tester inserted in the center of a muffin comes out clean, 20 to 25 minutes.

7. Transfer the pan to a wire rack to cool for 10 minutes. Use an offset spatula or table knife to gently lift and turn the muffins on their sides in the muffin cups. Let cool completely in the pan.

Zucchini, Carrot, and Cranberry Muffins

The tartness of the cranberries in these muffins complements the sweetness of the carrots. The addition of zucchini provides a moist texture. While these muffins are packed full of nutritious goodness, their lovely orange-gold color and hearty taste will make them irresistible to adults and kids alike. Try topping them with Cream Cheese Frosting (page 196) for an indulgent treat.

MAKES 12 MUFFINS

2 cups all-purpose flour
¾ teaspoon baking powder
¾ teaspoon coarse salt
¾ teaspoon ground cinnamon
½ teaspoon baking soda
1 cup sugar
1 cup canola oil
2 large eggs, at room temperature
¾ cup finely grated carrot (about 2 medium)
¾ cup finely grated zucchini (about 1 medium)
1½ teaspoons pure vanilla extract
1 cup whole fresh or frozen (unthawed) cranberries

TECHNIQUE TIP: Any of the muffins in this chapter can be made into a single breakfast cake by baking the batter in a loaf pan or Bundt pan. Just prepare the pan the same way you would a muffin pan, set it on a baking sheet, and bake until a tester comes out clean when inserted into the center of the cake (the baking time will vary depending on the batter and the shape of the pan). Remove from the oven and let the cake cool for a few minutes before removing it from the pan and cooling it completely on a wire rack.

1. Set the oven rack in the middle position. Preheat the oven to 375°F. Spray a standard 12-cup muffin pan with nonstick cooking spray, or generously butter with softened butter; set aside.

2. In a medium bowl, whisk together the flour, baking powder, salt, cinnamon, and baking soda; set aside.

3. In a large bowl, whisk together the sugar, oil, eggs, grated carrot and zucchini, and vanilla. Add the dry ingredients and fold with a rubber spatula until the flour has been absorbed. Fold in the cranberries.

4. Use a 2-inch (¼ cup) ice cream scoop to divide the batter evenly among the prepared muffin cups.

5. Bake, rotating the pan about two-thirds of the way through the baking time, until the muffins are golden brown, the tops spring back when touched, and a cake tester inserted in the center of a muffin comes out clean, 20 to 25 minutes.

6. Transfer the pan to a wire rack to cool for 10 minutes. Use an offset spatula or table knife to gently lift and turn the muffins on their sides in the muffin cups. Let cool in the pan. Serve warm or at room temperature.

Buttermilk Scones

My wife, Veronica, makes these light, flaky scones all the time at home. They are as simple to make as they are addictive to eat. Not too sweet, these are perfect to serve with breakfast or tea, and they make an ideal sandwich pairing for smoked ham and Swiss cheese. They are best served right out of the oven, although Veronica also prepares them and freezes them before baking, so she can have fresh-baked scones to serve or take on the go anytime.

MAKES 12 SCONES

2 cups all-purpose flour, plus more for dusting

2 tablespoons sugar

1 tablespoon baking powder

1 teaspoon coarse salt

½ teaspoon baking soda

6 tablespoons (¾ stick) cold unsalted butter, cut into small pieces

¾ cup buttermilk

TECHNIQUE TIP: Scones can be cut into a variety of shapes, including wedges (as with this recipe), rounds by using a biscuit cutter (Lemon Currant Scones, page 35), and triangles (Cheddar Chive Scones, page 36). Once cut, unbaked scones may be placed on a baking sheet, covered with plastic wrap, and frozen. Once frozen, stack the scones in resealable freezer bags and freeze for up to 1 month. Place frozen scones on a parchment-lined baking sheet, brush with heavy cream, sprinkle with sanding sugar, and bake while still frozen. Once baked, they are best eaten the same day.

1. Line a baking sheet with parchment paper; set aside.

2. In a large bowl, whisk together the flour, sugar, baking powder, salt, and baking soda.

3. Work the butter into the dry ingredients with your fingers until the mixture resembles coarse crumbs. Add ½ cup of the buttermilk and fold with a rubber scraper or your hands until the buttermilk has been absorbed. Then continue adding buttermilk, 1 tablespoon at a time, just until the dough comes together and there are no dry patches.

4. Turn out the dough onto a lightly floured work surface. Divide the dough into two balls and pat each ball into a 7-inch disk, ¾ to 1 inch thick. Using a bench scraper or a sharp knife, cut each disk into six equal wedges. Place the wedges on the prepared baking sheet and chill for 1 hour.

5. Set the oven rack in the middle position. Preheat the oven to 400°F.

6. Bake, rotating the baking sheet about two-thirds of the way through, until the scones are puffed and golden brown and the bottoms are lightly browned, 16 to 20 minutes.

7. Cool on the baking sheet on a wire rack for 10 minutes. Using a metal spatula, transfer to a wire rack to cool.

Sour Cherry Chocolate Scones

My young daughter Sophia is in elementary school, and it's hard to get her out the door in the morning without a bite of these favorite special-request quick breads. While most scones tend to be dense, these are light in texture but strong in flavor, with chunks of semisweet chocolate and sour cherries throughout. You can find dried sour cherries at most gourmet specialty stores and some supermarkets in the dried fruit or baking sections.

MAKES 12 TO 15 SCONES

5 cups all-purpose flour, plus more for cutting

2 tablespoons plus 2 teaspoons baking powder

¾ cup granulated sugar

½ teaspoon coarse salt
Grated zest of ½ orange

¾ cup dried sour cherries

¾ cup chopped (½-inch) semisweet chocolate

2¾ cups heavy cream, chilled, plus ¼ cup for brushing

2 to 3 tablespoons coarse sanding sugar, for finishing

1. Line a baking sheet with parchment paper or a nonstick silicone baking mat; set aside.

2. In a large bowl, whisk together the flour, baking powder, granulated sugar, salt, and zest. Stir in the sour cherries and chocolate chunks.

3. Add 2¼ cups of the cream and fold with a rubber scraper or your hands until the cream has been completely absorbed. Then continue adding cream by the tablespoon just until the dough comes together and there are no dry patches.

4. Turn the dough out onto a lightly floured work surface. With lightly floured hands, gently press and pat out the dough into a 1-inch-thick round. Using a 2¾-inch round cookie cutter, cut out as many rounds as possible, dipping the cutter into flour after each cut. Reroll the scraps and continue to cut out the dough. Place the cut scones about 2 inches apart on the prepared baking sheet. Refrigerate the scones until firm, about 1 hour.

5. Set the oven rack in the middle position. Preheat the oven to 375°F.

6. Lightly brush the top of scones with the remaining ¼ cup cream and sprinkle generously with the sanding sugar. Bake, rotating the baking sheet halfway through, until the tops are golden, 25 to 30 minutes. Use a metal spatula to transfer to a wire rack to cool.

Lemon Currant Scones

These traditional scones were inspired by time I spent in England. Lemon and currants are a classic flavor combination. Here, the lemon adds brightness while the currants offer a sweet, chewy fruit texture to these slightly sweet cream-based scones. Bake these scones one sheet at a time for even heating and best results.

MAKES ABOUT 18 SCONES

3 **cups all-purpose flour, plus more for dusting**

½ **cup granulated sugar**

1½ **tablespoons baking powder**

1½ **teaspoons coarse salt**

Grated zest of 2 lemons

1½ **cups dried currants**

1⅔ **cups heavy cream, chilled, plus ¼ cup for brushing**

2 **to 3 tablespoons sanding sugar, for finishing**

TECHNIQUE TIP: When sprinkling a dense item like a scone with sugar, try holding the scone upside down in your hand and dipping it in a bowl of cream and then a bowl of sanding sugar to evenly cover the most surface area. This is an especially handy tip if you're baking a large quantity of scones.

1. Line two baking sheets with parchment paper or nonstick silicone baking mats; set aside.

2. In a large bowl, whisk together the flour, sugar, baking powder, salt, and lemon zest. Stir in the currants.

3. Add 1½ cups of the cream and fold with a rubber scraper or your hands until the cream has been completely absorbed. Then continue adding cream by the tablespoon just until the dough comes together and there are no dry patches.

4. Turn out the dough onto a lightly floured work surface. With lightly floured hands, pat the dough to a 6½ by 11-inch rectangle, about 1 inch thick. Using a 2-inch round cookie or biscuit cutter, cut out the scones and place them on the prepared baking sheets. Combine the dough scraps, pat them together, and cut more scones, placing them on the baking sheets. Refrigerate the scones until firm, about 1 hour.

5. Set the oven rack in the middle position. Preheat the oven to 400°F.

6. Brush the tops of the scones with the remaining ¼ cup cream, and sprinkle with the sanding sugar. Bake one sheet at a time, rotating the sheet about two-thirds of the way through the baking time. Bake for 16 to 20 minutes, until the scones spring back when touched with a finger and the tops and bottoms are nicely browned. Repeat with the remaining scones.

7. Cool on the baking sheets on a wire rack for 10 minutes. Using a metal spatula, transfer to a wire rack to cool.

Cheddar Chive Scones

Perfect for any occasion, these basic savory scones can be served for breakfast, lunch, brunch, or tea. I like to use yellow Cheddar cheese for the color contrast, but you can use white Cheddar as well as any other favorite cheese, including Gruyère or fontina. For more variation, try substituting thyme or another favorite fresh herb for the chives.

MAKES 8 SCONES

2 **cups all-purpose flour**

1 **tablespoon baking powder**

1 **teaspoon coarse salt**

¼ **cup finely chopped fresh chives**

1 **cup (2 ounces) finely grated extra-sharp Cheddar cheese, plus about 1 tablespoon for sprinkling**

1¼ **cups heavy cream, chilled, plus ¼ cup for brushing**

TECHNIQUE TIP: In order to accurately measure ingredients, measure dry ingredients such as flour and sugar in a metal measuring cup (filled to the top and leveled off with the back of a knife, sweeping across the top) and wet ingredients such as milk in a glass measuring cup.

1. Line a baking sheet with parchment paper or a nonstick silicone baking mat; set aside.

2. In a large bowl, whisk together the flour, baking powder, salt, and chives. Stir in the cheese with a fork.

3. Add 1 cup of the cream and fold with a rubber scraper or your hands just until the cream has been completely absorbed. Then continue adding cream, 1 tablespoon at a time, just until the dough comes together and there are no dry patches.

4. Turn the dough out onto a heavily floured work surface. With lightly floured hands, pat the dough to a 3 by 10-inch rectangle, ¾ to 1 inch thick. Using a bench scraper or a sharp knife, cut the rectangle into eight equal triangles. Place on the prepared baking sheet and refrigerate until firm, about 1 hour.

5. Set the oven rack in the middle position. Preheat the oven to 400°F.

6. Brush the scones with the remaining ¼ cup cream, and sprinkle each with a pinch of grated cheese. Bake, rotating the baking sheet about two-thirds of the way through, until the scones are golden brown and puffed and the bottoms are lightly browned when you lift the scones with a metal spatula, 16 to 20 minutes. Using a metal spatula, transfer to a wire rack to cool.

Tart Tropezienne

This brioche-based buttery egg pastry is a combination bread, tart, and cream-filled dessert all wrapped in one. A round of brioche dough is sprinkled with pearl sugar (available at gourmet specialty stores), cut in half, and filled with vanilla pastry cream and sliced strawberries. I first made this pastry at my bakery Encore, in Manhattan, in the mid-1980s. The recipe has stuck with me ever since. In addition to a breakfast pastry, this makes a great dessert, brunch, or tea dish. The dough can also be cut into 4-inch rounds for individual presentations.

MAKES ONE 9½-INCH
PASTRY, SERVES 8

Brioche

- 3 tablespoons warm (105° to 110°F) milk (see Technique Tip, page 39)
- 1½ teaspoons active dry yeast
- 1⅓ cups all-purpose flour, plus more for kneading
- ⅓ cup bread flour
- 1½ tablespoons granulated sugar
- 1 teaspoon coarse salt
- 2 large eggs
- 1 large egg yolk
- 10 tablespoons (1 stick plus 2 tablespoons) cold unsalted butter, cut into tablespoons
- 1 large egg, beaten, for egg wash
- 1½ tablespoons pearl sugar

Vanilla Pastry Cream

- 2 large egg yolks
- ¼ cup granulated sugar
- 2 tablespoons cornstarch
- 1 cup milk
- ⅛ teaspoon coarse salt
- ½ vanilla bean, split in half lengthwise, or 1 teaspoon pure vanilla extract
- 1½ tablespoons cold unsalted butter, cut into ½-inch pieces

- 1 pint strawberries (you'll need about 11 large strawberries)

1. To make the brioche: In a medium bowl, pour the milk over the yeast and let proof (the act of adding a liquid to yeast to see if it's "alive" and active), 5 minutes.

2. In the bowl of a standing mixer fitted with the paddle attachment, mix the all-purpose and bread flours with the sugar and salt. When the yeast has proofed, add the whole eggs and yolk to the yeast and whisk; add to the mixer bowl. Beat on low speed, scraping down the sides of the bowl at least once, until the flour has been absorbed and the dough comes together, 1 to 2 minutes. With the mixer on low, add the butter, 1 tablespoon at a time, and beat until the butter has been absorbed. The dough will be very sticky.

3. To knead by machine, replace the paddle with the dough hook and beat on medium-low to medium speed until the dough is smooth, shiny, and elastic and completely cleans the sides of the bowl, 10 to 15 minutes. Add 1 to 2 tablespoons all-purpose flour as needed. (Or, to knead by hand, turn the dough out onto a lightly floured work surface. Knead by successively scooping the dough up from underneath with the thumb and the first two fingers of each hand, then slapping it down on the board as you pull your hands away. At first, the dough will stick to both board and hands, but as the gluten develops and the flour absorbs moisture, the dough will pull together into a ball and become less tacky. Knead a good 15 minutes, adding flour as needed, or until the dough no longer sticks to the work surface.)

4. Turn the dough into a buttered bowl, cover with oiled plastic wrap, and refrigerate overnight.

5. On a lightly floured work surface, roll the dough to a round about 10 inches in diameter and ⅓ inch thick. Using a pastry wheel, cut

RECIPE CONTINUES . . .

to a 9½-inch round. Place on a parchment-lined baking sheet, cover very loosely with plastic, and let rise in a warm place (at least 70°F), until very soft and doubled in bulk, about 3 hours.

6. Set the oven rack in the middle position. Preheat the oven to 375°F. Brush the risen dough round with the egg wash and sprinkle with the pearl sugar. Bake, rotating the baking sheet about two-thirds of the way through, until golden brown, 13 to 16 minutes. Transfer to a wire rack and let cool completely.

7. To make the pastry cream: In a medium bowl, whisk together the egg yolks, about half the sugar, all the cornstarch, and ¼ cup of the milk.

8. In a saucepan, combine the remaining sugar, the remaining ¾ cup milk, and the salt. If using a vanilla bean, scrape the tiny black seeds into the saucepan and add the pod. Bring to a simmer. Whisking constantly, gradually pour the hot milk into the egg mixture to temper it. Set a strainer over the saucepan. Strain the custard mixture back into the saucepan and bring to a boil over medium heat, whisking constantly. Boil for 10 seconds, while whisking (make sure the custard boils for 10 seconds in the center of the pan, not just around the sides). The mixture should thicken to a puddinglike consistency.

9. Transfer the pastry cream to the bowl of a standing mixer fitted with the paddle attachment and beat on medium speed for 2 to 3 minutes, to cool slightly. Beat in the vanilla extract, if using. With the mixer running, beat in the butter a little at a time. Beat until cooled, 5 to 10 more minutes. Press a piece of plastic wrap directly on the surface and refrigerate until chilled, about 1 hour.

10. When the bread round has cooled completely, use a long serrated knife to split it in half horizontally. Remove the top half. Spread the bottom half with half of the pastry cream. Slice enough strawberries, lengthwise and ⅛ to ¼ inch thick, to make a single layer of strawberry slices, and arrange cut side down in a single layer on top of the cream. Spread the remaining cream on top of the strawberries. Set the top of the brioche on top of the strawberries and cream. Cut into eight to ten wedges.

TECHNIQUE TIP: When using yeast, it is critical that the liquid you add to it, either water or milk, be between 105° and 110°F. Hotter than this and the yeast will die, cooler and it will be much slower to activate. To properly register the temperature, heat the liquid and pour it into a measuring cup. Immediately place an instant-read thermometer in the liquid. If it reads more than 110°F, let the liquid cool, testing often so as not to let it cool too much. If less than 105°F, reheat it slightly and continue to test until it falls between 105° and 110°F.

Apple Walnut Strudel

Making authentic strudel dough can be a hugely labor-intensive process. This much simpler, but no less delicious, version that calls for already-prepared filo dough was taught to me by Rudy Bader, fellow pastry chef at Encore Patisserie, a Manhattan bakery we owned together in the 1980s. For best results, be sure to use a baking apple that remains firm when cooked, such as a Rome or Cortland. You can also use pears instead of apples for a slightly different flavor.

MAKES ONE 14-INCH
STRUDEL, SERVES 6 TO 8

Filling

- ¼ cup (½ stick) unsalted butter
- ¼ cup granulated sugar
- ½ teaspoon ground cinnamon
- ¼ teaspoon ground nutmeg
  Pinch of ground cloves
  Pinch of ground allspice
  Pinch of coarse salt
- 2 pounds apples, peeled, cored, and cut into ½-inch dice
  Juice of ½ lemon
- ⅓ cup raisins

Pastry

- 1 tablespoon granulated sugar
- ⅛ teaspoon ground cinnamon
- 3 tablespoons unsalted butter, melted
- ½ cup finely chopped walnuts (see Technique Tip)
- 6 (9 by 14-inch) sheets frozen filo dough, thawed (see Technique Tip)
- 2 tablespoons sanding sugar, for finishing

TECHNIQUE TIP: Frozen filo dough should always be thawed in the refrigerator for 2 to 3 hours to allow for even thawing. Chop the nuts fairly fine (but not into a powder), so that they don't make holes in the filo.

1. To make the filling: In a large skillet, melt the butter over medium heat. Add the sugar, cinnamon, nutmeg, cloves, allspice, and salt. Cook, stirring to blend. Add the apples and lemon juice and cook, stirring often, until the apples are tender but not cooked into a puree and the juices are reduced and evaporated, 15 to 18 minutes. The apples should be moist, but there should be no excess liquid. Stir in the raisins and set aside to cool.

2. Set the oven rack in the middle position. Preheat the oven to 375°F. Line a baking sheet with parchment paper or a nonstick silicone baking mat.

3. To make the pastry: In a small bowl, mix the sugar with the cinnamon. Set up your work surface with the cinnamon sugar, the melted butter in another bowl, and the walnuts in a third bowl. Now layer two sheets of filo dough, with the long side facing you, on the work surface. Brush all over with melted butter and sprinkle with the cinnamon sugar and about one-third of the walnuts. Lay two more filo sheets on top, brush with butter, and sprinkle with another one-third of the walnuts. Top with the remaining two sheets filo, brush with butter, and sprinkle with the rest of the walnuts.

4. Spread the apple filling in a 3-inch-wide layer at the bottom of the dough, leaving about ½ inch pastry at each end and 1 inch at the bottom. Roll the strudel from the bottom into a flat log. Tuck in the edges. Set the strudel, seam side down, on the prepared baking sheet and pierce the top several times with a knife to allow the steam to escape. Brush with melted butter and sprinkle with the sanding sugar.

5. Bake until the filo is golden brown and crisp, 25 to 30 minutes. Let cool on the baking sheet on a wire rack for 10 minutes. Cut into six to eight slices, on the diagonal.

Cheese Danish

This traditional breakfast pastry features a sweetened cream cheese filling folded into flaky danish dough. At the bakery we finish all of our danish with an apricot glaze when they come out of the oven, to give them a little shine and to help seal in moisture. The glaze also adds another dimension of flavor.

MAKES 12 PASTRIES

Cheese Filling

- **8 ounces cream cheese, at room temperature**
- **⅓ cup sugar**
- **¼ teaspoon pure vanilla extract**
- **⅛ teaspoon coarse salt**
- **2 tablespoons all-purpose flour**

Pastry

- **½ recipe Danish Dough (see page 42)**
- **1 egg, beaten, for egg wash**
  Sliced almonds
- **1 cup apricot jam**

1. To make the filling: In the bowl of a standing mixer fitted with the paddle attachment, beat the cream cheese with the sugar, vanilla, and salt on medium-high speed until smooth. Reduce the speed to low and beat in the flour.

2. Line two baking sheets with parchment paper or nonstick silicone baking mats; set aside.

3. To make the pastry: On a lightly floured work surface, roll out the dough to a 17 by 13-inch rectangle. (If the dough is hard to roll, transfer it to one of the baking sheets and refrigerate for 15 to 20 minutes.) Using a ruler and a pizza wheel or pastry cutter, trim the edges of the dough to form a 16 by 12-inch rectangle. Then cut the dough into twelve 4-inch squares.

4. Using a tablespoon or a pastry bag fitted with a ½-inch round pastry tip, pipe 1½ to 2 tablespoons cheese filling onto the center of each square. Fold the upper right corner over the filling, about two-thirds of the way toward the opposite corner; press down firmly to seal. Bring the lower left corner up and over the first fold, pressing down to adhere. Repeat with the remaining corners to make a square. Place the pastries on the prepared baking sheets, folded sides up. Cover with plastic wrap and let rest in a warm place until the dough has increased by 1½ times and is very soft when you touch it, about 30 minutes.

5. Set the oven rack in the middle position. Preheat the oven to 375°F.

6. Brush the pastries with the egg wash and sprinkle with sliced almonds. Bake one sheet at a time, rotating the baking sheet about two-thirds of the way through baking, until evenly browned, about 20 minutes. Transfer to a wire rack.

7. While the pastries are still warm, in a small saucepan, warm the apricot jam over low heat until liquid. Strain through a fine strainer. Brush the top and sides of the pastries with the strained jam. Let cool completely and serve.

Danish Dough

In addition to the Cheese Danish on page 41, this traditional cardamom-flavored puff-pastry-like dough is used to make Sticky Buns (page 53), Raspberry Streusel Pinwheels (page 48), Hazelnut Chocolate Spirals (page 50), and Ginger Pear Danish (page 46). Be aware that this dough is a 2-day process. It is important to let the dough rest to relax the gluten before folding in the butter, or the pastry will be too tough to roll. Ideally, the butter should be the same consistency and temperature as the dough, so that the two will roll together into neat layers. This dough will keep frozen in double resealable bags for up to 1 month.

MAKES ENOUGH DOUGH
FOR 2 DOZEN DANISH

½ **cup water**

½ **cup milk**

5 **teaspoons (2 envelopes) active dry yeast**

4½ **cups all-purpose flour, plus extra for rolling and pounding the butter**

½ **cup sugar**

1 **tablespoon coarse salt**

½ **teaspoon ground cardamom**

6 **tablespoons (¾ stick) cold unsalted butter, cubed, plus 1½ cups (3 sticks) cold unsalted butter**

2 **large eggs**

2 **large egg yolks**

1. In a small saucepan, heat the water and milk to 110°F (use an instant-read thermometer to check the temperature). Pour over the yeast in a medium bowl and let proof for about 5 minutes.

2. In the bowl of a standing mixer fitted with the paddle attachment, sift the flour. Add the sugar, salt, cardamom, and the 6 tablespoons butter and beat on low speed until the butter breaks down and dissolves completely in the dry ingredients, 3 to 4 minutes.

3. Add the whole eggs and the yolks to the bowl with the yeast. Add the wet ingredients to the mixer bowl, and beat on the lowest speed just until the batter is completely blended and tacky, about 1½ minutes. Turn out onto a lightly floured work surface and knead very lightly for about 30 seconds, adding a little flour as needed, until the dough comes together and can be formed into a ball. Shape into a ball, wrap in plastic, and refrigerate overnight.

4. The next day, on a lightly floured work surface, lightly flour the remaining 3 sticks butter and pound with a rolling pin to flatten into a mass. Fold the mass of butter in half and continue pounding and rolling, sprinkling often with flour as needed to keep the butter from sticking to the pin and work surface, until the butter is malleable enough (but not melted) that you can roll it like pastry. Shape into a 9 by 9-inch square; set aside.

5. Roll the dough into an 18 by 10-inch rectangle, with one of the short sides facing you. Brush off excess flour with a pastry brush. Place the butter square on the bottom half of the dough. Fold over the unbuttered half so that it covers the butter. Press the edges together and pinch to seal.

RECIPE CONTINUES . . .

Apricot Danish
$2.50

6. Roll the dough out again into an 18 by 10-inch rectangle; the butter should roll easily with the dough. Brush off excess flour. Fold the bottom third up so that it covers half of the remaining dough, as if you were folding a letter. Brush off the flour. Fold the top third down to cover. (This is called a "turn.") Wrap in plastic and refrigerate for 1 hour. Mark the dough by pressing a finger into it, to designate one turn.

7. Remove the dough from the refrigerator. Place on the work surface with the seam on your left, and roll and fold as above to give it its second turn. Mark with two fingers to designate the second turn. Refrigerate for 1 hour.

8. Repeat to give the dough a third turn. Wrap the dough in plastic and refrigerate for at least 4 hours, or overnight.

Monkey Bread

When the SoNo Baking Company first opened, our croissant baker was Jana Adams. Trained at the Culinary Institute of America, Jana knew to let nothing in a commercial kitchen go to waste. She would use the scraps of the croissants she rolled to make this sweet, puffy breakfast pastry. One recipe of Croissant Dough will yield just enough scraps to make this recipe. You can also use scraps from Danish Dough (page 42) or Brioche Dough (page 37) as an alternative.

MAKES 8 PASTRIES

¾ **cup granulated sugar**
1 **teaspoon ground cinnamon**
¾ **teaspoon coarse salt**
1 **large egg, lightly beaten**
¼ **recipe Croissant Dough (see page 231), or about 1 pound dough scraps**
1 **cup confectioners' sugar**
   About 2 tablespoons milk

1. Spray 8 muffin cups in a nonstick muffin pan with nonstick cooking spray, or generously butter with softened butter; set aside.

2. In a medium bowl combine the sugar, cinnamon, salt, and lightly beaten egg; set aside.

3. Roll out the dough to form a rectangle ⅛ to ¼ inch thick (it doesn't matter if the edges aren't perfectly straight). Using a pizza cutter or pastry wheel, cut the dough into 1-inch square pieces. Toss the pieces of dough in the cinnamon-sugar mixture, using a rubber spatula to completely coat each piece. Fill each muffin cup with the dough up to the rim. Discard any excess cinnamon-sugar mixture left in the bowl. Spray a piece of plastic wrap large enough to cover the muffin pan with nonstick cooking spray. Cover the muffin pan with the oiled plastic wrap and let it sit in a warm place until the breads are soft and puffed up over the top of the pan, 30 to 40 minutes.

4. Set the oven rack in the middle position. Preheat the oven to 500°F. Line a baking sheet with parchment paper or a nonstick silicone baking mat.

5. Place the muffin pan on the prepared baking sheet and place in the oven. Immediately reduce the oven heat to 375°F. Bake, rotating the sheet about two-thirds of the way through the baking time, until the breads are well browned and bubbling, 20 to 30 minutes. Let rest in the muffin pan on a wire rack for 5 minutes—they need to firm up just enough that they don't pull apart when you unmold them, but not so long that the sugar hardens and they stick. Turn the pastries out of the pans and let stand upside down on the rack to cool.

6. Meanwhile, in a small bowl, whisk the confectioners' sugar with the milk, adding the milk gradually until the glaze is thick and white, but pourable (you'll use 1 tablespoon plus a little over 2 teaspoons milk). Stir until completely smooth. Drizzle the glaze over the cooled monkey bread and let set for 15 minutes before serving.

Ginger Pear Danish

*These seasonal fall favorites are soft, puffy, two-crusted "tartlets" made
with Danish Dough and filled with ginger pastry cream and pear. We
use canned pears because they are the ideal consistency, but feel free to
peel, core, halve, and poach your own in a poaching liquid of 1 part
sugar to 1 part water; simmer for 6 to 10 minutes (depending on
ripeness) until just soft. You'll need 4-inch round, straight-sided (¾-inch
sides) tartlet molds and a pastry wheel to make this pastry (you can
also use 4-inch pastry rings or large cookie cutters). Gather up any
scraps, chill, and use for Monkey Bread (page 45).*

MAKES 8 PASTRIES

Ginger Pastry Cream

- **2 large egg yolks**
- **¼ cup granulated sugar**
- **2 tablespoons cornstarch**
- **1 cup milk**
- **⅛ teaspoon coarse salt**
- **½ vanilla bean, split in half lengthwise, or 1 teaspoon pure vanilla extract**
- **1½ tablespoons cold unsalted butter, cut into ½-inch pieces**
- **2 teaspoons finely grated fresh ginger**

Pastry

- **4 canned pear halves, drained and cut in half lengthwise (8 quarters)**
- **½ recipe Danish Dough (page 42)**
- **1 large egg, beaten, for egg wash**
- **2 to 3 tablespoons sanding sugar, for finishing**

1. To make the pastry cream: In a medium, heatproof bowl, whisk together the egg yolks, half the sugar, all the cornstarch, and ¼ cup of the milk.

2. In a saucepan, combine the remaining sugar, the remaining ¾ cup milk, and the salt. If using a vanilla bean, scrape the tiny black seeds into the saucepan and add the pod. Bring to a simmer. Whisking constantly, gradually pour the hot milk into the egg mixture to temper it. Set a strainer over the saucepan. Strain the custard mixture back into the saucepan and bring to a boil over medium heat, whisking constantly. Boil for 10 seconds while whisking (make sure the custard boils for 10 seconds in the *center* of the pan—not just around the sides). The mixture should thicken to a pudding-like consistency.

3. Transfer the pastry cream to the bowl of a standing mixer fitted with the paddle attachment and beat on medium speed for 2 to 3 minutes, to cool slightly. Beat in the vanilla extract, if using. With the mixer running, beat in the butter, a little at a time. Beat until cooled, 5 to 10 more minutes. Beat in the ginger. Press a piece of plastic wrap directly on the surface, and refrigerate until chilled, about 1 hour.

4. Line two baking sheets with parchment paper or nonstick silicone baking mats; set aside. Spray eight 4-inch nonstick round, straight-sided tart molds with nonstick cooking spray, or coat with softened butter.

5. To make the pastry: Thinly slice each pear quarter lengthwise, leaving the top ½-inch of the pear quarter intact, and press gently to fan; set aside.

6. On a lightly floured surface, roll out the dough to a rectangle about 17 by 25 inches. The dough should be about ⅛ inch thick, or as thin as you can comfortably roll it. (If the dough fights you and contracts so much that it's hard to work with it, sprinkle it with flour, fold in half, transfer to a sheet pan, refrigerate for 1 hour, then try again.) Brush off excess flour with a pastry brush. Cut eight 5-inch rounds (you can get 3 across); these will form the bottoms of the pastries. With the remaining dough, cut eight 4-inch rounds; these will form the tops of the pastries. Gather up the scraps and refrigerate for Monkey Bread. If your kitchen is warm and the pastry is getting very soft, transfer the pastry "tops" to a parchment-lined baking sheet and refrigerate until you're ready to use them.

7. To assemble the pastries, fit the 5-inch rounds into the prepared molds; place on the prepared baking sheet. Pipe or spoon about 2 tablespoons pastry cream onto the center of each pastry. Place a fanned pear quarter on top. Brush the edges of the bottom crusts with egg wash. Set a pastry "top" on top of each and press around the edges gently to seal. Cover the tartlets with plastic wrap, and let rise in a warm place (at least 70°F) until the dough is doubled in bulk, puffy, and very soft when you touch it, 45 to 60 minutes.

8. Set the oven rack in the middle position. Preheat the oven to 375°F.

9. Brush the tops of the pastries with egg wash, sprinkle with sanding sugar, and with a sharp paring knife or kitchen shears, cut three ½-inch slits in the top of the pastries to act as vents during baking. Bake one sheet at a time, rotating the sheet two-thirds of the way through the baking time, until the pastries are golden brown, 20 to 25 minutes. Transfer to a wire rack to cool for 10 minutes. Using your fingertips, gently pull the pastry away from the sides of the molds to unmold, and let cool on the wire rack. Repeat with the remaining pastries.

Variation: Replace the Ginger Pastry Cream with Vanilla Pastry Cream (see pastry cream from Tart Tropezienne, page 37). Replace the pear quarter in each danish with 2 canned, drained apricot halves, each cut in half to yield 4 quarters. Arrange the quarters in a spiral fashion with each danish like the spokes of a wheel. Top with pastry rounds, glaze, sprinkle with sugar, vent, and bake as above.

Raspberry Streusel Pinwheels

We sell out of these light, flaky pastries every day. You can use any favorite seedless jam. Bake one sheet of pastries at a time, leaving the second sheet out at room temperature until ready to go into the oven.

MAKES 12 PASTRIES

Streusel Topping

- ½ **cup all-purpose flour**
- ½ **cup light brown sugar**
- ½ **teaspoon coarse salt**
- ¼ **teaspoon ground cinnamon**
- ¼ **cup (½ stick) cold unsalted butter, cut into small cubes**

Pastry

- ½ **recipe Danish Dough (page 42)**
- ¾ **cup seedless raspberry jam**

Milk Icing

- ½ **cup confectioners' sugar**
- 2 **to 3 teaspoons milk**

1. To make the streusel: In a medium bowl, use a fork to stir together the flour, brown sugar, salt, and cinnamon. Add the butter, and using your fingertips, quickly work it into the dry ingredients until pea-size crumbs form; set aside in the refrigerator.

2. Line two baking sheets with parchment paper or nonstick silicone baking mats; set aside.

3. To make the pastry: On a lightly floured work surface, roll out the dough to a 17 by 13-inch rectangle about ¼ inch thick. Using a ruler and a pizza wheel or pastry cutter, trim the edges of the dough to form a 16 by 12-inch rectangle. Then cut the dough into twelve 4-inch squares.

4. Use the pizza wheel to make diagonal cuts in each square, three-quarters of the way toward the center, leaving a 1-inch square in the middle. (Each piece should have eight points, two at each corner.) Fold every other point toward the center, pressing down to seal. Place on the prepared baking sheets.

5. Dot each pastry in the center with about 2 teaspoons jam. Sprinkle with streusel to cover. Cover the pastries with plastic wrap and let rise in a warm place (at least 70°F) until the dough is doubled in bulk, puffy, and very soft, about 30 minutes.

6. Set the oven rack in the middle position. Preheat the oven to 375°F.

7. Bake one sheet at a time, rotating it two-thirds of the way through the baking time, until the pastries are golden brown, 20 to 25 minutes. Transfer to a wire rack.

8. To make the icing: In a small bowl, stir the confectioners' sugar with enough milk to make a thin white glaze. Drizzle the icing over the pastries. Let cool completely on the rack.

Hazelnut Chocolate Spirals

This pastry is a variation on the traditional Pain aux Raisins (see Variation). The key to successfully rolling the dough is to make sure it is cold so you can roll it tightly to form the spirals. If your kitchen is warm and the dough gets soft and difficult to roll, transfer it to a baking sheet and refrigerate until it firms up. As with other pastries, bake one baking sheet at a time for best results and even baking. Hazelnut-praline paste can be found at gourmet specialty stores.

MAKES 12 PASTRIES

Vanilla Pastry Cream

- 3 **large egg yolks**
- 6 **tablespoons sugar**
- 3 **tablespoons cornstarch**
- 1½ **cups milk**
- ⅛ **teaspoon coarse salt**
- ½ **vanilla bean, split in half lengthwise, or ½ tablespoon pure vanilla extract**
- 2 **tablespoons cold unsalted butter**

Pastry

- 3 **tablespoons hazelnut-praline paste**
- ½ **recipe Danish Dough (page 42)**
- 1 **large egg, beaten, for egg wash**
- 8 **ounces bittersweet chocolate, chopped into ¼-inch pieces**
- 1 **cup apricot jam**

1. To make the pastry cream: In a medium bowl, whisk together the egg yolks, about half of the sugar, all the cornstarch, and ¼ cup of the milk.

2. In a saucepan, combine the remaining sugar, the remaining 1¼ cups milk, and the salt. If using a vanilla bean, scrape the tiny black seeds into the saucepan and add the pod. Bring to a simmer. Whisking constantly, gradually pour the hot milk into the egg mixture to temper it. Set a strainer over the saucepan. Strain the custard mixture back into the saucepan and bring to a boil over medium heat, whisking constantly. Boil for 10 seconds, whisking. (Make sure the custard boils for 10 seconds in the center of the pan—not just around the sides.) The mixture should thicken to a pudding-like consistency.

3. Transfer the pastry cream to the bowl of a standing mixer fitted with the paddle attachment and beat on medium speed for 2 to 3 minutes, to cool slightly. Beat in the vanilla extract, if using. With the mixer running, beat in the butter, a little at a time. Beat until cooled, 5 to 10 more minutes. Press a piece of plastic wrap directly on the surface of the pastry cream to help keep a skin from forming. Refrigerate until chilled, about 1 hour.

4. Line two baking sheets with parchment paper or nonstick silicone baking mats; set aside.

5. To make the pastry: In a small bowl, stir together 1½ cups of the pastry cream and the hazelnut-praline paste with a whisk; set aside.

6. On a lightly floured surface, roll out the dough to a 17 by 13-inch rectangle, with the 17-inch side facing you. Spread the hazelnut

pastry cream all over, leaving a ½-inch border along the bottom edge of the pastry. Brush the border with egg wash. Sprinkle the chocolate on top of the pastry cream. Arrange the dough so that the short side faces you, and roll it up tightly to form a log about 3 inches in diameter and 13 inches long. Place the log seam side down on one of the prepared baking sheets, cover with plastic wrap, and refrigerate for 30 minutes to firm.

7. Transfer the log to the work surface. Trim the ends and cut the log into twelve 1-inch slices. Place the slices on the baking sheets, cover with plastic wrap, and let rise in a warm place (at least 70°F) until the dough is doubled in bulk, puffy, and very soft—45 to 60 minutes.

8. Set the oven rack in the middle position. Preheat the oven to 375°F.

9. Brush the tops and sides of the pinwheels with egg wash. Bake one sheet at a time, rotating the sheet about two-thirds of the way through the baking time, until golden brown, 20 to 25 minutes. Transfer to a wire rack.

10. While the pastries are still warm, in a small saucepan, warm the apricot jam over low heat until liquid. Strain through a fine strainer. Brush the top and sides of the pastries with the strained jam. Let cool completely and serve.

Variation: PAIN AUX RAISINS

Follow directions exactly as described, replacing the hazelnut pastry cream with 1½ cups Vanilla Pastry Cream (page 37), and replacing the chocolate with 1 cup raisins.

Sticky Buns

These generous-size buns smeared with a honey–brown sugar mixture and sprinkled with pecans require jumbo muffin tins, preferably nonstick. Be very careful when inverting the muffin tins to remove the sticky buns—the sugar-butter filling is very hot.

MAKES 12 BUNS

Honey Glaze

- ½ cup (1 stick) unsalted butter, at room temperature
- 1¼ cups light brown sugar
- ¼ cup honey
- ¼ cup light corn syrup
- Pinch of coarse salt
- 2 tablespoons water

Pastry

- 2 cups chopped pecans
- ½ recipe Danish Dough (page 42)
- 1 large egg, lightly beaten, for egg wash

1. To make the glaze: In a standing mixer fitted with the paddle attachment, beat the butter, brown sugar, honey, corn syrup, and salt until blended, about 2 minutes. Beat in the water to thin.

2. Line a baking sheet with parchment paper or a nonstick silicone baking mat; set aside. Spray 12 jumbo muffin cups with vegetable spray.

3. Spoon 1½ tablespoons honey glaze into the bottom of each of the 12 muffin cups, and sprinkle each with 1 tablespoon pecans.

4. On a lightly floured work surface, roll the dough to an 18 by 14-inch rectangle, about ¼ inch thick, with the long side facing you. Spread all but a 1-inch border with the rest of the honey glaze. Sprinkle with the rest of the pecans. Brush the border with egg wash. Starting at the bottom, roll the dough tightly to make a log about 3 inches in diameter and 18 inches long. Place on a baking sheet lined with parchment paper, cover with plastic wrap, and chill for 30 minutes.

5. Slice the dough crosswise about 1½ inches thick, and place the slices cut side down in the muffin cups. Cover with plastic wrap and let rise in a warm place until the buns reach ½ inch above the tops of the muffin cups, 45 to 60 minutes.

6. Set the oven rack in the middle position. Preheat the oven to 350°F.

7. Place the muffin pan on the prepared baking sheet. Bake, rotating the sheet about two-thirds of the way through the cooking, until the buns are a dark golden brown, 25 to 30 minutes.

8. Line another baking sheet with parchment paper or a nonstick silicone baking mat. Immediately turn the hot buns out onto the lined baking sheet; be careful—the glaze will be very hot. Place the baking sheet on a wire rack and let the buns cool completely.

Sour Cream Coffee Cake

This rich and flavorful cake is topped with a crunchy cinnamon-brown sugar-pecan mixture. More of the mixture is hidden in its dense center. While good served with morning coffee, try slicing it thin and serving it with afternoon tea as well. For serving ease, use a pan with a removable bottom.

MAKES ONE 10-INCH TUBE CAKE, SERVES 12

Topping

- ½ cup firmly packed light brown sugar
- 2 teaspoons ground cinnamon
- 1 cup pecans, finely chopped

Cake

- 2 cups sour cream
- 2 teaspoons baking soda
- 3½ cups cake flour, sifted
- 1 tablespoon baking powder
- 1 cup (2 sticks) unsalted butter, at room temperature
- 2 cups granulated sugar
- 2 teaspoons coarse salt
- 4 large eggs, at room temperature
- 1½ tablespoons pure vanilla extract

1. To make the topping: In a small bowl, stir together the brown sugar, cinnamon, and finely chopped pecans with a fork until combined; set aside.

2. Set the oven rack in the middle position. Preheat the oven to 350°F. Spray a 10-inch tube pan (preferably with removable bottom) with nonstick cooking spray, or generously brush with softened butter; dust with flour and shake out the excess.

3. To make the cake: In a small bowl, stir together the sour cream and baking soda; set aside. Whisk together the cake flour and baking powder in another bowl; set aside.

4. In the bowl of a standing mixer fitted with the paddle attachment, beat the butter, sugar, and salt on medium-high speed until light and fluffy, 2 to 3 minutes, scraping down the sides of the bowl halfway through. Add the eggs one at a time, beating after each addition. Beat in the vanilla.

5. With the mixer on low speed, add the dry ingredients in three batches, alternating with the sour cream mixture and beating well after each addition.

6. Scrape half of the batter into the prepared pan. Sprinkle with half of the topping mixture, avoiding the edges of the pan so that the sides are smooth and the filling is hidden. Use a knife to gently swirl the topping mixture into the batter. Add the remaining batter and smooth the top. Sprinkle with the rest of the topping mixture.

7. Place the pan on a baking sheet and bake, rotating the sheet about two-thirds of the way through the baking time, until the top of the cake springs back when touched and a cake tester inserted in the center comes out clean, 50 to 60 minutes.

8. Transfer the tube pan to a wire rack and let the cake cool completely in the pan. Using a spatula, loosen the sides of the cake from the pan, then lift the cake up and off the center tube. Serve at room temperature.

Blueberry Tea Cake

When I worked as a pastry chef at the Helmsley Palace Hotel in New York City, afternoon tea service was a major part of the pastry department's daily creations. We would prepare this rich, buttery, fruit-filled Bundt cake in a smaller version and serve it alongside a variety of sweet and savory bites. This cake travels well and is a good choice for a picnic or potluck meal. Finish it with the lemon glaze as written below, or simply dust it with confectioners' sugar.

MAKES ONE 10-INCH
BUNDT CAKE, SERVES 12

Cake

2½ **cups all-purpose flour, plus 1 teaspoon for blueberries and zest**
2 **teaspoons baking powder**
1 **cup (2 sticks) unsalted butter, at room temperature**
1 **cup firmly packed light brown sugar**
1 **cup granulated sugar**
½ **teaspoon coarse salt**
4 **large eggs, at room temperature**
1 **teaspoon pure vanilla extract**
1 **cup buttermilk**
2 **cups blueberries**
2 **tablespoons grated lemon zest**

Glaze

2 **to 3 tablespoons lemon juice**
2 **cups confectioners' sugar**

1. Set the oven rack in the middle position. Preheat the oven to 350°F. Generously butter a 12-cup Bundt pan; set aside.

2. To make the cake: In a medium bowl, whisk the 2½ cups flour with the baking powder; set aside.

3. In the bowl of a standing mixer fitted with the paddle attachment, beat the butter, sugars, and salt on medium-high speed until light and fluffy, 2 to 3 minutes. Add the eggs one at a time, beating after each addition. Beat in the vanilla. On low speed, add the dry ingredients in three batches, alternating with the buttermilk, and beginning and ending with the flour. Beat just until the flour is absorbed.

4. In a bowl, toss the blueberries and lemon zest with the remaining 1 teaspoon flour, and fold into the batter with a rubber spatula. Scrape the batter into the Bundt pan and smooth the top. Place the pan on a baking sheet and bake, rotating the sheet about two-thirds of the way through the baking time, until a cake tester inserted into the center of the cake comes out clean, about 65 minutes. Cool in the pan on a wire rack for 20 minutes. Invert the pan on the rack to turn the cake out; let cool completely on the rack.

5. To make the glaze: In a small bowl, whisk the lemon juice into the confectioners' sugar, adding the second tablespoon gradually, so that the glaze is just liquid enough to pour easily but still opaque. Place a sheet pan under the cooling rack. Spoon the glaze over the cooled cake, allowing the excess to drip onto the baking sheet. Allow the glaze to cool completely for 30 minutes, then serve.

Cookies, Brownies, and Bars

Whenever I'm home for more than a few hours at a time, my kids beg me to make cookies with them. No matter how tired I am from a long day at the bakery, I really can't say no, as I have a team of helpers to assist with measuring, mixing, scooping, and of course licking! Many of the cookies we bake and sell at the SoNo Baking Company were first developed at home with the help of these little hands. Kitchen Sink Cookies (page 65) have been made with every possible mix-in combination. Try those we list in the recipe or any of your own favorites. Chocolate-filled Almond Macaroons (page 76) quickly became both a house and a bakery favorite, and Macadamia Butterscotch Bars (page 83) are usually gone before I've managed to transfer them from the baking pan to a serving platter.

The cookies and bars in this chapter can be served for a range of occasions from casual to formal. Big oversize cookies such as Chocolate Chip Oatmeal Coconut Cookies (page 82) and Lemon Drop Sugar Cookies (page 64) are great for after-school snacks, while sophisticated confections such as Sarah Bernhardts (page 78) and Spritz Cookies (page 80) can be the perfect after-dinner adult treat.

To produce the best cookies and bars, you must take a few simple steps to ensure success. First off, always make sure all of your ingredients are at room temperature, including the butter and eggs. They should be taken out of the refrigerator at least 4 hours in advance of baking. Second, space cookies at least 2 inches apart (3 inches, if possible, with the exception of meltaways and macaroons, which are smaller and need to be only 1 inch apart) on a baking sheet lined with parchment paper or a nonstick silicone baking mat. And third, whenever possible, try to bake cookies one sheet at a time in the middle of the oven to ensure overall evenness of baking and browning.

Most of the cookies and bars in this chapter can be kept in a resealable container for up to one week, with moist cookies separated from crisp ones.

Double Chocolate Chunk Cookies

These dense, chewy cookies are a chocolate lover's dream. Made with two kinds of chocolate, unsweetened and semisweet, they are pleasantly bitter and loaded with chunks. The texture is delicate and fudgy, almost like a brownie. Be careful not to overbake them. When buying chocolate chips, be sure to look for natural vanilla in the ingredients and make sure that the chocolate hasn't "bloomed" (developed a grayish coating on the outside), which can oftentimes mean the chocolate has been sitting around for a while. Serve with a large, cold glass of milk.

MAKES ABOUT 22 COOKIES

1 cup all-purpose flour

1 teaspoon coarse salt

¼ teaspoon baking soda

4 ounces unsweetened chocolate, chopped into ½-inch pieces

10 ounces semisweet chocolate chunks

6 tablespoons (¾ stick) unsalted butter, cut into tablespoon-size pieces

1 cup firmly packed light brown sugar

3 large eggs, at room temperature

1 tablespoon pure vanilla extract

TECHNIQUE TIP: When melting chocolate, always use a double boiler rather than a microwave, which might burn the chocolate. A double boiler is essentially two fitted saucepans, the larger one partially filled with 1 inch of water and brought to a simmer. The inner saucepan uses this indirect heat to melt chocolate and butter, warm egg whites, dissolve sugar, and cook custards. A double boiler can also be improvised with a large saucepan and a heatproof bowl.

1. Set the oven rack in the middle position. Preheat the oven to 350°F. Line two baking sheets with parchment paper or nonstick silicone baking mats; set aside.

2. In a medium bowl, whisk together the flour, salt, and baking soda; set aside.

3. Bring 1 inch of water to a simmer in the bottom of a double boiler. Combine the unsweetened chocolate, 6 ounces of the semisweet chocolate chunks, and the butter in the top of the double boiler, set it over (not in) the simmering water, and heat until the chocolate and butter melt, about 5 minutes. Stir to blend. Remove from the heat and let cool for 3 minutes.

4. Add the brown sugar and stir with a rubber spatula for 2 to 3 minutes until the sugar dissolves. Then add the eggs one at a time, stirring well after each addition. Stir in the vanilla. Add the dry ingredients and fold with a rubber spatula just until the flour has been absorbed. Fold in the remaining 4 ounces of the chocolate chunks.

5. Use a ¼ cup (2-inch-wide) ice cream scoop to scoop out the dough onto the prepared baking sheets, placing the scoops about 3 inches apart.

6. Bake one sheet at a time, rotating the sheet two-thirds of the way through the baking time, until the cookies are set on the edges but still soft in the center, 11 to 13 minutes. Do not overbake.

7. Let the cookies cool on the baking sheet on a wire rack for 10 minutes. Then remove with a metal spatula and let cool completely on the rack. Bake the remaining cookies in the same way.

Ginger Cookies

These cookies are the creation of Ed Schriver, one of SoNo Baking Company's original bakers. This recipe has been handed down through his family for generations. The cookies are crisp and thin like a snap, and full of ginger flavor with an almost caramelized taste. We serve these popular cookies year-round.

MAKES 60 COOKIES

2 **cups all-purpose flour**

2 **teaspoons baking soda**

¼ **teaspoon coarse salt**

1 **teaspoon ground cinnamon**

1 **teaspoon ground cloves**

1 **teaspoon ground ginger**

1 **cup sugar, plus ¾ cup for rolling**

¾ **cup (1½ sticks) unsalted butter, at room temperature**

1 **large egg, at room temperature**

¼ **cup unsulfured molasses**

- -

TECHNIQUE TIP: When baking at home, I like to have only one baking sheet of cookies in the oven at one time. This allows for more even heat distribution and proper browning. Prepare two baking sheets of cookies at a time so that the second one is waiting and ready to go into the oven as soon as the first sheet comes out. There are, however, a few exceptions to this rule, such as for meringues and other cookies that have an egg white component and may need longer baking times, or for high-volume baking when it may not be practical to bake one sheet at a time.

1. In a large bowl, whisk together the flour, baking soda, salt, cinnamon, cloves, and ginger; set aside.

2. In the bowl of a standing mixer fitted with the paddle attachment, beat together the sugar and butter on medium speed until light and fluffy, 2 to 3 minutes, scraping down the sides of the bowl halfway through. Beat in the egg and molasses until combined. Reduce the mixer speed to low and gradually add the flour mixture, beating until combined. Transfer the dough to a clean bowl, cover with plastic wrap, and refrigerate until well chilled, about 1 hour (and up to 24 hours).

3. Arrange the oven rack in the middle position. Preheat the oven to 350°F. Line two baking sheets with parchment paper or nonstick silicone baking mats; set aside. Place the extra sugar for rolling on a plate; set aside.

4. Use a 1½-inch ice cream scoop to scoop out the dough, and roll into balls between your hands. Roll the balls in the sugar to coat, and place about 2 inches apart on the prepared baking sheets.

5. Bake one sheet at a time, rotating the sheet two-thirds of the way through the baking time, until the cookies are deep golden brown and the centers are firm, 15 to 20 minutes.

6. Transfer the sheet to a wire rack to cool for 10 minutes. Use a spatula to transfer the cookies to the rack, and let cool completely. Continue to roll and bake the remaining cookies in the same way.

Uncle Bobby's Chocolate Chunk Cookies

This recipe is my wife's. Veronica's brother, Bobby, is infamous for breaking into our house and stealing these cookies. We keep them in the freezer not only because we like the cakey texture they get (which prevents them from freezing solid), but also because we're always looking for new places to hide them from Bobby. This recipe uses Lighter Bake (which can be found in the baking section of most grocery stores), a fruit-based fat-free replacement for butter or oil, which makes the cookies lighter than your usual chocolate chip cookies but still sweet and chocolaty. The almond flavor pairs well with the chocolate, and the soft cookie and hard chocolate chip is a great texture combination.

MAKES 16 OVERSIZE COOKIES

2¼ cups all-purpose flour

1 teaspoon baking soda

½ cup (1 stick) unsalted butter, at room temperature

¼ cup Lighter Bake (see above)

¾ cup granulated sugar

¾ cup light brown sugar

½ teaspoon coarse salt

2 large eggs, at room temperature

1 teaspoon almond extract

2 cups semisweet chocolate chunks

1. Set the oven rack in the middle position. Preheat the oven to 350F. Line two baking sheets with parchment paper or nonstick silicone baking mats; set aside.

2. In a medium bowl, whisk together the flour and baking soda; set aside.

3. In the bowl of a standing mixer fitted with the paddle attachment, beat the butter, Lighter Bake, granulated sugar, brown sugar, and salt on medium-high speed until light and fluffy, 2 to 3 minutes, scraping down the sides of the bowl halfway through. Add the eggs one at a time, beating after each addition. Beat in the almond extract.

4. With the mixer on low speed, add the dry ingredients, beating until the flour is absorbed. Gently fold in the chocolate chunks with a rubber scraper.

5. Use a ¼ cup (2-inch) ice cream scoop to scoop out the batter onto the prepared baking sheets, placing the scoops about 2 inches apart.

6. Bake one sheet at a time, rotating the sheet about two-thirds of the way through the baking time, until the cookies are set and browned on the edges but still very soft in the center, 14 to 16 minutes.

7. Transfer the sheet to a wire rack to cool for 10 minutes. Use a metal spatula to transfer the cookies to the rack and let cool completely.

Lemon Drop Sugar Cookies

These classic sugar cookies are enhanced with both lemon extract and lemon zest. Feel free to mix and match the citrus that you use—try orange and lime as well as lemon. Be careful not to overbake these cookies. They should remain a pale yellow color and not brown at all.

MAKES ABOUT 12 COOKIES

½ **cup sanding sugar, for rolling**

2 **cups all-purpose flour**

1½ **teaspoons baking powder**

½ **cup (1 stick) unsalted butter, at room temperature**

1 **cup granulated sugar**

½ **teaspoon coarse salt**

2 **large eggs, at room temperature**

2 **teaspoons grated lemon zest (from 2 lemons)**

1 **teaspoon pure lemon extract**

1. Set the oven rack in the middle position. Preheat the oven to 350°F. Line two baking sheets with parchment paper or nonstick silicone baking mats; set aside. Place the sanding sugar on a plate; set aside.

2. In a medium bowl, whisk together the flour and baking powder; set aside.

3. In the bowl of a standing mixer fitted with the paddle attachment, beat the butter, sugar, and salt on medium-high speed until light and fluffy, 2 to 3 minutes, scraping down the sides of the bowl halfway through. Add the eggs one at a time, beating after each addition. Beat in the lemon zest and extract.

4. With the mixer on low speed, add the dry ingredients, beating until the flour is absorbed. Use a ¼ cup (2-inch-wide) ice cream scoop to scoop out the dough and quickly roll into balls between your hands (the dough will be a little sticky but you shouldn't need to use flour). Roll the balls in the sanding sugar to coat, and place about 3 inches apart on the prepared baking sheet.

5. Bake one sheet at a time, rotating the sheet about two-thirds of the way through the baking time, until the cookies are set but not browned, slightly cracked on the top, and still soft in the center, 12 to 15 minutes.

6. Transfer the baking sheet to a wire rack to cool for 10 minutes. Use a spatula to transfer the cookies to the rack and let cool completely.

Kitchen Sink Cookies

As the name says, these oversize, overstuffed cookies are loaded with pretty much everything but the kitchen sink! Our version uses coconut, chocolate, pecans, raisins, and oats, but feel free to substitute some of your favorite mix-ins including dried cranberries, dried cherries, walnuts, candied orange peel, candied ginger, or even granola.

MAKES 24 COOKIES

2½ **cups all-purpose flour**
½ **teaspoon baking soda**
1 **teaspoon coarse salt**
1½ **cups (3 sticks) unsalted butter, at room temperature**
1 **cup light brown sugar**
1 **cup granulated sugar**
1 **large egg, at room temperature**
1 **teaspoon pure vanilla extract**
1 **cup sweetened shredded coconut**
6 **ounces semisweet chocolate, cut into ¼-inch chunks**
1 **cup pecans, coarsely chopped**
1 **cup raisins**
1 **cup old-fashioned rolled oats (not instant)**

- -

TECHNIQUE TIP: For freshly baked cookies anytime, make a double batch of cookie dough, scoop extra balls of dough, and freeze in a single layer on a baking sheet. Once frozen, store in a resealable freezer bag for up to 2 months. Thaw and bake as directed.

1. Set the oven rack in the middle position. Preheat the oven to 350°F. Line two baking sheets with parchment paper or nonstick silicone baking mats; set aside.

2. In a medium bowl, whisk together the flour, baking soda, and salt; set aside.

3. In the bowl of a standing mixer fitted with the paddle attachment, beat the butter, brown sugar, and granulated sugar on medium speed until light and fluffy, 2 to 3 minutes, scraping down the sides of the bowl halfway through. Add the egg and vanilla, and mix to combine.

4. With the mixer on low speed, add the flour mixture, beating until the flour is absorbed. Fold in the coconut, chocolate chunks, pecans, raisins, and oats. Mix until combined.

5. Use a ¼ cup (2-inch-wide) ice cream scoop to scoop out the dough onto the prepared baking sheets, placing the scoops about 3 inches apart.

6. Bake one sheet at a time, rotating the sheet about two-thirds of the way through the cooking time, until the cookies are golden brown, about 20 minutes.

7. Transfer the baking sheet to a wire rack to cool for 10 minutes. Use a spatula to transfer the cookies to the rack and let cool completely.

Traditional Anise Biscotti

These classic Italian cookies are dry and crisp, sweet with anise, and full of almonds. They remind me of dinners at my grandparents' house in Brooklyn, when I was a kid. My grandparents would serve biscotti alongside peaches soaked in red wine for a satisfying dessert. Stored in an airtight container, the cookies will last up to one week. Be careful not to store them with more moist cookies because the biscotti will absorb the moisture and lose the desired crispness. If you can't find blanched almonds, substitute whole unblanched almonds in the skin, or you can use any favorite nut, such as hazelnut or macadamia nut. For a more citrusy taste, add grated orange zest and substitute orange extract for the anise extract and anise seeds.

MAKES ABOUT 30 COOKIES

2½ **cups all-purpose flour**
2 **tablespoons coarse yellow cornmeal**
2 **teaspoons baking powder**
½ **cup (1 stick) unsalted butter, at room temperature**
¾ **cup granulated sugar**
1 **teaspoon coarse salt**
2 **large eggs, at room temperature, lightly beaten**
2 **teaspoons pure anise extract**
1 **tablespoon anise seeds**
1 **cup blanched whole almonds**
1 **egg, lightly beaten, for egg wash**
 Sanding sugar

1. Set the oven rack in the middle position. Preheat the oven to 350°F. Line a baking sheet with parchment paper or a nonstick silicone baking mat; set aside.

2. In a medium bowl, whisk together the flour, cornmeal, and baking powder; set aside.

3. In the bowl of a standing mixer fitted with the paddle attachment, beat the butter, sugar, and salt on medium-high speed until light and fluffy, 2 to 3 minutes, scraping down the sides of the bowl halfway through. Add the eggs and beat until blended. Beat in the anise extract.

4. With the mixer on low speed, add the dry ingredients and beat until the flour is absorbed. Fold in the anise seeds and almonds.

5. Divide the dough in half. On a lightly floured work surface, gently roll each half with lightly floured hands to a log about 17 inches long and 1½ to 2 inches wide. Using two spatulas, carefully transfer the logs to the prepared baking sheet. Press down on the tops of the logs with your palm to flatten. Brush with the egg wash and sprinkle with sanding sugar.

6. Bake, rotating the baking sheet about two-thirds of the way through, until the logs are a light golden brown and spring back when you press on them at the thickest point, about 20 minutes.

RECIPE CONTINUES . . .

7. Remove the logs from the oven (leave the oven on) and let cool on the baking sheet on a wire rack for 10 minutes. Using two spatulas, very carefully transfer one log at a time to a cutting board. Using a serrated knife and a sawing motion, cut the logs on the diagonal into slices about ¾ inch thick. Return the slices to the baking sheet, laying each one on its side, and bake until the biscotti are completely dried and browned on the edges, about 12 minutes.

8. Cool the biscotti for 10 minutes on the baking sheet on a wire rack. Then transfer them to the rack with a metal spatula and let cool completely.

Chocolate Hazelnut Biscotti

These biscotti have extra-deep chocolate flavor, as the recipe calls for both cocoa powder and bittersweet chocolate. The chocolate pairs nicely with the toasted hazelnuts. Serve with mixed berries or macerated oranges.

MAKES ABOUT 30 COOKIES

1 cup (4 ounces) hazelnuts
2⅔ cups all-purpose flour
½ cup Dutch-processed unsweetened cocoa powder
1 tablespoon baking powder
½ cup (1 stick) unsalted butter, at room temperature
¾ cup granulated sugar
1 teaspoon coarse salt
3 large eggs, at room temperature
2 ounces bittersweet chocolate, very finely chopped
1 large egg white, lightly beaten, for egg wash
Coarse sanding sugar

1. Set the oven rack in the middle position. Preheat the oven to 350°F. Line a baking sheet with parchment paper; set aside.

2. Place the hazelnuts in a single layer on a baking sheet and bake until they are are lightly colored and the skins are blistered and cracking, 10 to 15 minutes. Wrap in a kitchen towel and let steam for 1 minute. Rub the nuts in the towel to rub off as many of the skins as possible, but don't worry about the skins that stick; set aside to cool completely. Coarsely chop the hazelnuts.

3. In a medium bowl, whisk together the flour, cocoa powder, and baking powder; set aside.

4. In the bowl of a standing mixer fitted with the paddle attachment, beat the butter, sugar, and salt on medium-high speed until light and fluffy, 2 to 3 minutes, scraping down the sides of the bowl halfway through. Add the eggs one at a time, beating after each addition until blended.

5. With the mixer on low speed, add the dry ingredients and beat until the flour is absorbed. Fold in the chocolate and the chopped hazelnuts.

6. Divide the dough in half. On a lightly floured work surface, gently roll each half with lightly floured hands to a log about 17 inches long and 1½ to 2 inches wide. Carefully transfer the logs to the prepared baking sheet. Press down on the tops of the logs with your palm to flatten. Brush with the egg wash, and sprinkle with sanding sugar.

7. Bake, rotating the baking sheet about two-thirds of the way through, until the logs spring back when you press on them at the thickest point, about 20 minutes.

RECIPE CONTINUES . . .

8. Remove the logs from the oven (leave the oven on) and let cool on the baking sheet on a wire rack for 10 minutes. Using two spatulas, very carefully transfer one log at a time to a cutting board. Using a serrated knife and a sawing motion, cut the logs on the diagonal into slices about ¾ inch thick. Return the slices to the baking sheet, laying each one on its side, and bake until the biscotti are completely dried and crisp, about 12 minutes.

9. Cool the biscotti for 10 minutes on the baking sheet on a wire rack. Then transfer them to the rack with a metal spatula and let cool completely. Store in a covered container at room temperature for up to 1 week.

TECHNIQUE TIP: Store biscotti for up to two weeks in an airtight container. Bake on a lined baking sheet in a 250°F oven for 15 to 20 minutes to crisp up, if necessary.

Meringues

These light-as-air meringues will melt in your mouth in an instant. They make a perfect accompaniment to a cup of dark-roast coffee and are the perfect low-fat treat to wrap in cellophane bags and give as gifts (add a drop or two of food coloring for special occasions). They can also be served atop a bowl of your favorite ice cream or with a heaping spoonful of macerated berries.

MAKES 12 LARGE COOKIES

½ **cup (4 large) egg whites, at room temperature**
½ **cup granulated sugar**
¼ **teaspoon coarse salt**
1½ **teaspoons pure vanilla extract**
¼ **teaspoon almond extract**
1 **cup confectioners' sugar, sifted**
½ **cup sliced blanched almonds**

- - - - - - - - - - - - - - - - - - - -

TECHNIQUE TIP: Gently warming the egg whites and sugar before whipping helps add volume. Be careful to gently warm the egg whites *above* the simmering water of the double boiler, not letting the bottom of the top of the double boiler touch the simmering water; otherwise you will cook the egg whites, causing a grainy texture. Also, continue to whisk the whites and sugar while they are being heated.

1. Set two oven racks in the oven. Preheat the oven to 200°F. Line a baking sheet with parchment paper; set aside.

2. Bring 1 inch of water to a simmer in the bottom of a double boiler. Combine the egg whites, granulated sugar, and salt in the top of the double boiler, set it over (not in) the simmering water, and whisk to dissolve the sugar just until it melts, 1 to 2 minutes. (The mixture should feel just warm to the touch, and not gritty.)

3. Transfer the mixture to the bowl of a standing mixer fitted with the whisk attachment. Beat on medium-high speed until stiff peaks form when you lift the whisk. The egg whites will start off glossy and damp, like the inside of a marshmallow, and eventually get drier and stiffer. This will take about 3 minutes.

4. Fold in the vanilla and almond extracts. Set a fine sieve over the bowl of meringue, and sift the confectioners' sugar on top. Add the sliced almonds and fold just enough to incorporate the sugar and almonds, but no more. The meringue will deflate somewhat.

5. Drop the meringue mixture by rounded serving spoons (or just dollop them with a rubber spatula) onto the prepared baking sheet. Bake for 1 hour. Rotate the baking sheet top to bottom and back to front, and continue baking until the exterior of the cookies is dry and the interior is light and soft, 1½ to 2 hours. The meringues should brown only slightly. To test the meringues, remove one from the oven and let stand a few minutes to cool. Bite it—it should be dry enough that the insides don't stick to your teeth.

Meltaways

These are one of the simplest cookies to make and one of the most delicious to eat. As the name suggests, these small, crisp, buttery cookies melt in your mouth. They are by far one of my favorites, as I love any kind of shortbread. Using cornstarch in addition to flour makes them extra-delicate. If you don't have any sanding sugar, bake the cookies and toss them in confectioners' sugar.

MAKES ABOUT 60 COOKIES

1 cup all-purpose flour
½ cup cornstarch
¾ cup (1½ sticks) unsalted butter, at room temperature
¾ cup confectioners' sugar
½ teaspoon coarse salt
1 teaspoon pure vanilla extract
Grated zest of 1 lemon
½ cup sanding sugar, for rolling

1. In a medium bowl, sift the flour with the cornstarch; set aside.

2. In the bowl of a standing mixer fitted with the paddle attachment, beat the butter, confectioners' sugar, and salt on medium-high speed until light and fluffy, 2 to 3 minutes, scraping down the sides of the bowl halfway through. Beat in the vanilla extract and lemon zest.

3. With the mixer on low speed, add the dry ingredients, beating until the flour is absorbed.

4. Scoop about half of the dough onto a sheet of parchment paper and roll into a log about 8 inches long and about 1½ inches in diameter; wrap in the paper and twist the ends. Repeat to roll and wrap the other half. Refrigerate until firm, at least 4 hours.

5. Arrange two oven racks in the upper and lower thirds of the oven. Preheat the oven to 350°F. Line two baking sheets with parchment paper or nonstick silicone baking mats.

6. Roll one of the logs in the sanding sugar to coat the outside generously with sugar. Set the log on a cutting board and slice into ¼-inch-thick rounds. Repeat with the second log. Place the cookies about 1 inch apart on the prepared baking sheets.

7. Bake one sheet at a time, rotating the sheet about two-thirds of the way through the baking time, until the cookies are a pale blond color with a rim of gold around the edges, 12 to 15 minutes.

8. Transfer the baking sheet to a wire rack to cool for 10 minutes. Use a spatula to transfer the cookies to the rack and let cool completely.

Coconut Macaroons

These moist, chewy macaroons are delicious on their own, but for a more professional finish, dip them in chocolate as written below. Make sure to get coconut labeled "finely shredded" (or "dessicated") rather than "medium shred." This unsweetened dried coconut (a different product from the softer-textured sweetened coconut) is available in gourmet specialty stores and some grocery stores.

MAKES ABOUT 20 COOKIES

1 cup (6 to 7 large) egg whites, at room temperature

½ cup sugar

¼ cup light corn syrup

3 tablespoons unsalted butter

8 ounces (2⅔ cups) unsweetened finely shredded dried coconut

1½ tablespoons pure vanilla extract

½ teaspoon coarse salt

½ recipe Chocolate Glaze (page 78)

1. Bring 1 inch of water to a simmer in the bottom of a double boiler. Combine the egg whites, sugar, corn syrup, and butter in the top of the double boiler, set it over (not in) the simmering water, and heat, whisking constantly, until the mixture reaches 140° to 150°F on a candy thermometer or instant-read thermometer, about 15 minutes.

2. Transfer to the bowl of a standing mixer fitted with the paddle attachment. Add the coconut, vanilla extract, and salt. Beat on low speed until the mixture has cooled, 10 to 15 minutes. The mixture will have coalesced and will no longer be watery.

3. Set the oven rack in the middle position. Preheat the oven to 350°F. Line a baking sheet with parchment paper or a nonstick silicone baking mat.

4. Using a 1-inch (2-tablespoon) ice cream scoop, firmly pack the batter into the scoop, and press the flat side against the side of the bowl to flatten. Arrange the scoops 1 to 2 inches apart on the prepared baking sheet.

5. Bake until the macaroons are a speckled light golden brown color, 10 to 13 minutes. The macaroons should still be soft and moist in the center.

6. Cool on the baking sheet on a wire rack for 10 minutes. Then remove from the baking sheet with a metal spatula and let cool completely on the rack.

7. If the chocolate glaze needs to be warmed to return it to a liquid state, heat it in a double boiler until pourable. Transfer the glaze to a narrow container (such as a 1-cup measure). Line a baking sheet with parchment paper. Dip the bottoms of the cooled macaroons in the chocolate so that it coats the bottom ¼ inch of each cookie. Set the macaroons, bottoms down, on the parchment-lined sheet and let dry completely.

Chocolate-filled Almond Macaroons

My grown son Nikolai and younger daughter Sophia fight over these chocolate-filled almond-flavored sandwich cookies whenever I bring them home from the bakery. They have a chewy thin crust on the outside and a truffle-like filling on the inside. For best results, make the ganache (an icing, glaze, or filling for cakes and cookies, made by pouring warm cream over chocolate) at least 6 hours before you plan to make the cookies to give it time to set up and thicken. Store the ganache in an airtight plastic container in the refrigerator for up to a week. You'll have a little bit of ganache left over. Warm it up in a double boiler and drizzle over ice cream or on top of french toast.

MAKES ABOUT 36 COOKIES

¼ recipe Ganache (page 169)
1 (8-ounce) can almond paste (1 cup)
6 tablespoons sugar, plus extra for sprinkling
1 teaspoon almond extract
½ teaspoon coarse salt
2 large egg whites, at room temperature, lightly beaten with a fork to blend

1. Make the ganache and set aside for at least 6 hours, or overnight, to set up.

2. Line two baking sheets with parchment paper or nonstick silicone baking mats; set aside.

3. In a standing mixer fitted with the paddle attachment, beat the almond paste with the sugar on medium-high speed until the almond paste breaks down and combines with the sugar, 3 to 5 minutes. Scrape down the sides of the bowl. Add the almond extract and salt, and beat until combined.

4. With the mixer running, add the egg whites, about 1 teaspoon at a time, beating well and scraping down the sides of the bowl after each addition. The batter should be very smooth and thick enough to pipe.

5. Scoop the batter into a pastry bag fitted with a #4 (½-inch) pastry tip. Holding the pastry tip about ¾ inch above the parchment paper, pipe a quarter-size round of batter on one of the prepared baking sheets. Lift the bag off the batter with a little sideways jerking motion of your hand; we call this action "cutting" because the edge of the metal tip will "cut" the batter, producing a flat, rather than a pointy, top on the cookie. Continue piping cookies about 1 inch apart, trying to finish with as small a peak as possible to leave the tops rounded and smooth. Wet your finger with warm water to smooth out any remaining peaked tops. Sprinkle the macaroons generously with sugar. Let stand at room temperature for 15 to 20 minutes so that a thin, crisp crust develops on the outside of each cookie.

6. Preheat the oven to 325°F.

TECHNIQUE TIP: When it comes to piping cookies onto a baking sheet, the trick is to use a guide to help place them for consistency and size. For these cookies I like to use a quarter as my guide. Place the quarter on the parchment-lined baking sheet and draw around it with a pencil, making rows of quarter-size rounds about 1 inch apart. Turn the parchment over to protect the cookies from the pencil. Using the guide on the other side, pipe the dough so that it just reaches the edges of each round.

7. Bake the macaroons, rotating the baking sheets top to bottom and back to front two-thirds through, until set but not browned and still gooey in the centers, 18 to 20 minutes. Let cool for 10 minutes on the baking sheet on a wire rack. Then transfer the cookies to the rack and let cool completely.

8. To fill the cookies, spread about 1 teaspoon ganache on the bottom of a macaroon, making sure to keep the ganache in the center of the cookie (you don't want to see any ganache on the sides of the filled cookies). Press a second cookie, flat side down, on top of the ganache. Continue to fill all of the cookies.

Sarah Bernhardts

These traditional Danish cookies are named for the famous actress Sarah Bernhardt, who supposedly fell in love with them when she visited Copenhagen in the 1880s. Although considered a cookie, these decadent treats are more of a truffle to me, with their marzipan-like interior, pointed chocolate ganache "hat," and shiny chocolate glaze. The glaze is finished with vegetable oil, which not only keeps the chocolate shiny (preventing it from developing a grayish "bloom"—sugar crystals on the chocolate's surface) when chilled, but also keeps it fluid at room temperature, for easy dipping. Keep in mind that the ganache needs to be made at least 6 hours in advance, to give it time to thicken to the right consistency.

MAKES ABOUT 68 COOKIES

1 **recipe Ganache (page 169)**
1 **recipe batter for Chocolate-filled Almond Macaroons (page 76)**

Chocolate Glaze

12 **ounces semisweet chocolate, chopped into ½-inch pieces**
2 **tablespoons vegetable oil**

1. Make the ganache and let cool completely at room temperature, at least 6 hours or overnight.

2. Make the macaroons and let cool completely.

3. Fit a pastry bag with a #4 (½-inch) tip and fill with ganache. Arrange the macaroons on a parchment-lined baking sheet. Pipe a mound of ganache on top of each macaroon so that the ganache-topped cookie is about 2 inches tall and ends in a point, like a big Hershey's Kiss. Chill in the refrigerator until the ganache is firm, about 30 minutes.

4. To make the glaze: Place the chopped chocolate in the top of a double boiler set over (not in) simmering water and heat until melted. Remove from the heat and stir in the vegetable oil. Let stand until cool but still fluid. The glaze needs to be cool enough not to melt the ganache, but not so cold that it thickens and sets. Pour into a 1-cup measuring cup and set aside.

5. To assemble the cookies, remove them from the refrigerator. Holding each cookie by its macaroon base, quickly dip the cookies into the chocolate glaze to coat; the chocolate glaze will harden immediately over the chilled ganache. Return the glazed cookies to the baking sheet. If the chocolate glaze becomes too thick, warm it briefly in the double boiler and continue dipping.

6. Store the cookies in the refrigerator and bring to room temperature before serving.

Spritz Cookies

These tasty German butter cookies are so wonderful because one recipe can make a wide assortment of cookies. Try making little cookie sandwiches, filling the piped cookies with chocolate ganache (page 169), mint-chocolate ganache, Nutella, or raspberry jam; dip them in chocolate, or chocolate and ground nuts. Half the batter can also be flavored with cocoa powder, as written. Note that this recipe calls for one-fourth of an 8-ounce can of almond paste. You can freeze the remainder for up to 1 month.

MAKES 35 VANILLA AND
35 CHOCOLATE COOKIES

1¾ cups plus 2 tablespoons all-purpose flour

½ teaspoon baking powder

2 tablespoons unsweetened cocoa powder

¼ cup almond paste

6 tablespoons sugar

½ teaspoon coarse salt

1 large egg, at room temperature, lightly beaten

¾ cup (1½ sticks) unsalted butter, at room temperature

1 teaspoon pure vanilla extract

½ teaspoon almond extract

1. In a bowl, whisk together 1 cup of the flour and ¼ teaspoon of the baking powder; set aside. In a second bowl, whisk together the remaining ¾ cup plus 2 tablespoons flour, the remaining ¼ teaspoon baking powder, and the cocoa powder; set aside.

2. In the bowl of a standing mixer fitted with the paddle attachment, beat the almond paste, sugar, and salt on medium speed until the almond paste has broken down and there are no big lumps. It's important to thoroughly blend the mixture, making sure to not leave any large lumps of almond paste, because they can turn into brittle chunks when baked. Beat in a little of the egg. With the mixer running, add the butter a couple of tablespoons at a time. Beat in the remaining egg, and the vanilla and almond extracts until combined.

3. Remove half (a generous ¾ cup) of the batter to a small bowl and set aside; this will become your chocolate dough.

4. Add the flour–baking powder mixture to the batter remaining in the bowl and beat on low speed until the flour is absorbed; this is your vanilla dough.

5. Arrange three oven racks in the oven, and preheat the oven to 350°F. Line three baking sheets with parchment paper or nonstick silicone baking mats.

6. Scoop the vanilla dough a little at a time (enough to fit into the palm of your hand) into a pastry bag fitted with a star tip. Pipe ladyfingers on the prepared baking sheets, about ½ inch wide by 2 inches long and about 1 inch apart. Refill the pastry bag as needed.

7. Bake, rotating the sheets about two-thirds of the way into the cooking time, until the cookies are crisp and lightly golden brown around the edges, 12 to 18 minutes, based on which rack the cookies are baking on.

8. Transfer the sheets to wire racks to cool for 10 minutes. Use a spatula to transfer the cookies to the rack to cool completely.

9. Return the reserved batter to the mixer bowl, add the cocoa-flour mixture, and beat on low speed until the flour is absorbed. Pipe onto the prepared baking sheets and bake as for the vanilla cookies.

TECHNIQUE TIP: To keep the parchment paper from sliding around on the baking sheet while you're piping cookies, stick the paper onto the sheet with a tiny bit of dough in each corner.

Chocolate Chip Oatmeal Coconut Cookies

These cookies are without a doubt one of my all-time favorites, perfect for the cookie jar. Old-fashioned rolled oats give these cookies a tender bite and coconut lends a wonderful chewy texture. For crisper cookies, bake longer. Perfect for a lunchbox or alongside an afternoon cup of tea.

MAKES ABOUT 18 LARGE COOKIES

2 cups all-purpose flour

1 teaspoon baking soda

1 cup (2 sticks) unsalted butter, at room temperature

1 cup granulated sugar

½ cup firmly packed light brown sugar

1 teaspoon coarse salt

2 large eggs, at room temperature

1½ tablespoons pure vanilla extract

12 ounces best-quality semisweet chocolate chips

1 cup sweetened shredded coconut

1 cup old-fashioned rolled oats (not instant)

- -

TECHNIQUE TIP: When adding mix-in elements like oats, chocolate chips, nuts, or coconut to a dough, be sure to fold them in gently with a rubber spatula, rather than with a standing mixer. The force of the mixer can break these ingredients into smaller pieces, thus changing the overall desired texture of the cookie.

1. Set the oven rack in the middle position. Preheat the oven to 350°F. Line two baking sheets with parchment paper or nonstick silicone baking mats; set aside.

2. In a medium bowl, whisk together the flour and baking soda; set aside.

3. In the bowl of a standing mixer fitted with the paddle attachment, beat the butter, granulated sugar, brown sugar, and salt on medium-high speed until light and fluffy, 2 to 3 minutes, scraping down the sides of the bowl halfway through. Add the eggs one at a time, beating after each addition. Beat in the vanilla.

4. With the mixer on low speed, add the dry ingredients, beating until the flour is absorbed. Gently fold in the chocolate chips and shredded coconut with a rubber scraper. Gently fold in the oats.

5. Use a ¼ cup (2-inch-wide) ice cream scoop to scoop out the dough onto the prepared baking sheets, placing the scoops about 2 inches apart.

6. Bake one sheet at a time, rotating the sheet about two-thirds of the way through the baking time, until the cookies are set and browned on the edges but still very soft in the center, 15 to 18 minutes.

7. Transfer the baking sheet to a wire rack to cool for 10 minutes. Use a spatula to transfer the cookies to the rack and let cool completely.

Macadamia Butterscotch Bars

These rich and chewy bars take traditional blondies to a whole new level. Dense and packed with butterscotch flavor, they're filled with dried cherries, chocolate chunks, and macadamia nuts. Each bite offers a different texture and taste. Feel free to add any of your favorite mix-ins in addition to or as an alternative to those listed below.

MAKES 15 BARS

1 cup dried cherries

2 cups all-purpose flour

¾ teaspoon baking soda

1 cup (2 sticks) unsalted butter, melted

2 cups firmly packed light brown sugar

2 large eggs, at room temperature

2½ tablespoons pure vanilla extract

2 tablespoons light corn syrup

1 teaspoon coarse salt

1 cup coarsely chopped macadamia nuts

1 cup semisweet chocolate chunks

TECHNIQUE TIP: One of the easiest ways to break up nuts into small pieces is to place them on a cutting board and give them a good smack with the back of a heavy pan.

1. Set the oven rack in the middle position. Preheat the oven to 325°F. Spray a 9 by 13-inch baking dish with nonstick cooking spray, or brush with softened butter; set aside.

2. Bring 2 cups of water to a boil. Place the cherries in a small bowl and pour the boiling water over them. Let stand while you put the blondies together.

3. In a small bowl, whisk together the flour and baking soda.

4. Combine the butter and brown sugar in the top of a double boiler and heat over simmering water until the butter melts. Whisk until blended. Remove from the heat and let cool.

5. Whisk in the eggs, vanilla, corn syrup, and salt until blended. Fold in the flour mixture until absorbed. Fold in the nuts and chocolate chunks. Drain the cherries, discarding their soaking liquid, and fold into the batter.

6. Scrape the batter into the prepared pan and bake until a tester inserted in the center comes out clean except for a few crumbs adhering, 40 to 45 minutes. Let cool in the pan on a wire rack, then cut into bars.

Raspberry Chocolate Chip Rugelach

I developed this rugelach for a Martha Stewart Living *television segment around the Jewish holidays. Martha and I made it on air together, and after the cameras were turned off the crew descended on the platter of just-baked rugelach, leaving not a crumb on the plate. This versatile cookie can be made with any favorite jam and/or with nuts in place of the chocolate chips. The recipe requires that you work quickly with one disk of dough at a time, leaving the others in the fridge to stay cold.*

MAKES 45 COOKIES

Dough

- 2⅓ cups all-purpose flour
- ¼ teaspoon baking powder
- 1 cup (2 sticks) unsalted butter, at room temperature
- 8 ounces cream cheese, at room temperature
- ½ cup granulated sugar
- ½ teaspoon coarse salt
- 3 large egg yolks
- 1 teaspoon pure vanilla extract

Filling

- 6 tablespoons granulated sugar
- ⅜ teaspoon ground cinnamon
- ⅜ teaspoon ground allspice
- ¾ cup seedless raspberry jam
- ¾ cup semisweet mini chocolate chips

- 1 large egg, beaten, for egg wash
- ½ cup sanding sugar, for finishing

1. To make the dough: In a mixing bowl, whisk together the flour and baking powder; set aside.

2. In the bowl of a standing mixer fitted with the paddle attachment, beat the butter and cream cheese on medium-high speed until lightened and blended, about 1 minute. Add the sugar and salt and beat until light and fluffy, 1 to 2 more minutes, scraping down the sides of the bowl halfway through. Add the egg yolks, and beat until blended. Beat in the vanilla.

3. With the mixer on low speed, beat in the flour mixture until absorbed.

4. Turn the dough out onto a work surface and divide into three pieces. Shape each piece into a disk. Wrap each disk separately and refrigerate for at least 2 hours, or overnight.

5. Set two racks in the upper and lower thirds of the oven. Preheat the oven to 350°F. Line two baking sheets with parchment paper or nonstick silicone baking mats.

6. To make the filling: In a bowl, stir together the sugar, cinnamon, and allspice; set aside.

7. On a lightly floured work surface, roll out one of the chilled dough disks to a 12-inch round. Spread about ¼ cup of the jam and sprinkle ¼ cup of the chocolate chips over the dough. Sprinkle with about one-third of the sugar-cinnamon mixture. Use a pizza wheel or pastry cutter to cut the dough round into 16 wedges. (Quarter the round first, and cut each quarter into 4.) Starting at the wide base of each wedge, tightly roll up the dough into crescents. Place on the prepared baking sheets. Brush the cookies with egg wash in the same direction as you rolled the crescents so that the egg goes on smoothly and doesn't collect in the layers. Sprinkle generously with sanding sugar.

8. Bake one sheet at a time, rotating the sheet about two-thirds of the way through the baking time, until the cookies are puffed and golden brown, 20 to 25 minutes.

9. Transfer the sheet to a wire rack to cool for 10 minutes. Transfer the parchment paper to the wire rack and let the cookies cool completely.

10. Repeat with the remaining two disks of dough.

SoNo Brownies

Cousin John's was the name of the second bakery I opened, back in 1986. It was, and still is, located in Park Slope, Brooklyn, and is now owned and operated by my cousin Louis. It was there that I first came up with these brownies, which I later perfected at SoNo Baking Company. These dense, fudgy brownies offer a double blast of chocolate flavor from the chocolate chips added for sweetness and the cocoa used for intensity and color. Be sure to use the best quality chocolate available. For a turbo-boost of chocolate, try the Triple Chocolate Ganache variation below. The brownies are covered with a ganache icing and topped with three different types of chocolate—white, milk, and semisweet.

MAKES 16 BROWNIES

½ cup all-purpose flour

½ cup unsweetened cocoa powder

½ teaspoon coarse salt

¼ teaspoon baking powder
Pinch of baking soda

½ cup (1 stick) unsalted butter

1 cup sugar

1 tablespoon light corn syrup

2 large eggs, at room temperature

1 tablespoon pure vanilla extract

1 cup semisweet chocolate chips

1. Set the oven rack in the middle position. Preheat the oven to 350°F. Coat an 8-inch square baking dish with nonstick cooking spray, or brush generously with softened butter; set aside.

2. In a bowl, whisk the flour with the cocoa, salt, baking powder, and baking soda; set aside.

3. In a saucepan, melt the butter over low heat. Remove the pan from the heat. Add the sugar and corn syrup and whisk to combine. Whisk in the eggs one at a time, whisking until well blended after each addition. Whisk in the vanilla.

4. Add the dry ingredients and fold until the flour has been incorporated. Fold in the chocolate chips.

5. Pour the batter into the prepared baking pan and smooth the top with a rubber spatula. Bake until a cake tester inserted in the center comes out clean, about 30 minutes.

6. Let cool completely in the pan on a wire rack, then cut into 2-inch squares.

Variation: TRIPLE CHOCOLATE GANACHE BROWNIES

Bake the brownies and cool completely. Run a knife around the edge of the pan to release the brownies, and then turn the brownies out onto a wire rack.

Heat ¾ cup of Ganache (page 169) in a double boiler until just liquid enough to be spreadable. Pour the ganache over the brownies so that it runs down the sides, and smooth the top with an offset spatula. Let set for at least 1 hour.

In a double boiler, separately melt 1 ounce each semisweet chocolate, milk chocolate, and white chocolate, and transfer each to a separate bowl. Working with one chocolate at a time, dip a fork or spatula into the melted chocolate and wave it back and forth over the brownies to make lines of chocolate. Let set at least 1 hour, then cut into squares.

The Best Lemon Squares

These lush, citrusy bars are double-baked, offering a base layer of shortbread-like cookie flavored with the nutty taste of wheat germ and topped with a baked layer of lemon zest and almond-flavored filling, one of my favorite flavor pairings. The wheat germ was the clever addition of Torie Hallock, caretaker of Martha Stewart's Skylands home in Maine. She suggested adding it for a deeper, more complex flavor, and it makes these bars really stand out.

MAKES 20 SQUARES

Crust

2¼ cups all-purpose flour

⅓ cup toasted wheat germ

⅓ cup confectioners' sugar

¾ teaspoon coarse salt

1¼ cups (2½ sticks) cold unsalted butter, cut into small pieces

Filling

1¾ cups plus 2 tablespoons granulated sugar

⅓ cup all-purpose flour

¼ teaspoon salt

¾ cup lemon juice (from about 5 lemons), plus 1 tablespoon grated lemon zest

½ teaspoon almond extract

3 large eggs, at room temperature

1 egg yolk, at room temperature

3 to 4 tablespoons confectioners' sugar, for dusting

TECHNIQUE TIP: To get a nice, clean slice when you're cutting a dense, moist cake or bar such as a cheesecake, flourless chocolate cake, or lemon bar, dip a chef's knife into hot water and wipe off the moisture with a towel. Cut into the cake or bars, and continue dipping into hot water and toweling off after every cut.

1. Coat a 9 by 13-inch glass baking dish with nonstick cooking spray, or generously brush with softened butter; set aside.

2. To make the crust: In a large bowl, whisk together the flour, wheat germ, confectioners' sugar, and salt. Add the butter, and working quickly, use your fingers to work the butter into the dry ingredients until the mixture resembles coarse crumbs. Make sure the butter is broken down into very small pieces (no larger than pea-size).

3. Press the dough over the bottom and about one-third of the way up the sides of the baking dish. Refrigerate for 30 minutes.

4. Set the oven rack in the middle position. Preheat the oven to 350°F.

5. Bake, rotating the pan about halfway through the cooking, until the crust turns an even blond color and is cooked through and crisp, 15 to 17 minutes. Remove the pan from the oven. Keep the oven at 350°F.

6. To make the filling: In a large bowl, whisk the sugar with the flour and salt. Add the lemon juice and zest, and the almond extract. Whisk in the eggs and egg yolk. Pour over the warm crust.

7. Bake the bars until the filling sets and the very center still jiggles slightly, 18 to 20 minutes.

8. Cool completely in the pan on a wire rack. Sift confectioners' sugar over the top. Cut into squares.

Raspberry Linzer Bars

Created in Austria, Linzer cookies are now an American bakery standard. At the SoNo Baking Company we tried to mix it up a bit by making them into chewy bars. We save the sliced tops from chocolate cakes and add them to the Linzer dough when creaming the butter and sugar. The cake breaks down into crumbs that add flavor and give the cookie a nice color.

MAKES 20 BARS

1 recipe Linzer Pastry (page 92), chilled

1½ cups seedless raspberry jam

1 large egg white, beaten, for glaze

2 to 3 tablespoons sanding sugar, for finishing

1. Set an oven rack in the middle position. Preheat the oven to 350°F. Spray a 9 by 13-inch rimmed cookie sheet with nonstick cooking spray, or brush generously with butter.

2. Remove one dough piece from the refrigerator. On a lightly floured work surface, roll the dough out between two sheets of parchment paper to a rectangle about 10 by 14 inches. Fit the dough into the bottom and up the sides of the prepared cookie sheet. Spread with the jam.

3. Roll the second dough piece to a rectangle about 9 by 13 inches. Chill for a few minutes if the dough is warm. Use a pizza wheel or pastry cutter and a ruler to cut ½-inch-wide strips. Lay half of the strips lengthwise, about ½ inch apart, over the jam. Lay the remaining strips over the first strips at a right angle, cutting and piecing as necessary, to make a lattice design. Brush the pastry all over with egg white and sprinkle with sanding sugar.

4. Bake, rotating the cookie sheet about two-thirds of the way through the baking time, until the pastry has puffed and is lightly browned, 30 to 35 minutes.

5. Transfer the sheet to a wire rack to cool completely. Cut into squares with a sharp knife.

Linzer Pastry

If you don't want to bother skinning hazelnuts, you can either buy whole toasted, skinned hazelnuts, or use chopped raw hazelnuts and toast them yourself on a baking sheet at 375°F for 5 to 8 minutes, until golden brown and fragrant. Be careful to not let them burn.

MAKES ENOUGH FOR TWO
SINGLE-CRUST 9-INCH
TARTS OR ONE DOUBLE-
CRUST 9-INCH TART
(OR 20 BARS)

12 ounces (3 cups) hazelnuts
2¼ cups all-purpose flour
1 teaspoon baking powder
¾ teaspoon ground cinnamon
½ teaspoon grated nutmeg
1 cup plus 3 tablespoons sugar
1 cup (2 sticks) unsalted butter, at room temperature
¾ teaspoon coarse salt
2 large eggs, at room temperature
1½ teaspoons pure vanilla extract

1. Preheat the oven to 350°F.

2. Place the hazelnuts in a single layer on a baking sheet and bake until they are lightly colored and the skins are blistered and cracking, 10 to 15 minutes. Wrap in a kitchen towel and let steam for 1 minute. Rub the nuts in the towel to rub off as many of the skins as possible, but don't worry about the skins that stick; set aside to cool completely.

3. In a medium bowl, whisk together the flour, baking powder, cinnamon, and nutmeg; set aside.

4. In a food processor, pulse the toasted hazelnuts with 3 tablespoons of the sugar until finely ground. (Be careful not to overprocess, as the nuts will turn into an oily paste.) Transfer to the bowl of a standing mixer fitted with the paddle attachment. Add the butter, the remaining 1 cup sugar, and the salt, and beat on medium-high speed until light and fluffy, about 2 minutes, scraping down the sides of the bowl halfway through. Beat in the eggs one at a time, beating well after each addition. Beat in the vanilla.

5. Add the dry ingredients and beat on low speed until the flour is absorbed.

6. Scrape the dough onto a work surface and divide in half. Shape each half into a thin rectangle, wrap in plastic, and refrigerate until firm, at least 2 hours.

Coconut Chocolate Chip Bars

This recipe is SoNo Baking Company's take on traditional magic cookie bars. Our recipe features two distinct layers: the base, which consists of a brown sugar shortbread-like cookie crust, and the top layer, a rich, chewy oatmeal-coconut-chocolate-chip cookie. Use any favorite nut or dried fruit as a variation to what's listed below.

MAKES ABOUT 20 BARS

Crust

10 tablespoons (1 stick plus 2 tablespoons) unsalted butter, at room temperature

½ cup plus 2 tablespoons light brown sugar

¼ teaspoon coarse salt

2 teaspoons pure vanilla extract

1¾ cups all-purpose flour

Filling

1½ cups light brown sugar

½ teaspoon coarse salt

3 large eggs, at room temperature

1 tablespoon pure vanilla extract

2 tablespoons all-purpose flour

1½ cups sweetened shredded coconut

6 tablespoons old-fashioned rolled oats (not instant)

1½ cups macadamia nuts, coarsely chopped

1 cup semisweet chocolate chips

1. Set the oven rack in the middle position. Preheat the oven to 350°F. Butter a 9 by 13-inch baking dish; set aside.

2. To make the crust: In the bowl of a standing mixer fitted with the paddle attachment, beat the butter with the brown sugar and salt on medium speed until light and fluffy, about 3 minutes, scraping down the sides of the bowl halfway through. Beat in the vanilla. With the mixer on low speed, beat in the flour until absorbed.

3. Press the dough over the bottom of the prepared baking dish. Set on a baking sheet and bake, rotating the sheet about halfway through the cooking time, until the crust turns an even blond color and is cooked through and crisp, 10 to 12 minutes. Remove the baking dish from the oven. Do not turn off the oven.

4. To make the filling: In a large bowl, whisk the brown sugar with the salt. Add the eggs and vanilla and whisk to blend. Whisk in the flour. Fold in the coconut, oats, and nuts. Spread the filling over the crust. Sprinkle with the chocolate chips.

5. Bake, rotating the pan about two-thirds of the way through the baking time, until the filling is set to a soft, chewy, cookie-like texture, 20 to 25 minutes. Let cool completely in the pan on a wire rack. Cut into bars approximately 2¼ by 2½ inches.

Pecan Squares

I learned how to make these rich bars at the Culinary Institute of America, and I further mastered them at the Louis XVI restaurant in the Marie Antoinette hotel in New Orleans, where I worked during my baking externship. The bars are almost toffee-like with their praline caramel filling baked into a Pâte Sucrée crust. They are great as wrapped gifts during the holidays. They also travel well and will last up to 2 weeks in an airtight container.

MAKES 72 SQUARES

1 **recipe Pâte Sucrée (page 99)**
1 **cup (2 sticks) unsalted butter, cut into tablespoons**
1 **cup light brown sugar**
2 **tablespoons granulated sugar**
¾ **cup honey**
¼ **cup heavy cream**
¼ **teaspoon coarse salt**
4 **cups pecans, coarsely chopped**

1. Set the oven rack in the middle position. Preheat the oven to 350°F.

2. On a lightly floured work surface, use a rolling pin to roll out the dough to the dimensions of the baking sheet. Carefully transfer the dough to a rimmed sheet and with the back of a spoon or your fingers, press the dough into the pan from corner to corner. Bake until lightly golden, 20 to 25 minutes. Transfer the baking sheet to a wire rack to cool. Leave the oven on.

3. In a medium saucepan, bring the butter, sugars, honey, heavy cream, and salt to a boil, stirring constantly. Add the pecans and continue to stir until it is back to a boil, then cook 2 minutes longer. The caramel should be golden in color. Remove from the heat. Using an offset spatula, spread the caramel over the cooled crust. Bake until the filling is bubbling and jiggles slightly in the center, about 15 minutes.

4. Let cool in the baking sheet on a wire rack, then cut into 1½-inch squares.

Pies and Tarts

Pâte Brisée

Pâte Sucrée

Apple Handpies

Mile-high Apple Pie

Pumpkin Pie

Cranberry Pear Pie with
Streusel Topping

Chocolate Cream Pie

Individual Tarte Tatins

Apple Cranberry Crostata

Apple Pizzette

Plum Tart

French Blueberry Tartlets

Blueberry Coconut Tartlets

Banana Almond Tart

Lemon Meringue Tart

Jam Tartlets

Torta Della Nonna

Pasta Frolla

Maple Pecan Tart

Coconut Cream Tart

Chocolate Truffle Tart

Crème Brûlée Tartlets

The SoNo Baking Company and Café always offers a variety of seasonal pies and tarts. Maple Pecan Tart (page 127) in autumn, Coconut Cream Tart (page 128) in winter, Jam Tartlets (page 123) in spring, French Blueberry Tartlets (page 115) in summer are just a few examples. The combinations of sweet luscious fruits, nuts, or chocolate in a buttery, flaky pastry are limitless.

Regardless of what pie or tart you choose to bake, it all comes down to the crust. An overhandled crust or one that has too much flour or water will result in a less than perfect dessert. Most of the pies and tarts in this book call for a basic Pâte Brisée dough (page 98) or Pâte Sucrée dough (page 99). Pâte Brisée is made by incorporating little pebbles of chilled butter into flour and adding a touch of ice-cold water to combine, for a layered, flaky crust. Pâte Sucrée is made by beating room-temperature butter with sugar and salt, and eventually adding egg and flour. It produces a sweeter, richer dough. Once you make them, you'll never be able to go back to the store-bought version again!

A couple of tips to keep in mind for perfect pie and tart crusts: when it comes to pastry, coldness is essential. When making Pâte Brisée, make sure the butter is in the refrigerator until just before it's added to the flour. Don't overhandle it or it will warm the dough. Add ice water to the flour-butter mixture so that the dough forms a ball and then wrap it in plastic wrap and get it into the refrigerator immediately; chill it for at least an hour. Keep in mind that when making Pâte Sucrée, you'll need to refrigerate the dough at least 2 hours before using it. Refrigerate both doughs again after they are rolled out and fitted to the pie plate or tart pan. Either of these doughs can be frozen for up to one month before it is rolled out and baked; thaw the disk in the refrigerator for a few hours before rolling it.

For a nice accompaniment, all of these pies and tarts can be served with a scoop of vanilla or cinnamon ice cream or a dollop of whipped cream or crème fraîche.

Pâte Brisée

This rich, flaky, butter-based dough can be used for both savory and sweet pies, tarts, and quiches. Wrapped well, it can last for up to a month in the freezer.

MAKES ENOUGH FOR ONE
DOUBLE-CRUST OR TWO
SINGLE-CRUST 9-INCH PIES

2¼ cups all-purpose flour

2 teaspoons sugar

1 teaspoon coarse salt

1 cup (2 sticks) cold unsalted butter, cut into small pieces

¼ cup ice water

- - - - - - - - - - - - - - - - - -

TECHNIQUE TIP: When making dough, not only should the ingredients be cold (including dry ingredients), but so should your equipment, including the bowl and blade of your food processor or bowl and attachment of your standing mixer.

1. In the bowl of a food processor, combine the flour, sugar, and salt. Add the butter and pulse until the mixture resembles coarse crumbs, about 10 seconds. With the machine running, add the ice water through the feed tube in a slow and steady stream, a little bit at a time until the dough just comes together. The dough should not be wet or sticky. If the dough is too dry and does not hold together, add a little more water.

2. Turn the dough out onto a clean work surface. Divide in two and wrap each half in plastic wrap, shaping them into flattened disks. Chill at least 1 hour before using.

Pâte Sucrée

This sweet dough incorporates both egg and egg yolk to form a sweet and rich crust for pies and tarts.

MAKES ENOUGH FOR ONE
DOUBLE-CRUST OR TWO
SINGLE-CRUST 9-INCH PIES

- 2 **cups all-purpose flour**
- 1 **cup (2 sticks) unsalted butter at room temperature**
- ¼ **cup sugar**
- 1 **teaspoon coarse salt**
- 1 **large egg**
- 1 **large egg yolk**

- -

TECHNIQUE TIP: Roll sweet dough with as little flour as possible—too much flour makes the dough break and alters the recipe. Instead, when the dough starts to stick, slide an offset spatula or bench scraper underneath, freeing the dough, continuing to turn it as you do so.

1. In a bowl, whisk the flour to aerate it; set aside.

2. In the bowl of a standing mixer fitted with the paddle attachment, beat the butter, sugar, and salt on medium-high speed until light and fluffy, about 3 minutes, scraping down the sides of the bowl halfway through. Add the egg and yolk, and mix to combine. Add the flour and beat until it has been absorbed.

3. Scoop about half of the dough onto a sheet of plastic wrap, shape into a flattened disk, and wrap in the plastic. Do the same for the other half. Refrigerate until firm, at least 2 hours.

Apple Handpies

These turnovers offer two different textures of cooked Granny Smith apples wrapped in pillowy puff pastry. Here, they are made into half-moon shapes, but you can also make them into triangles, rectangles, or squares. You can also use a variety of fruits for these pies, including peaches, pears, plums, and berries. Use the best quality store-bought puff pastry you can find (Dufour makes a good one). And be sure to thaw it in the refrigerator, not on the counter, for 2 to 3 hours before using.

MAKES EIGHT 4-INCH
TURNOVERS

2 tablespoons unsalted butter

2 tablespoons granulated sugar

¼ teaspoon ground cinnamon
    Pinch of salt

2 Granny Smith apples, peeled, cored, and sliced
    Juice of ½ lemon

1 (14-ounce) sheet frozen puff pastry, thawed (13½" by 11½")

1 large egg, beaten, for egg wash

1 to 2 tablespoons coarse sanding sugar, for finishing

TECHNIQUE TIP: At the bakery we use two kinds of egg wash: basic egg wash, which consists of beaten whole egg (for most cookies), and deluxe egg wash, which consists of beaten egg combined with beaten egg yolk (for breads like Challah, page 229). When using egg wash to adhere one piece of dough to another (as with the Apple Handpies here), be sure to brush only one side of the dough with egg. If you brush both sides, they will fail to adhere to each other.

1. In a medium saucepan, combine the butter, sugar, cinnamon, and salt over medium-low heat and stir to melt the butter. Add the apple slices and the lemon juice. Cook, stirring often, until the apples are tender but not cooked into a puree, about 15 minutes. In the pan, use a potato masher or fork to mash about one-quarter of the apples, creating a chunky sauce to help bind the rest of the apple slices. Stir it all together; set aside to cool.

2. Set the oven rack in the middle position. Preheat the oven to 425°F. Line a baking sheet with parchment paper or a nonstick silicone baking mat; set aside.

3. On a lightly floured work surface, roll the dough to about ⅛ inch thick and smooth the folds. Use a pastry cutter to cut eight 4-inch rounds. Brush around half of the rim of each round with egg wash. Spoon a rounded tablespoon of the apple mixture into the center of each. Starting with the half that has not been egg-washed, fold half of the dough round over the filling to enclose it and make a half-moon-shaped package. Press the edges together with your fingers and press all the way along the folded edge with the tines of a fork to make a decorative edging. Place on the prepared baking sheet. Brush all over with egg wash. Sprinkle the tops of the turnovers with sanding sugar, and cut vents to allow the steam to escape.

4. Bake, rotating the baking sheet about two-thirds of the way through the baking time, until the pastries are golden brown and puffed, about 15 minutes. Transfer to a wire rack and let cool.

Mile-high Apple Pie

True to its name, this pie has a bounty of apples. The fruit is sliced thick, providing more texture per bite. This pie is my son Nikolai's favorite, and he boasts that he can eat this entire pie in one sitting. I've seen him come pretty close and have no doubt that he will soon achieve his goal! Use a 9-inch deep pie plate to accommodate this pie. Serve with a big scoop of vanilla bean ice cream.

MAKES ONE 9½-INCH
DOUBLE-CRUST PIE,
SERVES 10

3 pounds (about 7 medium) Granny Smith apples, peeled, cored, and cut into ½-inch-thick wedges
Juice of 1 lemon
½ cup granulated sugar
2 tablespoons all-purpose flour
1 teaspoon coarse salt
¾ teaspoon ground cinnamon
Pinch of grated nutmeg
1 recipe Pâte Brisée (page 98), chilled
3 tablespoons unsalted butter, cut into bits
1 large egg, lightly beaten, for egg wash
1 to 2 tablespoons sanding sugar, for finishing

1. In a large bowl, toss the apple slices with the lemon juice, sugar, flour, salt, cinnamon, and nutmeg (note: don't toss too far ahead of time, because the salt will draw the moisture out of the apples, leaving a lot of liquid).

2. Set the oven rack in the lower third of the oven. Preheat the oven to 425°F. Line a baking sheet with a nonstick silicone baking mat.

3. On a lightly floured work surface, roll out one dough disk to a 12-inch round and fit it into a deep 9-inch pie plate. Mound the apple mixture into the crust. Dot with the butter. Brush the rim of the pie shell with egg wash.

4. Roll the second dough disk to an 11-inch round. Place it on top of the apples, and press top and bottom edges together to seal. Trim the dough to a 1-inch overhang and crimp the edges. Brush the top crust all over with egg wash and sprinkle generously with sanding sugar. Cut an *X* (each cut about 2 inches long) in the center of the top crust, and gently fold back the corners to make a "chimney" to allow the steam to escape.

5. Set the pie plate on the prepared baking sheet. Bake for 20 minutes. Reduce the oven heat to 375°F and bake, rotating the baking sheet about two-thirds of the way through the baking time, until the crust is golden brown and the juices are bubbling through the slits cut in the top crust, 40 to 50 minutes longer.

6. Transfer the pie to a wire rack to cool, and let sit for at least 2 hours to let the juices be absorbed.

Pumpkin Pie

This traditional pie is Veronica's most-requested dessert. When I was courting her, it was this dessert that really won her over. Now she makes this failproof pie year-round. At the bakery we serve it mostly in the fall and winter. Serve with whipped cream, crème fraîche, or Greek yogurt, sprinkled with cinnamon.

MAKES ONE 9-INCH PIE, SERVES 10

2 **large eggs, at room temperature**

1 **(15-ounce) can pumpkin puree**

¾ **cup firmly packed light brown sugar**

1 **teaspoon coarse salt**

1 **teaspoon ground cinnamon**

½ **teaspoon ground ginger**

¼ **teaspoon ground cloves**

¾ **cup half-and-half**

½ **recipe Pâte Brisée (page 98), chilled**

- -

TECHNIQUE TIP: Always bake pies with a pastry crust in the lower third of the oven so that the bottom crust crisps up when cooking. Also, there's no need to butter pie pans because the pastry you're working with already has lots of butter in it.

1. In a large bowl, whisk the eggs until blended. Whisk in the pumpkin, brown sugar, salt, cinnamon, ginger, and cloves until smooth. Whisk in the half-and-half.

2. On a lightly floured work surface, roll the dough to a 12-inch round, about ⅛ inch thick. Fit the dough into a 9-inch fluted tart pan with a removable bottom, and trim the dough so that it comes slightly above the rim of the tart pan. Then press the excess dough against the sharp edge of the rim of the pan with your fingers to cut it level with the pan. Chill until firm, about 30 minutes.

3. Set the oven rack in the bottom third of the oven. Preheat the oven to 350°F. Line a baking sheet with parchment paper or a nonstick silicone baking mat.

4. Pour the pumpkin mixture into the pie shell. Set the tart pan on the prepared baking sheet. Bake, rotating the sheet about two-thirds of the way through the baking time, until the crust is golden brown and the custard has set so that a tester inserted into the center comes out clean, 55 to 60 minutes. Transfer the tart pan to a wire rack and let cool to room temperature.

Cranberry Pear Pie with Streusel Topping

Pears and cranberries make for a welcome autumn flavor combination. Here, the cranberries are cooked down into a sauce (that can also be served alongside roast turkey, chicken, and pork) and tossed with the pears. It's best to make the cranberry sauce the day before using, so that it has time to thicken. Use it cold or at room temperature. Serve with whipped crème fraîche.

MAKES ONE 9-INCH PIE, SERVES 10

Cranberry Sauce

- ½ cup granulated sugar
- ½ cup water
- 6 ounces (1¾ cups) fresh or frozen cranberries
- Pinch of coarse salt
- Grated zest of ½ orange
- 1 small cinnamon stick

- ½ recipe Pâte Brisée (page 98)

Streusel Topping

- 1 cup all-purpose flour
- 1 cup light brown sugar
- ½ teaspoon coarse salt
- ¼ teaspoon ground cinnamon
- ½ cup (1 stick) cold unsalted butter, cut into small cubes

Pie Filling

- 1 pound (6 to 7) Anjou or Bosc pears, peeled and cored, cut into 1-inch pieces
- ¼ cup granulated sugar
- ½ teaspoon ground cinnamon
- ¼ teaspoon grated nutmeg
- 2 tablespoons all-purpose flour

1. To make the cranberry sauce: In a medium saucepan, bring the sugar and water to a boil. Add the cranberries, salt, zest, and cinnamon stick. Simmer over medium to low heat until the cranberries begin to break down and become juicy, about 10 minutes.

2. Transfer to a small bowl. Remove the cinnamon stick. Cover with plastic wrap, pressing the wrap directly onto the surface of the sauce to prevent a skin from forming. Refrigerate overnight (or up to 1 week).

3. To prepare the crust: On a lightly floured surface, roll out the disk of dough to a 12-inch round and fit it into a 9-inch pie plate, pressing into the edges. Trim to a ½-inch overhang all around and use your fingertips to crimp the edges. Chill until firm, 30 minutes.

4. Set the oven rack in the bottom third of the oven. Preheat the oven to 425°F. Line a baking sheet with a nonstick silicone baking mat.

5. To make the streusel topping: In a medium bowl, use a fork to stir together the flour, brown sugar, salt, and cinnamon. Add the butter, and using your fingertips, quickly work it into the dry ingredients until pea-size crumbs form; set aside in the refrigerator.

6. To make the filling: In a medium bowl, toss together the pears, sugar, cinnamon, nutmeg, flour, and 1 cup of the cranberry sauce. Pour the mixture into the prepared pie shell. Sprinkle the streusel topping over the top, covering it completely.

7. Place the pie plate on the prepared baking sheet, and bake for 20 minutes. Reduce the heat to 375°F and continue baking until the streusel turns golden brown and the juices begin to bubble, 30 to 40 minutes. Transfer to a wire rack and let cool completely, at least 1 hour, to let the juices be absorbed. Serve at room temperature.

Chocolate Cream Pie

When I was young, anything made with chocolate pudding was always a favorite of my family's. I came from a family of eight boys, so we all had to make sure we were at the dinner table on time in order to get dessert—or even dinner, for that matter! No one was ever late to the table on the nights chocolate pudding was served. I'm sure my brothers and I would still fight to this day over the last slice of this velvety chocolate custard pie. While it is oftentimes made with a pastry crust, I prefer a graham cracker crust flavored with grated chocolate for extra chocolaty flavor in every bite. To save time, you can use store-bought graham cracker crumbs for easier preparation.

MAKES ONE 9-INCH PIE,
SERVES 10

Chocolate–Graham Cracker Crust

- 1¼ **cups graham cracker crumbs (7 graham crackers pulsed to crumbs in a food processor)**
- 5 **tablespoons unsalted butter, melted and cooled slightly**
- 3 **tablespoons granulated sugar**
- ⅛ **teaspoon coarse salt**
- 1⅔ **ounces semisweet chocolate, coarsely grated on the large holes of a grater (about ½ cup)**

Chocolate Pastry Cream

- 6 **large egg yolks**
- ¾ **cup granulated sugar**
- ⅓ **cup cornstarch**
- 3 **cups milk**
- ⅓ **cup unsweetened cocoa powder**
- 4 **ounces semisweet chocolate, finely chopped**
- ¼ **teaspoon coarse salt**
- 1 **vanilla bean, split in half lengthwise, or 1 tablespoon pure vanilla extract**
- 4 **tablespoons (½ stick) cold unsalted butter, cut into ½-inch pieces**

1. Set the oven rack in the middle position. Preheat the oven to 350°F. Line a baking sheet with parchment paper or a nonstick silicone baking mat; set aside. Brush the bottom and sides of a 9-inch pie plate with softened butter; set aside.

2. To make the graham cracker crust: In a large bowl, mix the crumbs, butter, sugar, and salt. Add the chocolate and mix thoroughly. Press the graham cracker mixture onto the bottom and up the sides of the prepared pie plate. Chill the crust for at least 20 minutes.

3. Set the chilled piecrust on the prepared baking sheet and bake until you can smell the chocolate and butter cooking, and the edges of the crust are browning gently, 18 to 20 minutes. Transfer the baking sheet to a wire rack and let cool.

4. To make the pastry cream: In a medium bowl, whisk together the egg yolks, about half of the sugar, all the cornstarch, and ½ cup of the milk.

5. In a saucepan, combine the rest of the sugar, the remaining 2½ cups milk, the cocoa, chocolate, and salt. If using a vanilla bean, scrape the tiny black seeds into the saucepan and add the pod. Bring to a simmer. Whisking constantly, gradually pour the hot milk into the egg mixture to temper it. Set a strainer over the saucepan. Strain the custard mixture back into the saucepan and bring to a boil over medium heat, whisking constantly. Boil for 10 seconds, whisking. (Make sure the custard boils for 10 seconds in the center of the pan, not just around the sides.) The mixture should thicken to a pudding-like consistency. Discard the vanilla bean, if using.

6. Transfer the pastry cream to the bowl of a standing mixer fitted with the paddle attachment and beat on medium speed for 2 to 3 minutes, to cool slightly. Beat in the vanilla extract, if using. With the mixer running, beat in the butter, a little at a time.

7. Pour the pastry cream into the pie shell and smooth the top. Refrigerate until very cold, 2 to 3 hours.

8. Combine the heavy cream and confectioners' sugar in the bowl of a standing mixer fitted with the whisk attachment and beat until soft peaks form (or beat by hand with a whisk). Spread over the chocolate cream. Refrigerate until ready to serve.

Whipped Cream

¾ cup heavy cream

2 tablespoons confectioners' sugar

Individual Tarte Tatins

I first learned to make this classic dessert at Le Cordon Bleu Cooking School in Paris. I later developed them into these sweet-looking individual apple pastries at the Elms Restaurant in Ridgefield, Connecticut. The classic version calls for puff pastry, which can be labor-intensive to make. Instead we use Pâte Brisée, which can be made more easily and more quickly. You can make this dessert with ripe, firm pears instead of apples, if you prefer. You will need four 6-inch individual slope-sided pans for this recipe.

MAKES FOUR 6-INCH TARTS

½ **recipe Pâte Brisée (page 98), chilled**

Caramel

¾ **cup sugar**
6 **tablespoons water**
¾ **teaspoon white vinegar**

8 **teaspoons unsalted butter**
3 **Granny Smith apples, cored, peeled, and quartered**

1. On a lightly floured work surface, divide the dough into four pieces and roll each to a round slightly larger than your pie pans. Place on a parchment-lined baking sheet; chill.

2. Set the oven rack in the middle position. Preheat the oven to 400°F. Generously butter four 6-inch slope-sided pie pans and place them on a baking sheet lined with a nonstick silicone baking mat; set aside.

3. To make the caramel: In a small saucepan, combine the sugar, 4 tablespoons of the water, and the vinegar. Bring to a boil over medium-high heat, swirling the pan to dissolve the sugar. Boil until the mixture turns a deep amber color, 5 to 10 minutes.

4. Remove from the heat and add the remaining 2 tablespoons water; stand back—the caramel will spit. Swirl to combine. Return to the heat if necessary to re-melt the caramel.

5. Divide the caramel evenly among the four prepared pie pans. Dot each surface with 2 teaspoons butter.

6. Arrange 3 apple quarters, rounded sides down, on top of the caramel in each pie pan. Top each pie with a round of pastry, tucking it around the apples to cover them entirely.

7. Bake until the crust is cooked through, you can see caramel bubbling up from the bottom, and the apples are tender when you peek under the dough and pierce with a tester, about 25 minutes. Remove from the oven and let stand for 5 minutes. Using tongs, carefully invert the pans onto a wire rack set over a sheet pan to catch the drippings; remove the pans with the tongs. Immediately place the tarts on serving plates and top with the remaining pan drippings.

Apple Cranberry Crostata

One of the best perks of working at Martha Stewart Living Television was getting to work side by side in the prep kitchen with hundreds of top chefs from around the world. George Germon and Johanne Killeen of Al Forno restaurant in Providence, Rhode Island, were two such chefs. This homey, rustic open-face tart was inspired by the fresh fruit crostata we made together for a show segment. It's a fall classic with a loose free-form shape for easy assemblage.

MAKES ONE 10-INCH
CROSTATA, SERVES 8

1½ **pounds Granny Smith apples (about 3), cored, peeled, and cut into ½-inch-thick slices**

1 **cup fresh or frozen (unthawed) cranberries**
Juice of ½ lemon

¼ **cup granulated sugar**

1 **tablespoon all-purpose flour**

½ **teaspoon coarse salt**

½ **teaspoon ground cinnamon**

⅛ **teaspoon ground allspice**
Pinch of grated nutmeg

½ **recipe Pâte Brisée (page 98), chilled**

2 **tablespoons cold unsalted butter, cut into ¼-inch bits**

1 **large egg, lightly beaten, for egg wash**

1 **to 2 tablespoons sanding sugar, for finishing**

1. Set the oven rack in the lower third of the oven. Preheat the oven to 425°F. Line a baking sheet with a nonstick silicone baking mat (do not use parchment paper, as the crostata will stick to it).

2. In a large bowl, toss the apple slices with the cranberries, lemon juice, sugar, flour, salt, cinnamon, allspice, and nutmeg.

3. On a lightly floured work surface, roll out the dough to a 14-inch round and place on the prepared baking sheet. Mound the apple-cranberry mixture in the center of the dough round. Dot with the butter. Fold the edges of the dough round in toward the center to make a 2-inch border of dough all around. Brush the dough with egg glaze. Sprinkle generously with sanding sugar.

4. Bake the crostata for 20 minutes. Reduce the oven heat to 375°F. Rotate the baking sheet and continue baking until the crust is golden brown and the apple mixture is bubbling, about 20 more minutes. Let cool fully on the baking sheet before transferring to a platter and serving.

TECHNIQUE TIP: When rolling out dough, instead of contorting your body and turning the rolling pin in various angles, which can be awkward, roll out dough from top to bottom, using an up-and-down motion with the rolling pin, turning the dough a quarter-turn every few rolls, for even pressure and roll-out.

Apple Pizzette

I started making this dessert when I worked at the renowned New York restaurant Le Bernardin. At the bakery we call this a pizzette because it is as thin as a Neapolitan pizza pie. The apples sit in ¼ inch of puff pastry layered with applesauce. They are topped with butter and confectioners' sugar, which helps to caramelize them in the oven as the pizzette bakes. At the restaurant we used to make individual portions, top them with spun-sugar cages, and serve them with caramel ice cream. Try also serving with whipped crème fraîche, vanilla ice cream, or whipped mascarpone cheese alongside.

MAKES ONE 12-INCH RECTANGULAR TART, SERVES 10

1 pound frozen puff pastry, thawed

½ cup good-quality applesauce

3 Granny Smith apples, peeled, cored, halved, and cut into ⅛-inch thick (vertical) slices

5 tablespoons unsalted butter, melted

3 to 4 tablespoons confectioners' sugar, for dusting

1 cup apricot jam

1. On a lightly floured work surface, roll out the puff pastry to a 12 by 10-inch rectangle, about ⅛ inch thick. Prick the dough all over with a fork. Transfer the dough to a baking sheet lined with a nonstick silicone baking mat. Chill for 30 minutes.

2. Set the oven rack in the middle position. Preheat the oven to 425°F.

3. Pour the applesauce onto the center of the dough, and using an offset spatula, spread the sauce over the dough, leaving a ½-inch border all around. Arrange the apple slices on top of the applesauce in four tight overlapping rows. Brush with the melted butter and dust heavily with confectioners' sugar.

4. Bake, rotating the sheet two-thirds of the way through the baking time, until golden brown, 25 to 30 minutes. Transfer to a wire rack.

5. While the pizzette is still warm, in a small saucepan, warm the apricot jam over low heat until liquid. Strain through a fine strainer. Brush the top of the pizzette with the strained jam. Using a pizza wheel, cut into squares and serve warm.

Plum Tart

When I worked with Martha Stewart, one of my jobs was to assist her with planning the menu for all of her weekend entertaining. One summer night Martha hosted a dinner party and asked me to serve a plum tart for dessert. We ended up using eight different varieties and hybrids of plums, including apricots, pluots, and plumcots, which produced a rainbow of lush purple and red hues. For the recipe below I would suggest using ripe black plums such as Santa Rosa or Black Beauty. They turn a beautiful purple color when you bake them. Feel free to experiment with different varieties of plums for a range of color. The combination of plums and almond cream is a variation of the traditional French apricot frangipane tart.

MAKES ONE 9-INCH TART (SERVES 10) OR EIGHT 3½-INCH TARTLETS

½ recipe Pâte Sucrée (page 99), chilled

Almond Cream

½ cup blanched whole almonds

6 tablespoons sugar

1 teaspoon coarse salt

6 tablespoons (¾ stick) unsalted butter, at room temperature

2 large eggs, at room temperature

1½ teaspoons almond extract

3 tablespoons all-purpose flour

¾ cup apricot jam, strained

1¼ to 1½ pounds (6 to 8) ripe plums, halved, pitted, and cut into ½-inch wedges

1 to 2 tablespoons sugar, for sprinkling

1. On a lightly floured work surface, roll the dough to a 12-inch round, about ⅛ inch thick. Fit the dough into a 9-inch fluted tart pan with a removable bottom, and trim the dough so that it comes slightly above the rim of the tart pan. Then press the excess dough against the sharp edge of the rim of the pan with the heel of your hand to cut it level with the pan. Chill until firm, about 30 minutes.

2. To make the almond cream: In a food processor, pulse the almonds with the sugar and salt for about 10 seconds, until finely ground. Add the butter and process to blend. Add the eggs, processing until blended and scraping the bowl after each addition. Add the almond extract. Add the flour and process until combined.

3. Set the oven rack in the bottom third of the oven. Preheat the oven to 375°F. Line a baking sheet with a nonstick silicone baking mat.

4. Use an offset spatula to spread the tart shell with ¼ cup of the apricot jam. Then spread with the almond cream. Arrange the plum wedges side by side, rounded sides down, on top of the cream, and press gently to settle them. Place the tart on the prepared baking sheet. Sprinkle all over with the sugar.

5. Bake, rotating the baking sheet about two-thirds of the way through the baking time, until the crust is cooked through and golden brown, and the almond cream is puffed and golden, 40 to 45 minutes. Transfer the tart pan to a wire rack.

RECIPE CONTINUES . . .

TECHNIQUE TIP: Some bakers like to trim pie and tart crusts by rolling the rolling pin over the pie plate or tart pan. I warn against this as it can damage a wooden rolling pan, causing small indentations from the metal rim of the pan. Instead, I prefer to chill the dough, including the overhang, and then use the base of my palm to "push" or "sweep" the excess dough away and off the edges of the pan.

6. While the tart is still warm, in a small saucepan, warm the remaining ½ cup apricot jam over low heat until liquid. Strain through a fine strainer. Brush the top of the tart with the strained jam. Allow the tart to cool completely.

7. Set the tart on top of a large can, and allow the sides of the tart pan to fall. Cut the tart into wedges and serve.

French Blueberry Tartlets

Piled high with fresh blueberries, these individual fruit tarts offer a sweet, creamy custard surprise in the center. Try making these with raspberries or strawberries, or an assortment of berries. Set one whole perfect berry in the center of each tart, and surround with berries (or halves, if strawberries), shingled slightly to entirely cover the pastry cream. When one bites into the tart, the cream comes as a surprise. Each tartlet uses very little pastry cream, so you'll have some left over, which can be used as a garnish and served alongside the tarts.

MAKES FIVE 3-INCH TARTLETS

½ **cup sliced almonds**

Pastry Cream

2 **large egg yolks**
¼ **cup sugar**
2 **tablespoons cornstarch**
1 **cup milk**
⅛ **teaspoon salt**
½ **vanilla bean, split in half lengthwise, or 1½ teaspoons pure vanilla extract**
2 **tablespoons unsalted butter**

½ **recipe Pâte Sucrée (page 99), chilled**
¼ **cup apricot jam**
3 **pints large, firm blueberries**

- -

TECHNIQUE TIP: Tart shells made with Pâte Sucrée dough don't need to be filled with pie weights during blind baking (a term used to describe baking a crust without a filling) because the dough is rich in fat with butter and eggs fully mixed into the flour, causing it to not puff up or shrink when baked. All it needs ahead of time is a good chilling in the refrigerator and some docking (a technique whereby you use the tines of a fork to gently create holes in the dough).

1. Preheat the oven to 350°F. Spread the almonds out in a single layer on a baking sheet. Bake for 3 to 5 minutes, until lightly browned. Set aside to cool.

2. To make the pastry cream: In a medium bowl, whisk together the egg yolks, about half of the sugar, all the cornstarch, and ¼ cup of the milk.

3. In a saucepan, combine the remaining sugar, the remaining ¾ cup milk, and the salt. If using a vanilla bean, scrape the tiny black seeds into the saucepan and add the pod. Bring to a simmer. Whisking constantly, gradually pour the hot milk into the egg mixture to temper it. Set a strainer over the saucepan. Strain the custard mixture back into the saucepan and bring to a boil over medium heat, whisking constantly. Boil for 10 seconds, whisking. (Make sure the custard boils for 10 seconds in the center of the pan, not just around the sides.) The mixture should thicken to a pudding-like consistency.

4. Transfer the pastry cream to the bowl of a standing mixer fitted with the paddle attachment and beat on medium speed for 2 to 3 minutes, to cool slightly. Beat in the vanilla extract, if using. With the mixer running, beat in the butter, a little at a time. Beat until cooled, about 5 more minutes. Press a piece of plastic wrap directly on the surface, and refrigerate until chilled, about 1 hour.

5. On a lightly floured surface, roll the dough to about ⅛ inch thick. Cut as many 5-inch rounds as possible. Re-roll the scraps and cut more rounds—you should get five rounds. Fit the rounds into 3-inch fluted tart shells; the dough should extend slightly over the tops of the molds. Prick each round of dough all over with a fork. Chill for 15 minutes.

RECIPE CONTINUES . . .

TECHNIQUE TIP: Fruit tarts are traditionally garnished with toasted, sliced almonds. At the bakery we also use coarsely chopped pistachios or pecans as well.

6. Set the oven rack in the middle position. Preheat the oven to 350°F. Line a baking sheet with parchment paper or a nonstick silicone baking mat; set aside.

7. Even the edges of the chilled pastry shells by pressing the excess dough against the sharp edge of the rims of the molds with the heel of your hand to cut it level with the molds. Set the molds on the prepared baking sheet and bake, rotating the sheet about two-thirds of the way through the baking time, until the pastry is completely cooked through, lightly browned, and crisp, 15 to 18 minutes. Transfer the tart shells to a wire rack and let cool completely in the molds. Remove the tartlet shells from the molds when cool.

8. When you are ready to fill the shells, warm the apricot jam with 1 to 2 teaspoons of water in a small saucepan to thin the jam slightly (it should be fluid, but not liquid) and strain through a fine sieve into a medium bowl. Add the berries, and toss gently to coat.

9. Break the almond slices between your fingers into smaller bits and set aside separately.

10. Using a spoon or a pastry bag, spoon or pipe a mound of pastry cream (you'll use about 2 tablespoons cream) into the center of each tartlet shell. The cream should not extend all the way to the edges of the shell. Mound the berries on top of the cream so that they completely cover the cream. Carefully press the almonds around the bottom edge of the berries, where they meet the pastry, to make a border. Refrigerate until ready to serve, or up to 24 hours.

Blueberry Coconut Tartlets

This tart is one of our all-time best-selling items. It is adapted from a recipe from City Bakery in New York City. Our version uses coconut milk and vanilla bean in the custard for extra flavor. These tartlets can be made in straight-sided or fluted tartlet molds. I like to keep a selection of different-shaped stainless steel molds with removable bottoms in a range of sizes on hand, so that I have different options for any of the tarts I'm making. Finely shredded unsweetened dried coconut can be found in many grocery stores and gourmet specialty stores.

MAKES FIVE 4-INCH
FLUTED TARTLETS

½ **recipe Pâte Sucrée (page 99), chilled**

½ **cup heavy cream**

6 **tablespoons coconut milk**

⅔ **cup sugar**

¼ **teaspoon coarse salt**

½ **vanilla bean, split in half lengthwise, or 1½ teaspoons pure vanilla extract**

1 **cup blueberries**

6 **ounces (about 2 cups) finely shredded unsweetened dried coconut**

1. On a lightly floured work surface, roll the dough to about ⅛ inch thick. Cut three or four 6-inch rounds (however many will fit), and gently press them into 4-inch tartlet molds, making sure to get the dough all the way down into the bottom edges of the pans. You'll have a ⅛- to ¼- inch overhang. Re-roll the scraps, and cut more rounds until you have lined five molds. Chill the tart shells for 15 minutes.

2. Set the oven rack in the middle position. Preheat the oven to 375°F. Line a baking sheet with parchment paper or a nonstick silicone baking mat; set aside.

3. Press the excess dough against the rims of the molds with the heel of your hand to cut the dough level with the mold. Prick the bottoms of the tartlets all over with the tines of a fork. Bake the pastry shells until the crust is golden brown, crisp, and completely cooked through, 15 to 18 minutes. Set aside on the baking sheet on a wire rack. Do not turn off the oven.

4. In a medium saucepan, bring the cream, coconut milk, sugar, salt, and vanilla bean, if using, to a boil. Reduce the heat and simmer for 5 minutes. Remove from the heat and let stand for 10 minutes to cool. Stir in the vanilla extract, if using. Fold in the blueberries and coconut.

5. Remove the pastry shells from the tartlet molds and return them to the parchment-lined baking sheet. Divide the blueberry mixture among the pastry shells and bake at 375°F until the coconut is lightly toasted and the juices are bubbling around the edges, 20 to 25 minutes. Transfer from the baking sheet to a wire rack to cool completely before serving.

Banana Almond Tart

This tart combines two of my favorite flavors. It is a variation on the classic pairing of pears and almonds. The bananas bake in the rum-and-almond-flavored cream to create a rich, multidimensional taste. Make sure to use ripe bananas, as they will need to almost melt into the cream when baked.

MAKES ONE 9-INCH TART, SERVES 8

½ **recipe Pâte Brisée (page 98), chilled**

2 **ounces semisweet chocolate, chopped into ½-inch pieces**

Rum-Almond Cream

½ **cup blanched whole almonds**

6 **tablespoons granulated sugar**

1 **teaspoon coarse salt**

6 **tablespoons (¾ stick) unsalted butter, at room temperature**

2 **large eggs, at room temperature**

1 **teaspoon almond extract**

1 **tablespoon dark rum**

¼ **cup all-purpose flour**

3 **ripe bananas, sliced ¼ inch thick on a gentle diagonal**

3 **to 4 tablespoons confectioners' sugar, for dusting**

TECHNIQUE TIP: The best way to insert dough into a tart pan is to push the dough against the inside walls of the pan with a metal measuring cup. This way you don't warm the pastry with the heat of your hands.

1. On a lightly floured work surface, roll the dough to a 12-inch round, about ⅛ inch thick. Fit the dough into a 9-inch fluted tart pan with a removable bottom and trim the dough so that it comes slightly above the rim of the tart pan. Then press the excess dough against the sharp edge of the rim of the pan with the heel of your hand to cut it level with the pan. Chill until firm, about 30 minutes.

2. Bring 1 inch of water to a simmer in the bottom of a double boiler. Place the chocolate in the top of the double boiler, set it over (not in) the simmering water, and heat until melted. Using an offset spatula, spread the bottom of the chilled tart shell with the chocolate. Refrigerate until firm, about 10 minutes.

3. To make the almond cream: In a food processor, pulse the almonds with the sugar and salt for about 10 seconds, until finely ground. Add the butter and process to blend. Add the eggs, processing to blend and scraping the bowl after each addition. Add the almond extract and the rum. Add the flour and process until combined.

4. Set the oven rack in the bottom third of the oven. Preheat the oven to 375°F. Line a baking sheet with parchment paper or a nonstick silicone baking mat; set aside.

5. Spread the tart shell with the almond cream. Place on the prepared baking sheet. Shingle the banana slices in overlapping concentric circles to cover the top of the tart. Bake, rotating the baking sheet about two-thirds of the way through the baking time, until the crust is cooked through and golden brown, and the almond cream is puffed and golden, about 40 minutes. Remove from the oven.

6. Preheat the broiler. Arrange the oven rack 5 to 6 inches below the broiler element. Sift confectioners' sugar generously over the tart and broil until the top is golden brown and lightly caramelized, 1 to 2 minutes. Careful—it burns quickly! Transfer the tart to a wire rack and let cool to room temperature before serving.

Lemon Meringue Tart

Unlike a traditional lemon meringue tart or pie, which uses lemon-flavored pastry cream, this recipe calls for a filling composed of rich and tangy lemon curd, stabilized with a bit of gelatin. The curd provides a more intense lemon experience. Martha Stewart taught me how to make the best lemon curd (offered here), using fresh-squeezed lemon juice and adding the butter at the end of the process. It is the only version we have ever used at the bakery. If you prefer, you can also make this tart in a 9-inch round tart pan with a removable bottom.

MAKES ONE 13¼-INCH
RECTANGULAR TART,
SERVES 8

Lemon Curd

- **2 tablespoons cold water**
- **1 teaspoon powdered unflavored gelatin**
- **6 large egg yolks**
  Grated zest of 4 lemons
- **½ cup freshly squeezed lemon juice**
- **¾ cup sugar**
- **⅛ teaspoon coarse salt**
- **½ cup (1 stick) cold unsalted butter, cut into ½-inch pieces**

- **½ recipe Pâte Brisée (page 98), chilled**
- **3 large egg whites**
- **½ cup sugar**
  Pinch of coarse salt

1. To make the lemon curd: In a small bowl, sprinkle the cold water over the gelatin; set aside. In a medium saucepan, combine the egg yolks, lemon zest, lemon juice, sugar, and salt, and whisk to combine. Set over medium heat and cook, stirring constantly, until the mixture has thickened enough to coat the back of a wooden spoon, about 5 minutes. Do not boil. Whisk in the gelatin.

2. Strain the curd through a fine sieve into the bowl of a standing mixer fitted with the paddle attachment. Beat until cool, about 5 minutes. Beat in the butter a little at a time, until smooth. Strain through a fine sieve into a bowl. Cover with plastic wrap, pressing it directly onto the surface of the curd to prevent a skin from forming. Refrigerate until chilled, at least 1 hour.

3. On a lightly floured work surface, roll the dough to a 7 by 17-inch rectangle, about ⅛ inch thick. Fit the dough into a 4 by 13¼-inch fluted rectangular tart pan with a removable bottom, and trim the dough so that it comes slightly above the rim of the tart pan. Then press the excess dough against the sharp edge of the rim of the pan with the heel of your hand to cut it level with the pan. Chill until firm, about 30 minutes.

4. Set the oven rack in the bottom third of the oven. Preheat the oven to 350°F. Line a baking sheet with parchment paper or a nonstick silicone baking mat; set aside.

5. Place the chilled tart shell on the prepared baking sheet and line it with parchment paper, leaving a 1-inch overhang. Fill with pie weights. Bake until the edges of the tart shell are firm and are just beginning to turn golden, 15 to 20 minutes. Remove the parchment paper and pie weights. Return the tart shell to the oven and continue to bake until the surface is golden all over, about 10 more minutes. Remove from the oven. Transfer to a wire rack and let cool.

6. Whisk (or beat in a standing mixer) the lemon curd to loosen. Spread the curd over the bottom of the cooled tart shell. Refrigerate.

7. Bring about 1 inch of water to a simmer in the bottom of a double boiler. Combine the egg whites, sugar, and salt in the top of the double boiler, set it over (not in) the simmering water, and whisk to dissolve the sugar just until it melts, 1 to 2 minutes. (The mixture should feel just warm to the touch, and not gritty.) Transfer to the bowl of a standing mixer fitted with the whisk attachment, and beat on medium-high speed until the meringue is glossy and stiff peaks form when you lift the whisk.

8. Preheat the broiler and arrange an oven rack 5 to 6 inches from the broiler element. Spread the meringue over the lemon curd. Place the tart on a parchment-lined baking sheet, and broil until the meringue is nicely browned, 1 to 2 minutes.

TECHNIQUE TIP: When it comes to pie weights (baking weights that help hold a crust in place during blind baking in order to keep its shape and avoid puffing up or shrinkage), I prefer using ceramic or metal weights rather than dried beans. The weights are heavier, conduct and retain heat better, and do a better job with helping to cook the top of the pastry.

Jam Tartlets

It's easy to underestimate just how delicious these easy little tartlets are. The crust is crisp and buttery, the jam a little sharp, and the streusel nice and sweet. They are perfect little mouthfuls. They were inspired by a visit to a L.A. Burdick Bakery in Walpole, New Hampshire, where I stopped on my way back home from bread-baking classes at the King Arthur Flour Baking Education Center in Norwich, Vermont. These tartlets are excellent served as an after-school snack, for tea, or for a picnic, as they travel quite well and don't need to be refrigerated. Try them with any favorite jam. You will need 2-inch mini tart pans or rings, as shown here, to make these individual tartlets.

MAKES ABOUT 16 MINI TARTLETS

½ recipe Pâte Sucrée (page 99), chilled

Streusel

½ cup all-purpose flour

½ cup firmly packed light brown sugar

¼ teaspoon coarse salt

⅛ teaspoon ground cinnamon

¼ cup (½ stick) cold unsalted butter, cut into ¼-inch cubes

½ cup seedless raspberry jam

3 to 4 tablespoons confectioners' sugar, for dusting

1. Line a baking sheet with parchment paper or a nonstick silicone baking mat; set aside. Butter sixteen 2-inch tart molds; set aside.

2. On a lightly floured work surface, roll the dough to about ⅛ inch thick. Cut as many 2½-inch rounds as possible, and fit them into the prepared molds. Chill and reroll the scraps, cut out the remaining rounds, and fit them into the remaining molds; you should be able to line 16 tartlet molds. Arrange the molds on the prepared baking sheet, and chill for 20 minutes.

3. To make the streusel: In a medium bowl, use a fork to stir together the flour, brown sugar, salt, and cinnamon. Add the butter, and using your fingertips, quickly work into the dry ingredients until pea-size crumbs form; set aside in the refrigerator.

4. Set the oven rack in the bottom third of the oven. Preheat the oven to 350°F.

5. Spoon about 1 teaspoon jam into each tart shell. Mound 1 rounded tablespoon of streusel on top of each tartlet, bunching the crumbs together in order to make large crumbs and give the topping texture.

6. Bake, rotating the baking sheet about two-thirds of the way through the cooking time, until the edges of the tarts are golden brown and the streusel is cooked, 20 to 25 minutes. Remove from the oven and let cool on a wire rack.

Torta Della Nonna

Translated, the name of this Italian-inspired pie means "Grandmother's Torte." This recipe is a variation of the Neapolitan one my great-grandfather Giuseppe Barricelli—who owned a turn-of-the-century panetteria *in Brooklyn—used to make. His* torta della nonna, *made without a top crust, included pine nuts and was more rustic than the lighter one we sell today at SoNo Baking Company.*

MAKES EIGHT 3½-INCH TORTES

Filling

- 4 **egg yolks**
- 1 **cup granulated sugar**
- 2 **cups milk**
- ½ **vanilla bean, split lengthwise, seeds scraped**
- ½ **cup durum wheat flour**
- ½ **teaspoon coarse salt**
- 4 **tablespoons (½ stick) unsalted butter, cut into small pieces**

- 1 **recipe Pasta Frolla (page 126)**
- 1 **large egg, beaten, for egg wash**
- 3 **to 4 tablespoons sanding sugar, for finishing**

1. In a medium heatproof bowl, whisk together the egg yolks and ½ cup of the sugar until thick and light in color; set aside.

2. In a medium saucepan, combine the milk, vanilla bean and seeds, remaining ½ cup sugar, flour, and salt. Bring to a simmer. Whisking constantly, gradually pour the hot milk into the egg mixture to temper it. Set a strainer over the saucepan. Strain the custard mixture back into the saucepan and bring to a boil over medium heat, whisking constantly. Boil for 10 seconds, whisking. (Make sure the custard boils for 10 seconds in the center of the pan, not just around the sides.) The mixture should thicken to a pudding-like consistency. Discard the vanilla bean, if using.

3. Transfer the pastry cream to the bowl of a standing mixer fitted with the paddle attachment and beat on medium speed for 2 to 3 minutes, to cool slightly. With the mixer running, beat in the butter, a little at a time. Continue beating for 5 minutes until cool. Transfer to a bowl and cover with plastic wrap, placing it directly on the custard to prevent a skin from forming. Refrigerate for 2 hours.

4. Line two baking sheets with parchment paper or nonstick silicone baking mats; set aside.

5. On a lightly floured work surface, roll out one of the Pasta Frolla disks to about ⅛ inch thick. With a knife and something to guide you, such as a saucer or a small plate, cut out eight 5-inch rounds. Fit the rounds into 3½-inch tart pans with removable bottoms and trim the dough so that it comes slightly above the rim of each tart pan. Then press the excess dough against the sharp edge of the rim of the pan with the heel of your hand to cut it level with the pan. Chill in the refrigerator for 30 minutes.

6. Roll out the second disk of dough in the same manner and cut out eight 5-inch rounds. Transfer to one of the prepared baking sheets and chill until firm, about 30 minutes.

7. Set the oven rack in the middle position. Preheat the oven to 350°F.

8. Remove the tart shells and the dough rounds from the refrigerator. Place the tart shells on the second prepared baking sheet. Using a small offset spatula, divide the custard evenly among the tart shells. Top each tart shell with a round of dough and trim flush with the edge of the tart pan to fit within the tart shell. Brush with egg wash and sprinkle with sanding sugar.

9. Bake, rotating the sheet two-thirds of the way through the baking time, until golden brown, about 45 minutes. Transfer to a wire rack and let cool for 20 minutes. Remove the tarts from the tart pans and let cool completely. Dust with confectioners' sugar.

Pasta Frolla

Pasta Frolla is similar to a tart dough in recipes in this section. My grandfather Tony taught me this recipe, which I've changed a bit here, for our Easter wheat grain pie.

MAKES ENOUGH DOUGH FOR EIGHT 3½-INCH TARTS OR ONE 10-INCH TART

4⅔ cups all-purpose flour
2 teaspoons baking powder
1 teaspoon coarse salt
1 cup (2 sticks) unsalted butter, at room temperature
1 cup sugar
2 large eggs, at room temperature
2 egg yolks, at room temperature
Grated zest of 1 orange

1. In a medium bowl, whisk together the flour, baking powder, and salt. Set aside.

2. In a bowl of an electric mixer fitted with the paddle attachment, beat the butter and sugar on medium speed until light and fluffy, about 3 minutes, scraping the sides down halfway through. Add the eggs, yolks, and orange zest, beating until fully incorporated. Reduce to low speed and add the flour mixture. Beat until the dough comes together.

3. Divide the dough into two equal pieces, flatten into disks, and wrap separately in plastic wrap. Refrigerate for 30 minutes or up to 3 days, or freeze for up to 3 months.

Maple Pecan Tart

Most pecan pies or tarts are filled with sugar and can be cloyingly sweet. This version uses only natural maple syrup to add not only a touch of sweetness but also a more complex taste. For more robust maple flavor, try using Grade B Dark Amber maple syrup. This tart should never be refrigerated. Serve at room temperature with whipped cream, whipped crème fraîche, or cinnamon ice cream.

MAKES ONE 9-INCH TART, SERVES 8

½ **recipe Pâte Sucrée (page 99), chilled**
1 **cup maple syrup**
3 **large eggs, at room temperature**
2 **tablespoons unsalted butter, melted**
1 **teaspoon pure vanilla extract**
  Pinch of coarse salt
1½ **cups (6 ounces) chopped pecans**

TECHNIQUE TIP: When using nuts in a baking recipe, buy them already chopped. When you chop them yourself, you end up with some nut "flour," which changes the intended texture of what you're making.

1. On a lightly floured work surface, roll the dough to a 12-inch round, about ⅛ inch thick. Fit the dough into a 9-inch fluted tart pan with a removable bottom, and trim the dough so that it comes slightly above the rim of the tart pan. Then press the excess dough against the sharp edge of the rim of the pan with the heel of your hand to cut it level with the pan. Chill until firm, about 30 minutes.

2. Set the oven rack in the bottom third of the oven. Preheat the oven to 350°F. Line a baking sheet with parchment paper or a nonstick silicone baking mat; set aside.

3. Place the chilled tart shell on the prepared baking sheet and line it with parchment paper, leaving a 1-inch overhang. Fill with pie weights. Bake until the edges of the tart are firm and are just beginning to turn golden, 15 to 20 minutes. Remove the parchment paper and pie weights. Return the pie shell to the oven and continue to bake until the surface is golden all over, about 10 more minutes. Remove from the oven, but leave the oven on.

4. In a medium bowl, whisk together the maple syrup, eggs, butter, vanilla, and salt.

5. Spread the pecans over the bottom of the pie shell and pour in the maple syrup mixture. Return the tart to the oven and bake until the custard puffs and sets, 30 to 35 minutes. Transfer from the baking sheet to a wire rack and cool completely.

Coconut Cream Tart

We use a considerable amount of coconut in this dessert, so it packs a lot more flavor than most classic coconut cream pies. We start with a Pâte Sucrée crust for the base, coated with a thin layer of melted chocolate, followed by a layer of coconut pastry cream, topped off with a layer of whipped cream garnished with toasted coconut. The hidden chocolate adds an element of surprise and combines nicely with the coconut.

MAKES ONE 9-INCH TART,
SERVES 8

Coconut Pastry Cream

- **4 egg yolks**
- ½ **cup granulated sugar**
- ¼ **cup cornstarch**
- **2 cups milk**
- ½ **vanilla bean, split lengthwise, seeds scraped**
  Pinch of coarse salt
- **3 tablespoons cold unsalted butter, cut into small pieces**
- **1 cup sweetened shredded coconut**

- ½ **recipe Pâte Sucrée (page 99)**
- ½ **cup sweetened shredded coconut**
- **4 ounces bittersweet chocolate, chopped into ½-inch pieces**

Whipped Cream

- **1 cup heavy cream**
- ¼ **cup confectioners' sugar**
- ½ **teaspoon pure vanilla extract**

1. To make the pastry cream: In a medium bowl, whisk together the egg yolks, ¼ cup of the sugar, all of the cornstarch, and ½ cup of the milk; set aside.

2. In a medium saucepan, combine the remaining 1½ cups milk, the remaining ¼ cup sugar, the vanilla bean and seeds, and the salt. Bring to a simmer. Whisking constantly, gradually pour the hot milk into the egg mixture to temper it. Set a strainer over the saucepan. Strain the custard mixture back into the saucepan and bring to a boil over medium heat, whisking constantly. Boil for 10 seconds, whisking. (Make sure the custard boils for 10 seconds in the center of the pan, not just around the sides.) The mixture should thicken to a pudding-like consistency. Discard the vanilla bean.

3. Transfer the pastry cream to the bowl of a standing mixer fitted with the paddle attachment and beat on medium speed for 2 to 3 minutes, to cool slightly. With the mixer running, beat in the butter, a little at a time. Add the coconut. Continue beating for 5 minutes until cool. Transfer to a bowl. Cover with plastic wrap, pressing it directly onto the surface to prevent a skin from forming. Refrigerate until chilled, about 3 hours.

4. On a lightly floured work surface, roll out the dough into a 12-inch round, ⅛ inch thick. Fit the dough into a 9-inch fluted tart pan with a removable bottom, pressing the dough into the corners, and trim the dough so that it comes slightly above the rim of the tart pan. Then press the excess dough against the sharp edge of the rim of the pan with the heel of your hand to cut it level with the pan. Prick the bottom of the dough with a fork. Chill until firm, about 30 minutes.

5. Preheat the oven to 375°F. Line the chilled tart shell with parchment paper, leaving a 1-inch overhang. Fill with pie weights. Bake until the edges of the tart are just beginning to turn golden, 15 to 20 minutes. Remove the parchment paper and weights. Return the crust to the oven and continue to bake until the surface is golden all over, about 20 minutes. Transfer to a wire rack and cool completely.

6. Meanwhile, place the ½ cup shredded coconut on a baking sheet, place in the oven, and toast until golden, 5 to 8 minutes; set aside.

7. Place the chopped chocolate in the top of a double boiler, set it over (not in) 1 inch of simmering water, and heat until melted. Stir until smooth.

8. Using a pastry brush, coat the bottom of the tart shell all over with half of the melted chocolate. Place in the refrigerator until the chocolate is set, about 15 minutes. Reserve the remaining chocolate.

9. Using an offset spatula, spread the custard evenly into the tart shell. Refrigerate the tart for 2 to 3 hours.

10. Just before serving, make the whipped cream: In the bowl of an electric mixer fitted with the whisk attachment, combine the cream, confectioners' sugar, and vanilla extract. Beat until soft peaks form.

11. Spread the whipped cream on top of the custard. Reheat the reserved melted chocolate in the top of a double boiler. Using a fork, streak chocolate over the entire top of the tart. Sprinkle the toasted coconut around the outer edges of the tart, and serve.

TECHNIQUE TIP: Most pastry cream recipes call for butter to be added to the saucepan the pastry cream is made in. I prefer to beat the cold butter into the pastry cream as it cools while being beaten in a standing mixer, to help emulsify and lighten the custard.

Chocolate Truffle Tart

This tart is inspired by Claudia Fleming's individual Chocolate Caramel Tartlets that she first made when she was pastry chef at Gramercy Tavern restaurant in New York City. It is the unique pairing of chocolate, caramel, and a hint of salt that makes it so alluring. The key to making this elegant dessert look great is to heat the ganache so that it's liquid enough to pour, but not so hot that it breaks through the pie shell. When you get it right, it is absolutely smooth and when it firms up, it looks like glass. Both the caramel and the ganache can be made a few days ahead and rewarmed to a pourable consistency. (Heat the caramel in a saucepan over low heat and heat the ganache in the top of a double boiler, 1 to 2 minutes, until both are a liquid consistency.)

MAKES ONE 9-INCH TART, SERVES 10

½ **recipe Pâte Sucrée (page 99), chilled**

Caramel

1 **cup sugar**
¼ **cup water**
1 **teaspoon white vinegar**
¾ **cup heavy cream, preferably at room temperature**
¼ **teaspoon coarse salt**

½ **recipe (about 1¾ cups) Ganache (page 169), warmed until just liquid (see Technique Tip) Fleur de sel**

1. On a lightly floured work surface, roll the dough to a 12-inch round, about ⅛ inch thick. Fit the dough into a 9-inch fluted tart pan with a removable bottom and trim the dough so that it comes slightly above the rim of the tart pan. Press the excess dough against the sharp edge of the rim of the pan with the heel of your hand to cut it level with the pan. Chill until firm, about 30 minutes.

2. Set the oven rack in the middle of the oven. Preheat the oven to 350°F. Line a baking sheet with parchment paper or a nonstick silicone baking mat.

3. Place the chilled tart shell on the prepared baking sheet and line it with parchment paper, leaving a 1-inch overhang. Fill with pie weights. Bake until the edges of the tart shell are firm and are just beginning to turn golden, 15 to 20 minutes. Remove the parchment paper and pie weights. Return the tart shell to the oven and continue to bake until the surface is golden all over, about 10 more minutes. Remove from the oven.

4. To make the caramel: In a small saucepan, combine the sugar, water, and vinegar. Bring to a boil over medium-high heat, swirling the pan to dissolve the sugar. Boil until the mixture turns a deep amber color, 5 to 10 minutes. Remove the pan from the heat and gradually add the cream; stand back—the caramel will spit and the cream will boil up. Return the pan to medium heat and cook, stirring with a wooden spoon or whisking, until the caramel melts

again and the mixture is smooth. Add the salt. Strain into a heat-proof container and set aside to cool slightly.

5. Pour the warm caramel sauce into the tart shell to cover the bottom. Refrigerate until well chilled, about 30 minutes.

6. Place 1¼ cups of the ganache in the top of a double boiler, set it over (not in) 1 inch of simmering water, and heat until melted. Warm until just liquid, stirring gently to keep air bubbles from forming (see Technique Tip). Pour over the caramel and set aside to firm up at room temperature, about 2 hours. Sprinkle with fleur de sel before serving.

TECHNIQUE TIP: To test the consistency of warmed ganache for this recipe, pour out a little onto a flat surface and let it set up. If it makes a ribbon when you pour, it is not quite hot enough and should be reheated. Then stir as little as possible while heating so that you don't get air bubbles.

Crème Brûlée Tartlets

Eggy vanilla custard set in a buttery crust and topped with torched sugar, this dessert is the ultimate end to any meal. You will need five 4-inch, straight-sided pastry rings for this recipe and a kitchen blowtorch for finishing. It's important to chill the cooked tarts before they are brûléed so they stand up to the heat from the torch. Brûlée just before serving.

MAKES FIVE 4-INCH TARTS

½ recipe **Pâte Sucrée (page 99), chilled**

Custard

1⅔ **cups heavy cream**

6 **tablespoons granulated sugar**
Pinch coarse salt

½ **vanilla bean, split lengthwise, or 1½ teaspoons pure vanilla extract**

4 **large egg yolks**

3 **tablespoons light brown sugar**

3 **tablespoons granulated sugar**

1. Set the oven rack in the middle position and preheat the oven to 375°F. Line a baking sheet with parchment paper or a nonstick silicone baking mat. Set five 4-inch rings on the baking sheet.

2. On a lightly floured work surface, roll the dough to about ⅛ inch thick. Cut three or four 6-inch rounds (as many as you can manage). Line the rings with the pastry rounds, making sure to get the dough all the way down into the bottom edges of the rings—you'll have a ⅛- to ¼-inch overhang. Re-roll the scraps, and cut more rounds until you have lined the five rings. Chill the rings for 15 minutes.

3. Press the excess dough against the rims of the molds with the heel of your hand to cut the dough level with the mold. Prick the bottoms of the tartlets all over with the tines of a fork. Bake the pastry shells until the crust is golden brown, crisp, and completely cooked through, 15 to 18 minutes. Set aside on the baking sheet on a wire rack. Reduce the oven temperature to 300°F.

4. To make the custard: In a medium saucepan, bring the cream to a simmer with about two-thirds of the sugar, all the salt, and the vanilla bean, if using.

5. Meanwhile, bring 1 inch of water to a simmer in the bottom of a double boiler. Combine the egg yolks and the remaining sugar in the top of the double boiler, set it over the simmering water, and cook, whisking constantly, until a ribbon forms when you lift the whisk from the bowl, 7 to 10 minutes.

6. Remove the top pan from the heat. Whisk in the hot cream. Replace the pan over the simmering water and whisk until thickened, enough to coat the back of a spoon, 3 to 5 minutes. Strain the custard through a fine strainer into a bowl, and whisk in the vanilla extract, if using.

7. Remove the pastry shells from the tartlet molds and place on the parchment-lined baking sheet. Ladle the custard mixture into the pastry shells. Return to the oven and bake until the custard is just set but jiggles when you shake the pan, 15 to 17 minutes. Do not overbake or the custard will curdle. Remove the tartlets from the oven. Let cool on a wire rack, and then refrigerate for 1 hour until the custard is chilled.

8. Just before serving, combine the light brown sugar and granulated sugar and sift through a fine sieve over the custard filling in the chilled tartlets, using 1 to 1½ tablespoons per tartlet. Following the manufacturer's directions, ignite a kitchen blowtorch. Move the flame evenly back and forth just above the top of the tartlets, avoiding the crust, until the sugar is caramelized and slightly browned. Serve immediately.

Cobblers, Crisps, and Buckles

Nothing is more welcoming in a home than the smell of a fresh-baked fruit cobbler or crisp coming out of the oven. Bake them often, as they are easy to make, require little time, can be made with a variety of seasonal fruits, and best of all, can be made a few hours in advance and reheated for serving for 30 minutes at 250°F.

Delicious ripe fruit is the key to these desserts. SoNo Baking Company participates in a number of local Fairfield County and New Haven County farmers' markets. When I'm not selling goods from the bakery, I walk around the markets looking for the best, juiciest, seasonal, locally grown fruit. I'll buy a large amount of whatever looks good—strawberries, peaches, nectarines, plums, apricots, blueberries, apples—to bring home or to the bakery to make a cobbler, crisp, betty, or buckle. I make them in large serving dishes as well as individual servings. They are as welcome at a formal dinner party as they are at a backyard clambake.

The recipes in this chapter are just a few of my favorites. Feel free to swap out peaches for nectarines, raspberries for blueberries, pears for apples. Anything goes when it comes to these luscious spoon desserts. Top each serving with a scoop of vanilla ice cream and the result is pretty much perfection.

Blueberry Nectarine Buckle

A buckle is an old-fashioned dessert in which the fruit is folded into a buttery, eggy batter and baked with a streusel topping. The weight of the topping makes the cake "buckle" in places. Use fruit that's ripe, but not too soft, so that it holds its shape when baked. This dessert can also double as a breakfast cake. It's best served the day it's made.

SERVES 8 TO 10

Streusel Topping

- 1 cup all-purpose flour
- 1 cup light brown sugar
- 1 teaspoon coarse salt
- ½ teaspoon ground cinnamon
- ½ cup (1 stick) cold unsalted butter, cut into small cubes

- 1¼ cups all-purpose flour
- 2 teaspoons baking powder
- 1 cup (2 sticks) unsalted butter, at room temperature
- 1 cup granulated sugar
- ½ teaspoon coarse salt
- 4 large eggs
- 2 teaspoons pure vanilla extract
- 2 cups blueberries
- 2 cups diced (½-inch) nectarines (about 2 nectarines)
- Confectioners' sugar

TECHNIQUE TIP: Always bake fruit crisps, cobblers, buckles, bettys, and pies on a nonstick silicone–lined baking sheet (parchment paper won't work as well, as the juices will burn, causing the paper to adhere to the bottom of the baking dish). Not only does baking on a lined baking sheet make for easier cleanup, it's also easier to maneuver the dish in and out of the oven.

1. To make the streusel: In a medium bowl, use a fork to stir together the flour, brown sugar, salt, and cinnamon. Add the butter, and using your fingertips, quickly work it into the dry ingredients until pea-size crumbs form; set aside in the refrigerator.

2. In a medium bowl, whisk together the flour and baking powder; set aside.

3. Set the oven rack in the middle position. Preheat the oven to 350°F. Butter a 9 by 13-inch baking dish; set aside. Line a baking sheet with a nonstick silicone baking mat; set aside.

4. In the bowl of a standing mixer fitted with the paddle attachment, beat the butter, sugar, and salt on medium-high speed until light and fluffy, 2 to 3 minutes. Beat in the eggs one at a time, and then the vanilla. On low speed, beat in the dry ingredients just until absorbed. Fold in the fruit. Transfer to the prepared baking dish. Sprinkle the streusel over the top.

5. Set the baking dish on the prepared baking sheet. Bake, rotating the sheet about two-thirds of the way through the cooking time, until a cake tester inserted into the thickest part of the buckle comes out clean and the topping is nicely browned and crisp, 30 to 35 minutes. Transfer to a wire rack to cool for 10 minutes. Dust with confectioners' sugar and cut into squares.

Pear Ginger Brown Betty

A traditional "betty," which dates back to colonial times, uses a bread-cube topping, as opposed to a crumble or a crisp, which uses more of a streusel topping. Here, the mellowness of pear combines with the sharp, clean taste of ginger and the sour yeasty taste of sourdough bread for a satisfying and complex combination of flavors.

MAKES SIX 4-INCH BETTYS

2 cups cubed (½-inch) sourdough bread

6 tablespoons (¾ stick) unsalted butter, melted

8 Bartlett pears, peeled and cored, cut into ¼-inch slices

⅓ cup sugar

1 tablespoon grated fresh ginger

½ teaspoon ground cinnamon

⅛ teaspoon grated nutmeg

¼ teaspoon coarse salt

2 tablespoons freshly squeezed lemon juice

1. Set the oven rack in the middle position. Preheat the oven to 250°F.

2. Place the bread cubes on a rimmed baking sheet. Bake until crisp, tossing halfway through, about 30 minutes. Let cool completely. Transfer to a bowl.

3. Raise the oven temperature to 375°F and line a baking sheet with a nonstick silicone baking mat; set aside.

4. Combine the bread cubes with the butter in a medium bowl and toss to coat; set aside. Combine the pears, sugar, ginger, spices, salt, and lemon juice in a large bowl and toss to coat; set aside.

5. Place ½ cup of the pear mixture into each of six 4-inch ramekins. Top each with ⅓ cup buttered bread cubes, top with the remaining pears, then remaining bread cubes, completing two layers of both pear and bread cubes.

6. Place the ramekins on the prepared baking sheet. Bake for 40 to 45 minutes, until the topping is golden and the juices are bubbling. Cover with foil if bread cubes are getting too browned. Transfer to a wire rack and let cool. Serve warm.

Cherry Rhubarb Cobbler

This is the perfect summer dessert for late June, when rhubarb and cherries are overlapping in season. Tart rhubarb pairs nicely with the mellow sweetness of cherries, all nestled beneath a rich, buttery biscuit topping. You can make this cobbler with frozen cherries, but make sure to buy individually quick-frozen cherries (not the kind frozen in syrup).

SERVES 8

1 **pound rhubarb, trimmed and cut into ½- to ¾-inch pieces**

2 **pints (2 pounds) fresh cherries, pitted, or frozen cherries**

1¼ **cups granulated sugar**

6 **tablespoons cornstarch**

1 **teaspoon coarse salt**
 Grated zest of ½ orange

Biscuit Dough

1⅓ **cups all-purpose flour**

⅓ **cup granulated sugar**

1½ **teaspoons baking powder**

1 **teaspoon baking soda**

½ **teaspoon coarse salt**

6 **tablespoons (¾ stick) cold unsalted butter, cut into ½-inch pieces**

½ **cup buttermilk, plus extra for brushing**

 Sanding sugar, for finishing

1. In a large bowl, toss the fruit with the sugar, cornstarch, salt, and orange zest; set aside.

2. Set the oven rack in the lower third of the oven. Preheat the oven to 375°F. Line a baking sheet with a nonstick silicone baking mat; set aside.

3. Make the biscuit dough: In a large bowl, whisk together the flour, sugar, baking powder, baking soda, and salt.

4. Working quickly so as not to warm the butter, work the butter into the dry ingredients with your fingers until the mixture resembles coarse crumbs. Add the buttermilk and fold with a rubber scraper or your hands until the buttermilk has been absorbed and there are no dry patches. Do not overwork. The dough will be wet.

5. Divide the fruit among eight 8-ounce ramekins or other ovenproof dishes and spoon dollops of the biscuit dough on top. Brush the dough with buttermilk and sprinkle with sanding sugar. Bake until the pastry is lightly browned and cooked through, about 25 minutes. Serve warm or at room temperature.

Apricot Blackberry Cobbler

Fruit cobblers are topped with a biscuit-like dough that bakes up flaky and light while the fruit underneath cooks in its own juices. We make individual versions of these desserts at many of our catering events, changing the fruit seasonally. Adjust the amount of sugar in this dessert based on the sweetness of the fruit you're using. Try any favorite combination of summer fruits here, such as peaches and raspberries or nectarines and blueberries.

SERVES 6 TO 8

2 pounds apricots, pitted and sliced

3 (6-ounce) baskets blackberries (about 3 cups)

⅓ to ½ cup granulated sugar (depending on ripeness of fruit)

½ teaspoon coarse salt

Juice of ½ lemon

2½ tablespoons cornstarch

Biscuit Dough

1⅓ cups all-purpose flour

⅓ cup granulated sugar

1½ teaspoons baking powder

1 teaspoon baking soda

½ teaspoon coarse salt

6 tablespoons (¾ stick) cold unsalted butter, cubed

½ cup buttermilk, plus extra for brushing

Sanding sugar, for finishing

1. In a large bowl, toss together the fruit, sugar, salt, lemon juice, and cornstarch. Transfer to a 13 by 9-inch oval gratin dish.

2. Set the oven rack in the middle position. Preheat the oven to 375°F. Line a baking sheet with a nonstick silicone baking mat.

3. To make the biscuit dough: In a large bowl, whisk together the flour, sugar, baking powder, baking soda, and salt.

4. Working quickly so as not to warm the butter, work the butter into the dry ingredients with your fingers until the mixture resembles coarse crumbs. Add the buttermilk and fold with a rubber scraper or your hands until the buttermilk has been absorbed and there are no dry patches. Do not overwork. The dough will be wet.

5. Spoon dollops of biscuit dough on top of the fruit. (The dollops will spread and join with one another as the cobbler cooks.) Brush the dough with buttermilk, and sprinkle with sanding sugar. Bake until the biscuit topping is lightly browned and cooked through, 30 to 35 minutes. Serve warm or at room temperature.

Plum Crisp

A fruit crisp offers a "crisp" streusel-like topping. This version browns up quite nicely when baked and includes oats in the streusel for a chewy texture. Use ⅓ to ½ cup sugar depending on sweetness of the plums you are using.

SERVES 6

Streusel Topping

- 1 cup all-purpose flour
- 1 cup firmly packed light brown sugar
- ½ teaspoon coarse salt
- ¼ teaspoon ground cinnamon
- ½ cup (1 stick) cold unsalted butter, cut into ¼-inch cubes
- ½ cup old-fashioned rolled oats (not instant)

- 2¾ to 3 pounds black plums, pitted and sliced into ½-inch-thick wedges (about 9 cups)
- ⅓ to ½ cup granulated sugar
- 3 tablespoons cornstarch
  Juice of ½ lemon
- 1 teaspoon coarse salt

1. Set the oven rack in the middle position. Preheat the oven to 375°F. Set a 13 by 9-inch oval gratin dish on a baking sheet lined with a nonstick silicone baking mat.

2. To make the streusel topping: In a medium bowl, use a fork to stir together the flour, brown sugar, salt, and cinnamon. Add the butter, and using your fingertips, quickly work it into the dry ingredients until pea-size crumbs form. Add the oats and toss. Set aside in the refrigerator.

3. In a medium bowl, toss together the plums, sugar, cornstarch, lemon juice, and salt. Transfer to the gratin dish. Sprinkle the streusel mixture over the top.

4. Bake, rotating the baking sheet about two-thirds of the way through the cooking, until the juices bubble up and the topping is golden brown and very crisp, 60 to 65 minutes. The crisp will still be very juicy when you take it out of the oven, but some of the juices will be reabsorbed as it stands. Let cool for 15 minutes before serving.

Strawberry Rhubarb Crisp

This homey, satisfying dessert is one of the first things I make in late spring when rhubarb comes into season. Serve with a big scoop of cinnamon or vanilla ice cream.

Streusel Topping

- ½ cup all-purpose flour
- ½ cup firmly packed light brown sugar
- ¼ teaspoon coarse salt
- ⅛ teaspoon ground cinnamon
- ½ cup (1 stick) unsalted butter, cut into ¼-inch cubes
- 3 tablespoons old-fashioned rolled oats (not instant)

- 1¼ pounds rhubarb, cut into 1-inch pieces (about 2½ cups)
- 1 pint strawberries, stemmed, then halved or quartered, depending on size (about 2½ cups)
- ½ cup granulated sugar
- 2 tablespoons cornstarch
- Juice of 1 lemon
- Grated zest of ½ orange
- ¼ teaspoon coarse salt

1. Set the oven rack in the middle position. Preheat the oven to 375°F. Butter an 8-inch square glass baking dish and set it on a baking sheet lined with a nonstick silicone baking mat.

2. To make the streusel topping: In a medium bowl, use a fork to stir together the flour, brown sugar, salt, and cinnamon. Add the butter, and using your fingertips, quickly work it into the dry ingredients until pea-size crumbs form. Add the oats and toss. Set aside in the refrigerator.

3. In a medium bowl, toss together the fruit, sugar, cornstarch, lemon juice, orange zest, and salt. Transfer to the prepared baking dish. Sprinkle the streusel mixture all over the top.

4. Bake, rotating the baking sheet about two-thirds of the way through the cooking, until the juices bubble up and the topping is golden brown and very crisp, 40 to 45 minutes. Serve warm or at room temperature.

Apple Date Crisp

This crisp is reminiscent of an old-time classic dessert. The addition of dates to the filling gives sweetness without adding extra sugar. When baked, they soften up nicely with the juice of the apples. Use a baking apple, such as Cortland, Winesap, or Rome, for the dish (Granny Smiths are too firm), as the apples will need to soften and fall apart during cooking. In contrast, the walnut-streusel topping is very crisp. A perfect dessert to help ease into fall.

MAKES FOUR 4-INCH
CRISPS

Streusel Topping

- ½ cup all-purpose flour
- ½ cup firmly packed light brown sugar
- ¼ teaspoon coarse salt
- ¼ teaspoon ground cinnamon
- ¼ cup (½ stick) cold unsalted butter, cut into ¼-inch cubes
- ⅓ cup chopped walnuts

- 1¼ pounds baking apples, such as Cortland, Winesap, or Rome, cored, peeled, and cut into coarse dice (about 4 cups)
- ½ cup coarsely chopped pitted dried dates
- 2 tablespoons granulated sugar
- 1 tablespoon cornstarch
- ¼ teaspoon ground cinnamon
- ⅛ teaspoon grated nutmeg
- ⅛ teaspoon coarse salt
- Juice of ½ lemon

1. To make the streusel topping: In a medium bowl, use a fork to stir together the flour, brown sugar, salt, and cinnamon. Add the butter, and using your fingertips, quickly work it into the dry ingredients until pea-size crumbs form. Add the walnuts and toss. Set aside in the refrigerator.

2. In a large bowl, toss the apples with the dates, sugar, cornstarch, cinnamon, nutmeg, salt, and lemon juice.

3. Set the oven rack in the middle position. Preheat the oven to 375°F. Butter four 4-inch ramekins (or any ovenproof dishes that hold about 1 cup) and set them on a baking sheet lined with a nonstick silicone baking baking mat.

4. Divide the apple mixture among the prepared ramekins. Top with the streusel. Bake, rotating the baking sheet about two-thirds of the way through the cooking, until the apples are cooked and bubbling and the topping is golden brown and very crisp, about 45 minutes. Serve warm or at room temperature.

Apple Pandowdy

I first started making this dessert while working with chef Brendan Walsh at the Elms Restaurant and Tavern in Ridgefield, Connecticut, which had an early American, colonial-themed menu. Originally named for its plain or "dowdy" appearance, this dessert is anything but! In a traditional pandowdy, the crust is cut halfway through the baking so that the filling is allowed to bubble up over the crust. Here, instead, we poach a variety of seasonal apples in wine and then bake them in shallow 6-inch ramekins topped and sealed with Pâte Sucrée pastry.

MAKES 4

½ recipe **Pâte Sucrée (page 99), chilled**

½ cup **light brown sugar**

½ teaspoon **ground cinnamon**

⅛ teaspoon **grated nutmeg**

⅛ teaspoon **coarse salt**

6 tablespoons **white wine**

2½ to 2¾ pounds **combination of Cortland, Rome, and Granny Smith apples, peeled, cored, and sliced**

¼ cup **raisins**

1 large egg, **whisked, for egg wash**

Sanding sugar, for finishing

1. On a lightly floured surface, cut the dough disk into four equal pieces. Roll each piece to a round about ⅛ inch thick, and cut from each one a round slightly larger than your ramekins (see above). Place on a parchment-lined baking sheet and chill.

2. Set the oven rack in the middle position. Preheat the oven to 375°F. Line a second baking sheet with a nonstick silicone baking mat.

3. In a medium saucepan, combine the brown sugar, cinnamon, nutmeg, salt, and wine. Bring to a simmer over medium-low heat, stirring to dissolve the sugar, about 3 minutes. Add the apples and raisins, raise the heat to medium, and cook, stirring often, until the apples are tender but not cooked into a puree, 10 to 12 minutes; set aside.

4. Divide the apples among the ramekins and top each with a round of dough, tucking the edges of the dough into the ramekins and around the apples. Cut a vent in the center of each crust with scissors or a small knife. Brush the dough with egg wash, and sprinkle generously with sanding sugar.

5. Bake until the dough is golden brown and cooked through, 30 to 35 minutes. Serve warm.

OPPOSITE: Chris, Andres, Roberto, and Felix early in the morning.

Trifles, Mousses, and Puddings

Smooth and elegant, or chunky and satisfying, these spoon desserts are as fitting at a formal dinner party as they are for a comfy night on the couch watching a movie.

I've always made these spoon desserts at every place I worked. Trifles were the dessert cornerstone of every banquet table at the Helmsley Palace, traditional English puddings were always in demand at the Elms Restaurant and Tavern, and to this day my wife, Veronica, still can't get enough Rice Pudding (page 159), so it's become a weekly regular at home.

Don't be intimidated by the word *trifle*. It is essentially a fancy English word for "layered dessert." Here, we layer different-flavored pastry creams, mousses, and whipped creams with fresh raspberries for two velvety desserts that will no doubt get "ooohs" and "aaahs" when you set them down on the table.

Mousse is a classic light and airy French dessert whose billowy texture is achieved by adding whipped cream or beaten egg whites to chocolate or to fruit purees stabilized with gelatin. It is wonderful eaten plain, on its own, in a trifle, or used in a cake, as with White Chocolate Mousse Roulade (page 204).

Pudding, always a favorite of kids but just as easily enjoyed by adults, runs the gamut in this chapter from smooth Chocolate Pudding Icebox Cake (page 158) and Butterscotch Pudding (page 161) to the heartier baked Date Nut Pudding (page 165) and Caramel Bread Pudding (page 162).

I invite you to grab some spoons and indulge!

Raspberry Coconut Trifle

Sweet, soft, and airy, this multitiered dessert combines layers of sponge cake, fresh raspberries, and chewy coconut mousse. At New York's Helmsley Palace Hotel, we used to make these as individual trifles and serve them during teatime. This dessert can be eaten immediately, or kept for several hours in the refrigerator. Be sure to let it come to room temperature for 30 minutes before serving. A trifle bowl is usually a round, clear glass vessel (to allow the layers inside to be seen), with tall sides and a pedestal base.

SERVES 8 TO 10

Coconut Pastry Cream

- 6 large egg yolks
- ¾ cup sugar
- 6 tablespoons cornstarch
- 3 cups milk
- ¼ teaspoon coarse salt
- 1 vanilla bean, split in half lengthwise, or 1 tablespoon pure vanilla extract
- ¼ cup (½ stick) cold unsalted butter
- 2½ cups sweetened shredded coconut

- 2 cups heavy cream
- 6 tablespoons raspberry puree (from a 10-ounce package frozen raspberries in syrup, thawed and pressed through a fine strainer)
- ¼ cup cream of coconut
- 1 Yellow Sponge Cake (page 172), trimmed and cut into 3 equal layers
- 2 (½-pint) containers raspberries

1. To make the pastry cream: In a medium bowl, whisk together the egg yolks, about half of the sugar, all the cornstarch, and ½ cup of the milk.

2. In a saucepan, combine the remaining sugar, the remaining 2½ cups milk, and the salt. If using a vanilla bean, scrape the seeds into the saucepan and add the pod. Bring to a simmer. Whisking constantly, gradually pour the hot milk into the egg mixture, slowly at first to temper it and then more quickly. Set a strainer over the saucepan. Strain the custard mixture back into the saucepan and bring to a boil over medium heat, whisking constantly. Boil for 10 seconds, whisking. (Make sure the custard boils for 10 seconds in the center of the pan, not just around the sides.) The mixture should thicken to a pudding-like consistency. Discard the vanilla bean, if using.

3. Transfer the pastry cream to the bowl of a standing mixer fitted with the paddle attachment and beat on medium speed for 2 to 3 minutes, to cool slightly. Beat in the vanilla extract, if using. With the mixer running, beat in the butter a little at a time. Beat in 1½ cups of the coconut. Transfer to a bowl, press a piece of plastic wrap directly on the surface to prevent a skin from forming, and refrigerate until cold, 1 to 2 hours.

4. Preheat the oven to 325°F. Spread the remaining 1 cup coconut out in a single layer on a baking sheet. Bake for 5 to 8 minutes, until lightly browned. Set aside to cool.

5. In the bowl of a standing mixer fitted with the whisk attachment, beat the cream to medium-stiff peaks. Divide between two bowls. Fold the raspberry puree into the cream in one bowl; fold the cream

RECIPE CONTINUES . . .

TECHNIQUE TIP: Use a pastry bag fitted with a large plain tip to pipe the pastry cream and whipped cream into the trifle dish. This will result in a cleaner presentation against the glass of the dish.

of coconut into the whipped cream in the other bowl. Set both bowls aside.

6. To assemble the trifle, stir the chilled pastry cream with a wooden spoon or rubber spatula to loosen it. Spread half of the pastry cream over the bottom of a 9-inch glass trifle bowl. Sprinkle with about one-quarter of the raspberries and one-quarter of the toasted coconut. Set one of the cake layers on top and spread with all of the raspberry whipped cream. Sprinkle with another quarter of the raspberries and another quarter of the toasted coconut. Top with a second cake layer and spread with the coconut whipped cream. Sprinkle with another quarter of the raspberries and a quarter of the toasted coconut. Add the third cake layer, and spread with the remaining coconut pastry cream. Top with the remaining raspberries and toasted coconut. Serve chilled.

White Chocolate Mousse and Raspberry Parfait

This dessert is wonderfully light in texture. The airiness is due to a combination of egg whites, whipped cream, and melted white chocolate. Make sure to use the best quality chocolate you can find. When buying white chocolate, never buy chips or chunks, as they won't melt properly. Couverture chocolate, which is used for finishing and confections, can also be used. It can be found at gourmet specialty stores. Try serving with a slice of toasted pound cake or Yellow Sponge Cake (page 172).

SERVES 6

1½ cups heavy cream

½ vanilla bean, cut in half lengthwise and scraped, or 1½ teaspoons pure vanilla extract

6 ounces white chocolate, chopped

4 large egg whites, at room temperature

¼ cup sugar

1 to 1½ cups raspberries

- - - - - - - - - - - - - - - - - - - -

TECHNIQUE TIP: When making mousse, be sure to underwhip the cream so that it forms medium, not stiff, peaks. If whipped too stiff, the cream may break when the rest of the mixture is folded in.

1. In a small saucepan, bring ½ cup of the cream to a simmer with the vanilla bean and seeds, if using. Pour the cream over the white chocolate in a heatproof bowl and let stand for 5 minutes to melt. Remove the vanilla bean, if using. Stir until smooth. Let cool. Stir in the vanilla extract, if using.

2. Bring 1 inch of water to a simmer in the bottom of a double boiler. Combine the egg whites and sugar in the top of the double boiler, set it over (not in) the simmering water, and whisk to dissolve the sugar just until it melts, 1 to 2 minutes. (The mixture should feel just warm to the touch, and not gritty.)

3. Transfer to the bowl of a standing mixer fitted with the whisk attachment and beat until stiff peaks form. Whisk about one-quarter of the meringue into the cooled chocolate mixture to lighten it, then fold in the rest with a rubber spatula.

4. Add the remaining 1 cup cream to the mixer bowl, and beat with the whisk attachment until medium peaks form. Gently fold into the white chocolate mixture. Cover the mousse with plastic wrap and refrigerate overnight.

5. Layer into individual bowls or parfait glasses, starting with a layer of raspberries, followed by a layer of mousse. Repeat one more layer of each, and top with one final layer of raspberries.

Classic Chocolate Mousse

Rick Steffann, one of my first mentors, taught me how to make the lightest, most intensely flavored chocolate mousse when we worked together at the New York restaurant Le Colombe d'Or. We would serve the mousse in martini glasses garnished with decadent chocolate shavings. SoNo Baking Company's version, which is similar to Rick's, uses bittersweet chocolate for an extra-dark chocolate flavor. It is deeply satisfying and rich, without being overly sweet. To make a parfait, try layering the mousse with Ganache (page 169) or between layers of fresh raspberries.

SERVES 4

5 ounces bittersweet
   chocolate, finely chopped
3 large eggs, separated
3 tablespoons sugar
   Pinch of coarse salt
1 cup heavy cream

1. Put the chocolate in a medium heatproof bowl; set aside.

2. Bring about 1 inch of water to a boil in the bottom of a double boiler. In the top of the double boiler, whisk the egg yolks with the sugar and the salt. Set the pan over (not in) the simmering water and whisk until warm to the touch, about 2 minutes. Transfer to the bowl of a standing mixer fitted with the whisk attachment.

3. Place the chocolate over the simmering water and heat until melted.

4. Beat the egg yolk mixture until the mixture is thick and pale yellow, and forms a ribbon when the whisk is lifted from the bowl, about 3 minutes.

5. Remove the mixer bowl from the stand. Add the warm melted chocolate and whisk by hand until smooth. Add the egg whites and whisk until smooth. Using a rubber spatula, scrape the chocolate mixture back into the bowl in which you melted the chocolate and set aside.

6. Wash and dry the mixer bowl. Pour the cream into the mixer bowl and beat with the whisk attachment until medium peaks form. Fold into the chocolate mixture until there are no visible streaks of white. Spoon into one large or four individual serving bowls and chill until set, at least 2 hours.

Lemon Mousse

There is plenty of intense lemon flavor in this lemon curd lightened with whipped cream. Serve with fresh seasonal berries.

2 tablespoons cold water

1 teaspoon powdered unflavored gelatin

6 large egg yolks
Grated zest of 4 lemons (about 4 teaspoons)

½ cup lemon juice (from about 4 lemons)

¾ cup sugar

⅛ teaspoon coarse salt

½ cup (1 stick) cold unsalted butter, cut into ½-inch pieces

½ cup heavy cream

1. In a small bowl, sprinkle the cold water over the gelatin; set aside.

2. In a medium saucepan, combine the egg yolks, lemon zest, lemon juice, sugar, and salt, and whisk to combine. Set over medium heat and cook, stirring constantly, until the mixture has thickened enough to coat the back of a wooden spoon, about 5 minutes. Do not boil. Whisk in the gelatin.

3. Strain through a fine strainer into the bowl of a standing mixer fitted with the paddle attachment. Beat until slightly cooled, 2 to 3 minutes. Beat in the butter a little at a time, and continue beating until smooth and completely cooled. Transfer to a large bowl and let stand until the gelatin just begins to set, about 10 minutes.

4. Wash and dry the mixer bowl. Add the cream and beat with the whisk attachment until medium peaks form. Fold into the cooled lemon mixture and refrigerate until very cold and the mousse is set, 2 to 3 hours.

Passionfruit Mousse

This tart and creamy tropical mousse sits atop a thin base of sponge cake. It is incredibly simple to make and incredibly elegant to serve. Be sure to use passionfruit puree, not nectar or juice, as the consistency will be different. Freeze any extra mousse in an airtight container for up to 2 weeks, for a snack later on.

SERVES 6

3 tablespoons cold water

1 tablespoon powdered unflavored gelatin

1 cup passionfruit puree

½ cup sugar

2 teaspoons lemon juice

1 (¼-inch-thick) 9-inch Yellow Sponge Cake (page 172) round

1 cup heavy cream, plus more for garnish

½ cup apricot jam

6 raspberries, for garnish

1. In a small bowl, sprinkle the cold water over the gelatin and let stand for 5 minutes.

2. In the top of a double boiler, combine the passionfruit puree, sugar, and lemon juice. Set over (not in) 1 inch of simmering water and heat, stirring every now and then, until the mixture is warm and the sugar dissolves. Add the gelatin and stir to dissolve. Remove from the heat and let stand at room temperature until cool to the touch, 15 to 20 minutes.

3. Line a baking sheet with parchment paper or a nonstick silicone baking mat. Use six 2¼-inch-wide by 2¼-inch-tall pastry rings to stamp out rounds of sponge cake; transfer the rings to the prepared baking sheet, leaving the cake inside each ring; set aside.

4. In the bowl of a standing mixer fitted with the whisk attachment, beat the cream to medium peaks. Fold a dollop of whipped cream into the cooled passionfruit mixture, then fold in the rest of the whipped cream until well combined. Pour the passionfruit mixture into each of the rings, all the way to the top. Cover with plastic wrap and freeze until set, at least 2 hours.

5. When the mousse has set, in a small saucepan, heat the apricot jam until liquid. Strain through a fine strainer into a bowl. Remove the mousses from the freezer. Spoon a little of the warm strained jam on top of each, using the back of the spoon to spread the jam evenly to cover. Return to the freezer.

6. To unmold, wrap a warm towel around one of the rings and let stand for 1 to 2 minutes. Place the mousse, still in the ring, on top of a small can, the diameter of which is smaller than the ring (a can of tomato paste works well). Slide the ring down and off the mousse. Repeat to unmold all of the mousses. Set each on a serving plate.

7. To garnish, on the top of each, pipe a small round of whipped cream, then add a fresh raspberry.

Chocolate Pudding Icebox Cake

My mother, Mary Ann, used to make her famous icebox cake all the time when we were kids. Her version came mostly from the back of a box and was topped with Cool Whip, but my brothers and I loved it and would beg her to make it. She somehow found the time, even with eight boys to take care of. The version below is more sophisticated but just as enjoyable, featuring layers of dark, bittersweet pudding layered with graham crackers and topped with (real!) whipped cream. We use cocoa in addition to bittersweet chocolate to intensify the chocolate flavor.

SERVES 8

3¾ cups milk

1½ cups half-and-half

1¼ cups granulated sugar

½ teaspoon coarse salt

1 vanilla bean, halved lengthwise and scraped, or 1 tablespoon pure vanilla extract

8 large egg yolks

⅓ cup Dutch-processed unsweetened cocoa powder

4½ tablespoons cornstarch

9 ounces bittersweet chocolate, finely chopped

3 tablespoons cold unsalted butter, cut into pieces

15 whole, rectangular graham crackers

¾ cup heavy cream

2 tablespoons confectioners' sugar

1. In a saucepan, combine 3 cups of the milk, the half-and-half, about half of the sugar, all the salt, and the vanilla bean and seeds, if using, and bring the mixture to a simmer.

2. Meanwhile, in a heatproof bowl, whisk the egg yolks with the rest of the sugar, the cocoa, cornstarch, and the remaining ¾ cup milk.

3. Whisking constantly, pour the hot milk mixture into the egg yolk mixture, gradually at first to temper the yolks and then more quickly. Set a strainer over the saucepan and strain the custard mixture back into the pan. Bring to a boil over medium heat, whisking constantly. Boil for 10 seconds, whisking. (Make sure the custard boils for 10 seconds in the center of the pan, not just around the sides.) The mixture should thicken to a pudding-like consistency. Discard the vanilla bean, if using.

4. Transfer to the bowl of a standing mixer fitted with the paddle attachment. Add the chocolate. Beat on medium speed to melt the chocolate and cool slightly, 2 to 3 minutes. Beat in the vanilla extract, if using. Beat in the butter a little at a time and continue beating until the chocolate is entirely melted and the mixture is cool, 5 to 10 more minutes.

5. Layer the bottom of an 8-inch square baking dish with one-third of the graham crackers, breaking up the crackers as needed to create a snug single layer. Spoon about one-third of the pudding on top and smooth the top. Make another layer using another one-third of the graham crackers, and spoon more pudding on top. Repeat one more time, to use all of the pudding. Refrigerate until chilled, 2 to 3 hours.

6. Combine the heavy cream and confectioners' sugar in the bowl of a standing mixer fitted with the whisk attachment and beat until medium peaks form (or beat by hand with a whisk). Spread the whipped cream over the chilled pudding, and serve.

Rice Pudding

This dessert is another favorite of my wife's. Veronica can't stay mad at me for long (after spending most of my day at the bakery) when I come home with a pint of this comforting pudding. Far from your typical drab diner dessert, this pudding can accommodate any favorite dried fruit, including apricots, cherries, cranberries, and golden raisins. Top with whipped cream and a sprinkle of cinnamon for an extra treat.

SERVES 6

1 **quart milk**

½ **cup long-grain rice, such as Carolina, or any other long-grain that isn't converted**

½ **cup sugar**

½ **teaspoon coarse salt**

1 **vanilla bean, split lengthwise and scraped, or 1 tablespoon pure vanilla extract**

1 **cinnamon stick**

2 **large egg yolks**

½ **cup heavy cream**

¼ **cup (½ stick) unsalted butter**

½ **cup dried apricots, diced (optional)**

½ **cup dried cherries (optional)**

1. In a medium saucepan, bring the milk to a simmer with the rice, sugar, salt, vanilla bean and seeds, if using, and cinnamon stick. Reduce the heat and simmer until the rice is tender, 15 to 20 minutes.

2. In a medium heatproof bowl, whisk the egg yolks with the cream. When the rice is tender, pour the mixture into the bowl with the yolks, gradually at first to temper the yolks and then more quickly, whisking constantly. Return the mixture to the saucepan and cook over medium heat, stirring, until the custard thickens enough to leave a trail when you run your finger across the back of the spoon, about 2 minutes. Remove from the heat. Remove and discard the vanilla bean and cinnamon stick. Whisk in the vanilla extract, if using, and then the butter. Fold in the dried fruits, if desired.

3. Transfer to a clean bowl, cover with plastic wrap, and chill. If you like, spoon the pudding into individual glasses before serving.

Butterscotch Pudding

I like to think of this pudding as a lighter version of crème brûlée. It can even be "brûléed" by sprinkling it with sugar and torching the top. But then you wouldn't get to enjoy my very favorite part of the pudding—the skin! Growing up, my brothers and I used to fight over it, all trying to elbow our way to the bowl with our spoons. My brother Peter once said, "If I were rich, I'd hire someone just to make pudding skin for me because I love it so much!" Serve topped with whipped cream.

4 large egg yolks, at room temperature

¼ cup cornstarch

3¼ cups half-and-half

¼ teaspoon coarse salt

1 cup firmly packed dark brown sugar

1 vanilla bean, split lengthwise and scraped, or 1 tablespoon pure vanilla extract

½ cup (1 stick) unsalted butter, cut into tablespoons

1. In a medium heatproof bowl, whisk together the egg yolks, cornstarch, ¼ cup of the half-and-half, and the salt; set aside.

2. In a saucepan, combine the remaining 3 cups half-and-half, ¼ cup of the dark brown sugar, and the vanilla bean and seeds, if using. Bring to a simmer.

3. Meanwhile, in a second saucepan, combine the remaining ¾ cup brown sugar and the butter. Cook over medium-low heat, stirring often, until the butter melts and the mixture is smooth and bubbly and smells a little nutty, about 2 minutes. Pour into the saucepan with the hot half-and-half and whisk until smooth.

4. Whisking constantly, pour the hot mixture into the egg mixture, gradually at first to temper it and then more quickly. Place a strainer over the saucepan and strain the custard mixture back into the saucepan. Bring to a boil over medium heat, whisking constantly. Boil for 10 seconds, whisking. (Make sure the custard boils for 10 seconds in the center of the pan, not just around the sides.) The mixture should thicken to a pudding-like consistency. Discard the vanilla bean, if using.

5. Fit a standing mixer with the paddle attachment and pour the pudding mixture into the bowl. Beat on medium speed for 2 to 3 minutes to cool slightly. Add the vanilla extract, if using. Transfer to a bowl, cover with plastic wrap, and refrigerate until chilled, 3 to 4 hours.

Caramel Bread Pudding

Flecked with vanilla beans and flavored with dark rum and a layer of caramel on top, this homey dessert is similar to a tarte tatin; the caramel is poured onto the bottom of the pan and when the bread pudding is inverted after baking, the caramel coats the top. If you don't have day-old bread, cut the bread into cubes and bake on a baking sheet at 250°F for 1 hour. Serve with or without the Crème Anglaise.

MAKES ONE 9-INCH ROUND PUDDING, SERVES 10

Caramel

- ¾ cup sugar
- ½ teaspoon white vinegar
- 7 tablespoons water

Pudding

- 6 large eggs
- ¾ cup sugar
- 3 cups milk
- 1 vanilla bean, split lengthwise and scraped, or 1 tablespoon pure vanilla extract
- ¾ teaspoon coarse salt
- 3 tablespoons dark rum or brandy
- 1 day-old (9-ounce) baguette with crusts intact, cut into 1-inch cubes (about 9 cups)
- 2 tablespoons unsalted butter, cut into pieces
- 1 recipe Crème Anglaise (page 164)

1. Brush a 9-inch round cake pan generously with softened butter; set aside.

2. To make the caramel: In a small saucepan, combine the sugar, vinegar, and 4 tablespoons of the water. Bring to a boil over medium-high heat, swirling the pan to dissolve the sugar. Boil until the mixture turns a deep amber color, about 10 minutes. Immediately add the remaining 3 tablespoons water off the heat. Stand back; the mixture will spit. Return the pan to the heat to re-melt the caramel.

3. Pour the caramel into the prepared cake pan. Tilt the pan to coat the bottom with the caramel; set aside to let the caramel firm and cool.

4. To make the pudding: In a heatproof bowl large enough to hold the bread cubes, whisk the eggs with the sugar; set aside.

5. In a large saucepan, bring the milk, vanilla bean and seeds, if using, and salt to a simmer. Pour into the bowl with the eggs, gradually at first to temper the eggs and then more quickly, whisking constantly. Add the rum or brandy and the vanilla extract, if using. Add the bread and let soak for 45 minutes, pushing the bread occasionally to keep it submerged, until all the liquid has been absorbed.

6. Set the oven rack in the middle position. Preheat the oven to 350°F. Bring a kettle of water to a boil. Dot the caramel with the butter.

7. Discard the vanilla bean, if using. Transfer the bread-custard mixture to the prepared pan and level the top. Cover with a round of parchment paper and place in a roasting pan. Place the roasting pan in the preheated oven, and pour in the boiling water to come about ½ inch up the sides of the pan.

8. Bake the pudding until firm to the touch, 55 to 60 minutes. Carefully remove it from the water bath and let it cool on a wire rack for 10 minutes. Run a knife around the edges (wearing oven mitts to protect your hands from being burned by the caramel), carefully invert onto a serving plate, and serve with Crème Anglaise.

Crème Anglaise

Crème Anglaise is a classic sauce for many desserts. Try freezing it in your ice-cream machine for the best vanilla ice cream.

MAKES ABOUT 2 CUPS

 5 **large egg yolks**

 ½ **cup plus 2 tablespoons sugar**

1⅔ **cups half-and-half (can also use half milk and half heavy cream)**

 1 **vanilla bean, cut in half lengthwise and scraped, or 1 tablespoon pure vanilla extract**

 ¼ **teaspoon coarse salt**

1. In a medium heatproof bowl, whisk the egg yolks with the ½ cup of sugar.

2. In a saucepan, combine the remaining 2 tablespoons sugar, the half-and-half, the vanilla bean and seeds, if using, and the salt. If using a vanilla bean, scrape the tiny black seeds into the saucepan and add the pod. Bring to a simmer over medium-low heat. Whisking constantly, gradually pour the hot mixture into the egg mixture to temper it. Return the mixture to the saucepan and cook, stirring, for 1 minute, or until the custard is thickened enough to coat the back of a spoon. Do not boil. Remove from the heat and serve.

Date Nut Pudding

This chewy toffee pudding is more like a small, moist cake than a pudding. It is a very traditional English dessert, in both technique and flavor. Serve with clotted cream or crème fraîche on the side. Or, serve with Armagnac-flavored whipped cream.

MAKES 8 INDIVIDUAL PUDDINGS

1½ cups all-purpose flour

1 teaspoon baking soda

½ teaspoon baking powder

½ teaspoon coarse salt

1½ cups (about 10 ounces) pitted dried dates, coarsely chopped

1½ cups plus 8 tablespoons boiling water

4 tablespoons (½ stick) unsalted butter, cut into 8 pieces

2 cups light brown sugar

1 large egg

1 teaspoon pure vanilla extract

1 cup walnuts, coarsely chopped

1. Place an oven rack in the middle position. Preheat the oven to 350°F. Butter eight 6-ounce plain or slope-sided ramekins, and place on a baking sheet; set aside.

2. In a medium bowl, combine the flour, baking soda, baking powder, and salt; set aside.

3. In another bowl, combine the dates, the 1½ cups boiling water, and the butter. Stir until the butter is melted and the dates are soft. Add 1 cup of the brown sugar, the egg, and the vanilla. Mix to combine. Add the flour mixture and combine. Add the walnuts and mix to combine.

4. Sprinkle 1 tablespoon of the remaining brown sugar on the bottom of each ramekin. Divide the date batter evenly among the ramekins, and top each with 1 tablespoon of brown sugar. Drizzle 1 tablespoon boiling water over the top of each ramekin.

5. Bake until a cake tester inserted in the center comes out clean, about 30 minutes.

6. Run a knife around the rim of each ramekin. Invert the ramekins immediately onto a rack, unmold the puddings, and serve.

Cakes

SoNo Chocolate Ganache Cake

Classic Yellow Sponge Cake with
Chocolate Buttercream Frosting

Yellow Sponge Cake

Chocolate Bavarian Torte

Individual Boston Cream Pies

Lemon Pound Cake

Orange Chiffon Cake

Vanilla Angel Food Cake

Chocolate Angel Food Cake

Hazelnut Cake with Praline and Milk
Chocolate Buttercream Frosting

Apple Spice Cake with Brown Sugar
Frosting

Strawberry Shortcake

Coconut Cake

Red Velvet Cupcakes

Carrot Cake Cupcakes

SoNo Cheesecake

Pumpkin Cheesecake

Citrus Icebox Cheesecake

White Chocolate Mousse Roulade

Flourless Chocolate Cake

Chapter Six

C akes are the perfect way to celebrate any occasion. Tall layer cakes such as SoNo Chocolate Ganache Cake (page 169), Coconut Cake (page 190), and Strawberry Shortcake (page 189) signify an important day, such as a birthday, anniversary, or first day of school. Sophisticated and elegant cakes such as the decadent Chocolate Bavarian Torte (page 173) and the White Chocolate Mousse Roulade (page 204) reveal you to be the true master baker you always believed you could be!

Finally there are the classics—Red Velvet Cupcakes (page 193), Carrot Cake Cupcakes (page 196), and SoNo Cheesecake (page 199). Ideal to bring to a potluck dinner or to serve during Sunday football or any night of the week.

No matter which of the nineteen cakes you make from this chapter, there are a few tips to keep in mind for best results. First, always serve cakes at room temperature unless otherwise directed. If cakes are placed in the refrigerator to set up, be sure to take them out at least 30 minutes before serving to get to full room temperature. Second, buttercream frosting should never be refrigerated. Once it hardens it's difficult to spread and use for decorating (it will hold up to five days unrefrigerated, in a cool place). Third, there's nothing worse than a slice of cake that has been cut jaggedly and delivered to the plate in a heap. All varieties of cake should be cut into clean, compact slices. Cut dense or flourless cakes with a sharp knife dipped in hot water and wiped off on a kitchen towel. Dip and repeat as often as needed. Cut layer cakes neatly and efficiently with a wide cake server. Cut angel food cakes with a serrated bread knife or an angel food cake cutter.

All of these cakes require a little time, some patience, and a touch of skill. Start with the pound cake, angel food cakes, and cupcakes to build up your confidence. From there you'll be able to conquer the layer cakes and flourless cakes. And finally you'll be ready for the more technical, more involved composed cakes such as the roulades and Chocolate Bavarian Torte. Whichever cake you try, at whatever level, I hope you enjoy the journey and the results.

SoNo Chocolate Ganache Cake

This classic, French-inspired, signature cake has been in my repertoire for nearly thirty years. I created it in the early 1980s while working at The Commissary, a very popular restaurant in New York's TriBeCa neighborhood (I worked there at the same time Madonna did, only she was a coat-check girl back then, not a superstar!). There has always been a high demand for this cake even from places like New York's Bloomingdale's department store, which used to ask me to ship them dozens of these cakes every week. With its alternating layers of choco-late cake and chocolate ganache, its no surprise that it is SoNo Baking Company's #1 most requested chocolate cake. Store any extra ganache in the refrigerator for up to one week.

MAKES ONE 9-INCH
FOUR-LAYER CAKE,
SERVES 12

Ganache

- **1 pound semisweet chocolate, very finely chopped**
- **1 pound bittersweet chocolate, very finely chopped**
- **4 cups heavy cream**
- **¼ cup good-quality honey**
- **½ teaspoon coarse salt**
- **1 vanilla bean, split in half lengthwise, or 1 tablespoon pure vanilla extract**

Chocolate Sponge Cake

- **2 cups all-purpose flour**
- **1⅓ cups good-quality unsweetened cocoa powder, plus extra for dusting**
- **2⅔ cups granulated sugar**
- **1½ teaspoons baking powder**
- **2½ teaspoons baking soda**
- **½ teaspoon coarse salt**
- **4 large eggs**
- **2 teaspoons pure vanilla extract**
- **11 tablespoons (1 stick plus 3 tablespoons) unsalted butter, melted**
- **1⅓ cups buttermilk**
- **1⅓ cups brewed American coffee**

1. To make the ganache: Place all the chocolate in a heatproof bowl; set aside. In a medium saucepan, combine the cream, honey, and salt. Scrape the tiny black seeds from the vanilla bean pod, if using, into the cream, and add the pod. Bring the cream to a boil, pour over the chocolate, and let stand for 5 minutes to melt the chocolate. Whisk until smooth. Strain through a fine strainer into a bowl. Discard the vanilla bean. Stir in the vanilla extract, if using. Cover with plastic wrap and let stand at room temperature until the ganache stiffens, at least 6 hours or overnight. (Or, place in the refrigerater and chill, stirring every 20 to 30 minutes, until the ganache stiffens.)

2. Preheat the oven to 350°F. Butter two 9 by 2-inch round cake pans. Line the bottoms with a round of parchment paper and dust with a little bit of cocoa powder, tapping out any excess.

3. To make the cake: In a bowl of an electric mixer fitted with the paddle attachment, sift in the flour, cocoa, sugar, baking powder, baking soda, and salt. Mix on low speed to combine.

4. Add the eggs, vanilla, melted butter, buttermilk, and coffee. Mix on low speed until fully combined. Pour the batter into prepared cake pans. Bake on a baking sheet until a cake tester inserted in the middle comes out clean, 35 to 40 minutes. Transfer to a wire rack and let cool in the pans for 10 minutes. Then unmold the cakes onto the rack and let cool completely.

RECIPE CONTINUES . . .

5. Using a serrated knife, slice the top ⅛ to ¼ inch off each cake to level it, if necessary. Discard the top pieces. Splice each cake horizontally into two layers for a total of four layers. Place the bottom layer on a 9-inch cake round, a turntable, or a platter, and using an offset spatula, spread thickly with about 1½ cups of the ganache. Repeat with the second and third layers, spreading another 1½ cups ganache over each layer. Add the final cake layer and spread it with a very thin layer of ganache (this is your crumb layer). Place the cake in the refrigerator until the crumb layer is set, about 30 minutes.

6. Remove the cake from the refrigerator and place it on a wire rack set over a sheet pan. In the top of a double boiler set over simmering water, heat the reserved ganache just until liquid. Pour the ganache over the top of the cake, allowing it to run down the sides. Using a large offset spatula, help spread the ganache from the center to the edges so the cake is completely covered. Smooth the top and sides. Refrigerate to set, about 30 minutes. Serve at room temperature.

Classic Yellow Sponge Cake with Chocolate Buttercream Frosting

This cake gives me reason to celebrate! It's the perfect dessert for any occasion, including birthday parties (we use it as our standard birthday cake at the bakery), family dinners, or rewarding the winning goal. The cocoa-infused buttercream is both simple to make and easy to work with, making for effortless decorating. Try using a pastry bag and plain tip to pipe a border around the top and bottom for an extra decorative touch.

MAKES ONE 9-INCH THREE-LAYER CAKE, SERVES 12

Chocolate Buttercream

- **5 large egg whites**
- **1⅓ cups sugar**
- **Pinch of coarse salt**
- **1 pound unsalted butter, firm but not chilled, cut into cubes**
- **½ teaspoon pure vanilla extract**
- **1 pound bittersweet chocolate, finely chopped**
- **¼ cup Dutch-processed unsweetened cocoa powder mixed with ¼ cup warm water**

- **1 (9-inch) Yellow Sponge Cake (page 172), cooled**

TECHNIQUE TIP: Do not refrigerate buttercream before using or it will harden. Instead, keep it at room temperature (in a cool room). It will keep for up to 5 days unrefrigerated.

1. To make the buttercream: Bring 1 inch of water to a boil in the bottom of a double boiler. In the top of the double boiler, whisk the egg whites with the sugar and the salt over (not in) the simmering water until warm to the touch and the sugar has dissolved, 1 to 2 minutes (make sure the bottom of the top of the double boiler doesn't touch the water). Transfer to the bowl of a standing mixer fitted with the whisk attachment and beat until stiff peaks form. With the machine running, gradually beat in the butter, piece by piece. By the time all the butter is added, the mixture will break, but it will become smooth again as you continue to beat. Beat in the vanilla.

2. Melt the chocolate in a heatproof bowl set over the bottom of the double boiler. While it is still warm but not hot, beat the chocolate into the buttercream. Add the cocoa mixture, and beat until the buttercream is cool—about 5 minutes.

3. Using a long serrated knife, trim the top of the cake if necessary to level it. Cut the cake into even thirds. Place one layer on a 9-inch cake round and spread with ⅓ to ½ inch buttercream. Set the second layer on top and spread with the same amount of buttercream. Add the final cake layer and spread a thin layer of buttercream over the top and sides of the cake—this is called a "crumb" layer, and its purpose is to glue the crumbs to the cake so that they don't end up in the frosting on the outside of the cake. Refrigerate the cake for 15 minutes, until the crumb layer is set. Then spread the cake with the rest of the buttercream.

Yellow Sponge Cake

At the bakery, we make our layer cakes in 3-inch-high cake pans. If you have a 3-inch cake pan, use the 4-egg recipe below. If you only have a 2-inch-high pan, use the 3-egg recipe. The oil called for in this recipe helps make the cake extra moist, more so than a typical genoise (sponge cake). Add the oil by slowly drizzling it and folding it into the cake batter to help the cake retain its airy quality. This sponge cake is the base for several desserts in this book, including Strawberry Shortcake (page 189) and Passionfruit Mousse (page 156).

MAKES ONE 9-INCH CAKE

4-Egg Sponge

- ¾ cup cake flour
- ½ cup cornstarch
- 4 large eggs, at room temperature
- 4 large egg yolks, at room temperature
- ⅔ cup sugar
- 1 teaspoon coarse salt
- 1 tablespoon pure vanilla extract
- 1 cup vegetable oil

3-Egg Sponge

- 9 tablespoons cake flour
- 6 tablespoons cornstarch
- 3 large eggs, at room temperature
- 3 large egg yolks, at room temperature
- ½ cup sugar
- ¾ teaspoon coarse salt
- 2 teaspoons pure vanilla extract
- ¾ cup vegetable oil

1. Set the oven rack in the middle position. Preheat the oven to 375°F. Spray a 9 by 2-inch (or 9 by 3-inch) round cake pan with vegetable spray. Line a baking sheet with parchment paper or a nonstick silicone baking mat; set aside.

2. In a medium bowl, sift together the flour and cornstarch; set aside. In the bowl of a standing mixer fitted with the whisk attachment, beat the whole eggs, the yolks, the sugar, salt, and the vanilla on high speed until thick and pale yellow colored, and the mixture holds a thick ribbon when the whisk is lifted from the bowl, 7 to 8 minutes.

3. Remove the bowl from the stand. Add the dry ingredients and quickly and gently fold them into the batter with a rubber spatula. Gradually add (drizzling, if possible) the oil, while folding.

4. Pour the batter into the prepared cake pan, set it on the prepared baking sheet, and bake until a tester comes out clean when inserted into the center of the cake, about 25 minutes for the 3-egg cake, 25 to 30 minutes for the 4-egg cake.

5. Remove from the oven and turn the cake out immediately on a wire rack (don't let it cool in the pan, as the steam may collapse it). Let cool completely, at least 1 hour.

Chocolate Bavarian Torte

This rich Bavarian contains a chocolate layer cake filled with chocolate mousse and is topped with a smooth, shiny layer of ganache. A chocolate lover's dream, this was created and developed by Valerie Denner, one of SoNo Baking Company's most talented and exacting pastry chefs. Warm any leftover ganache and serve alongside or with ice cream.

MAKES ONE 8-INCH
THREE-LAYER CAKE,
SERVES 8

1 (9-inch) Chocolate Sponge
Cake (page 169)

Chocolate Mousse

⅓ cup cold water
1 tablespoon plus ¾ teaspoon
powdered unflavored gelatin
5 large egg yolks
½ cup plus 2 tablespoons sugar
1⅔ cups milk
1 vanilla bean, cut in half
lengthwise and scraped, or
1 tablespoon pure vanilla
extract
5 ounces bittersweet
chocolate, finely chopped
3 tablespoons plus
1 teaspoon Dutch-processed
unsweetened cocoa powder
¼ teaspoon coarse salt
1⅔ cups heavy cream

Chocolate Ganache

2 ounces semisweet chocolate,
finely chopped
2 ounces bittersweet
chocolate, finely chopped
½ cup heavy cream
½ tablespoon honey
¼ teaspoon coarse salt
1 teaspoon pure vanilla extract

1. Using a long serrated knife, trim the cake to level the top if necessary. Cut the cake into three equal layers. Place one layer on a work surface, and stamp out a round with an 8 by 3-inch pastry ring; discard the excess inch of cake. Leaving the cake in the ring, place cake and ring on an 8-inch cardboard cake round. Using a 7-inch round as a guide, cut the remaining two cake layers into 7-inch rounds. Set the ring and two 7-inch cake layers aside.

2. To make the mousse: In a small bowl, sprinkle the cold water over the gelatin and let stand to soften.

3. Meanwhile, in a medium heatproof bowl, whisk the egg yolks with the ½ cup of sugar.

4. In a saucepan, combine the remaining 2 tablespoons sugar, the milk, the vanilla bean and seeds, if using, the chocolate, cocoa, and salt. Bring to a simmer over medium-low heat, whisking to blend the chocolate. Whisking constantly, gradually pour the hot milk mixture into the egg mixture to temper it. Return the mixture to the saucepan and cook, stirring, for 1 minute. Do not boil. Remove from the heat, and stir in the gelatin until smooth. Strain through a fine strainer into a large bowl. Stir in the vanilla extract, if using. Let stand at room temperature until cool to the touch, 15 to 20 minutes.

5. Meanwhile, in the bowl of a standing mixer fitted with the whisk attachment, beat the cream to medium peaks. Refrigerate until ready to use.

6. Fold a dollop of whipped cream into the cooled chocolate mixture to lighten it, then fold in the rest of the whipped cream until the mousse is fully combined.

RECIPE CONTINUES . . .

7. To assemble the cake, spoon about one-third of the chocolate mousse over the 8-inch cake layer in the ring. Gently center one of the 7-inch rounds on top. Carefully pour over another third of the chocolate mousse to cover the cake. Center the third cake round on top. Pour in enough of the chocolate mousse so that it comes all the way to the top of the ring (you'll have a little mousse left over). Cover with plastic wrap and freeze until set, at least 4 hours, or overnight.

8. Make the Chocolate Ganache (using the instructions on page 169); set aside at room temperature.

9. When the cake has set, in the top of a double boiler, warm the ganache over simmering water until just liquid. Pour over the frozen cake. Quickly draw a long palette knife over the ganache to smooth it level with the top of the ring; the chocolate will set immediately.

10. To unmold, wet a kitchen towel with hot water and wring it out, then wrap it around the ring for a minute to warm the mousse. Set the cake on top of a can and ease the ring down and off. If the ring doesn't slide off easily, repeat with the warm towel until it does.

11. Place the cake in the refrigerator for 2 hours. Let cake stand at room temperature for 10 minutes before serving.

Individual Boston Cream Pies

These little cakes, strangely called pies, were invented at Boston's Parker House Hotel in the 1850s. I made a George Washington Pie, a variation of Boston Cream Pie, using chocolate cake instead of yellow cake and adding cherries, and served it the Elms Restaurant in Ridgefield, Connecticut. This was the first dessert of mine that Martha Stewart tried when she came to the restaurant, and then she asked me to come work with her. Individual Boston Cream Pies are ideal for making ahead of time. The cake, pastry cream, and ganache (which needs at least 6 hours to thicken) can all be made a day or two in advance and then assembled the day of and refrigerated before serving. Be sure to let the fully assembled refrigerated dessert stand for 30 minutes at room temperature before serving.

MAKES 4 INDIVIDUAL 4-INCH PIES

½ **recipe Ganache (page 169)**

Vanilla Pastry Cream

- 3 **large egg yolks**
- 6 **tablespoons sugar**
- 3 **tablespoons cornstarch**
- 1½ **cups milk**
- ½ **vanilla bean, split in half lengthwise, or 1½ teaspoons pure vanilla extract**
- ¼ **teaspoon coarse salt**
- 2 **tablespoons cold unsalted butter, cut into small pieces**

Sponge Cake

- ½ **cup cake flour**
- ½ **teaspoon baking powder**
- 2 **large eggs, at room temperature**
- 1 **large egg yolk, at room temperature**
- ½ **cup sugar**
- ¼ **teaspoon coarse salt**
- ¼ **teaspoon almond extract**
- ½ **teaspoon pure vanilla extract**
- ½ **cup milk**

1. Make the ganache; cover with plastic wrap and let stand for at least 6 hours or overnight.

2. To make the pastry cream: In a medium bowl, whisk together the egg yolks, 2 tablespoons of the sugar, all the cornstarch, and ¼ cup of the milk; set aside.

3. In a medium saucepan, combine the remaining 1¼ cups milk, remaining 4 tablespoons sugar, the vanilla bean and seeds, if using, and the salt. Bring to a simmer. Whisking constantly, gradually pour the hot milk into the egg mixture to temper it. Set a strainer over the saucepan. Strain the custard mixture back into the saucepan and bring to a boil over medium heat, whisking constantly. Boil for 10 seconds, whisking. (Make sure the custard boils for 10 seconds in the center of the pan, not just around the sides.) The mixture should thicken to a pudding-like consistency. Discard the vanilla bean.

4. Transfer the pastry cream to the bowl of a standing mixer fitted with the paddle attachment and beat on medium speed for 2 to 3 minutes, to cool slightly. With the mixer running, beat in the butter, a little at a time. Add the vanilla extract, if using. Continue beating for 5 minutes until cool. Transfer to a bowl. Cover with plastic wrap, pressing it directly onto the surface to prevent a skin from forming. Refrigerate until chilled, about 3 hours.

5. Set the oven rack in the middle position. Preheat the oven to 350°F. Brush four 4-inch ramekins generously with softened butter and dust with flour; place on a baking sheet lined with parchment paper or a nonstick silicone baking mat.

6. To make the cake: In a small bowl, sift together the cake flour and baking powder; set aside. Combine the eggs, egg yolk, sugar, salt, and vanilla and almond extracts in the bowl of a standing mixer fitted with the whisk attachment and beat on medium-high speed until light colored and thickened, and a thick ribbon forms when you lift the whisk from the batter, about 5 minutes. Meanwhile, in a saucepan, bring the milk just to a simmer over medium heat. Fold the dry ingredients into the ribboned egg mixture. Fold in the hot milk.

7. Divide the batter evenly among the prepared ramekins. Bake, rotating the baking sheet about halfway through the cooking, until the cake springs back in the center when you touch it, 23 to 28 minutes.

8. Remove the cakes from the oven and run a knife around the rims to loosen the cakes. Invert them immediately onto a wire rack. Let cool completely.

9. To assemble, whisk the chilled pastry cream to loosen it. Split the sponge cakes in half through the centers with a serrated knife. Place each of the top halves, rounded side down, on a serving plate. Spread each with about ½ cup pastry cream, making sure that it extends all the way to the edges of the cake (you want to be able to see the custard between the layers). Set the top halves on top.

10. Warm the ganache in the top of a double boiler set over simmering water just until it is soft enough to spread easily. Use a large serving spoon to spoon the ganache over the tops of the cakes; use the bottom of the spoon to spread the ganache from the center out, so that it reaches the edge of the cake and drips over the sides.

Lemon Pound Cake

My daughter Nola loves this ultimate melt-in-your-mouth pound cake. Beautiful, with a fine texture, this buttery lemon cake is brushed with warm apricot jam as soon as it comes out of the oven and then drizzled with a confectioners' sugar glaze that is clear and shiny.

MAKES ONE 10-INCH
BUNDT CAKE, SERVES 12

3 **cups cake flour, sifted**
¼ **teaspoon baking soda**
¼ **teaspoon baking powder**
1½ **cups (3 sticks) unsalted butter, at room temperature**
2½ **cups granulated sugar**
1 **teaspoon coarse salt**
5 **large eggs, at room temperature**
2 **tablespoons lemon juice**
1 **tablespoon lemon extract**
1 **cup buttermilk**
¾ **cup apricot jam**

Glaze

1 **cup confectioners' sugar**
3½ **tablespoons lemon juice**

- -

TECHNIQUE TIP: When applying a jam glaze to cakes, always apply warm jam to a warm cake in order for the cake to best absorb the jam. It won't absorb as well if either the jam or the cake is cool.

1. Set the oven rack in the middle position. Preheat the oven to 325°F. Generously butter a 10-inch nonstick Bundt pan. Line a baking sheet with parchment paper or a nonstick silicone baking mat.

2. In a medium bowl, whisk together the flour, baking soda, and baking powder; set aside.

3. In the bowl of a standing mixer fitted with the paddle attachment, beat the butter with the sugar and salt on medium-high speed until light and fluffy, scraping down the sides of the bowl about halfway through, 2 to 3 minutes.

4. Add the eggs one at a time, beating after each addition. If the mixture curdles, beat in a little of the flour mixture, 1 tablespoon at a time; the flour will absorb the excess moisture and the batter will smooth out again. (If the batter stays curdled, you run the risk of having butter lumps in your cake.) Beat in the lemon juice and lemon extract.

5. With the mixer on low speed, beat in half of the dry ingredients until absorbed. Beat in the buttermilk. Beat in the remaining dry ingredients until absorbed.

6. Scrape the batter into the prepared pan and bake on the prepared baking sheet. Bake until a cake tester comes out clean when inserted into the center of the cake and the cake springs back when gently touched, 65 to 70 minutes.

7. Let cool in the pan on a wire rack for 10 minutes. Invert the pan onto the rack and remove the pan.

8. Heat the jam in a saucepan over medium-low heat until liquid. Strain through a fine strainer into a bowl.

9. Place the wire rack over a parchment-lined sheet pan to catch any drips. Using a pastry brush, while the cake is still hot, paint it all over with the hot strained jam. Let stand until partially dried, about 10 minutes. In a medium bowl, stir together the confectioners' sugar and lemon juice. Spoon over the cake and let cool completely.

Orange Chiffon Cake

This wonderfully tall, airy orange cake first came onto the scene in the early twentieth century. It fell out of popularity in recent decades, but we've reinvented it at the bakery with delicious results. It looks like an angel food cake but has a texture closer to a sponge cake. Beaten egg whites add a lightness to the sponge and oil adds moistness. At the bakery we always have a vast number of egg whites on hand, and this cake, along with angel food cakes, is the perfect way to utilize them. Try it the next time you have leftover egg whites. Serve with your favorite fresh fruit and a dollop of whipped cream or crème fraîche.

MAKES ONE 10-INCH TUBE CAKE, SERVES 12

Cake

- 2¾ cups cake flour
- 1⅔ cups sugar
- 1 teaspoon coarse salt
- 1 tablespoon baking powder
- ⅔ cup vegetable oil
- 6 large egg yolks
- ⅔ cup orange juice
  Grated zest of 1 orange
- 1 teaspoon orange extract
- ⅓ cup water
- 10 large egg whites
- ½ teaspoon cream of tartar

Grand Marnier Pastry Cream

- 3 large egg yolks
- 6 tablespoons sugar
- 3 tablespoons cornstarch
- 1½ cups milk
- ⅛ teaspoon coarse salt
- 2 tablespoons Grand Marnier
- 1 teaspoon pure vanilla extract
- 2 tablespoons unsalted butter, cut into pieces

- 10 orange sections (from 1 to 2 oranges), pith removed, for garnish

1. Set the oven rack in the middle position. Preheat the oven to 350°F. Line a baking sheet with parchment paper or a nonstick silicone baking mat.

2. To make the cake: In the bowl of a standing mixer, sift the flour with 1 cup of the sugar, the salt, and the baking powder. Fit the mixer with the paddle attachment and beat on low speed to combine. With the mixer running, gradually add the oil, egg yolks, orange juice, orange zest, orange extract, and water and beat until blended. Transfer the batter to a large bowl.

3. Wash and dry the mixer bowl. Fit the mixer with the whisk attachment. Add the egg whites and the cream of tartar to the bowl, and beat on medium speed until frothy. With the mixer running, gradually add the remaining ⅔ cup sugar and beat until the meringue is glossy and stiff peaks form, about 5 minutes. Fold the meringue into the batter with a rubber scraper just until incorporated. Scrape into an unbuttered 10-inch tube pan with removable bottom, preferably nonstick, and smooth the top.

4. Bake on the prepared baking sheet until a cake tester inserted into the cake comes out clean and the cake springs back when gently touched, 50 to 55 minutes. Invert the pan over a wire rack (the cake will remain in the pan) and let cool for 1 hour.

5. To unmold, set the pan back on its bottom and use your fingers to gently pull the cake away from the sides of the pan to release it. Invert the pan on the rack, and remove the rim. Gently pull the cake away from the bottom and from around the center tube, and then gently remove the tube.

RECIPE CONTINUES . . .

6. To make the pastry cream: In a medium bowl, whisk together the egg yolks, about half of the sugar, all the cornstarch, and ¼ cup of the milk.

7. In a saucepan, combine the remaining sugar, the remaining 1¼ cups milk, and the salt. Bring to a simmer. Whisking constantly, pour the hot milk into the egg mixture, gradually at first to temper it, and then more quickly. Set a strainer over the saucepan. Strain the custard mixture back into the saucepan and bring to a boil over medium heat, whisking constantly. Boil for 10 seconds, whisking. (Make sure the custard boils for 10 seconds in the center of the pan, not just around the sides.) The mixture should thicken to a pudding-like consistency.

8. Transfer the pastry cream to the bowl of a standing mixer fitted with the paddle attachment and beat on medium speed for 2 to 3 minutes, to cool slightly. Beat in the Grand Marnier and the vanilla. With the mixer running, beat in the butter a little at a time. Beat until cooled, 5 to 10 more minutes. Press a piece of plastic wrap directly on the surface to keep a skin from forming, and refrigerate until chilled, about 1 hour.

9. Slice the cooled cake in half horizontally. Spread the bottom half with half of the pastry cream. Place the top half back on. Fill a pastry bag, fitted with a large plain tip, with the remaining pastry cream. Pipe 12 quarter-size dollops of pastry cream in a circle, about 1 inch in from the outside of the cake so they are centered. Place an orange segment in each dollop of cream, pointing toward the center.

Vanilla Angel Food Cake

Served on its own or as the base to a multitude of desserts, angel food cake is one of the most versatile of all cakes. Virtually fat-free, but completely satisfying, this is one of my favorite cakes to indulge in. The key to a successful angel food cake lies in beating the egg whites to just the right consistency for fluffiness, not overbeating them into dry peaks, which will make for a more dense, less airy cake. Vanilla paste can be found in gourmet specialty stores.

MAKES ONE 10-INCH TUBE CAKE, SERVES 12

12 **large egg whites (1½ to 1¾ cups)**

1½ **cups sugar**

1 **teaspoon lemon juice**

½ **teaspoon cream of tartar**

½ **teaspoon coarse salt**

1 **vanilla bean, cut in half lengthwise and scraped, or 1 tablespoon vanilla paste, or 1 tablespoon pure vanilla extract**

1 **cup cake flour, sifted**

TECHNIQUE TIP: Make sure when you heat egg whites in the top of a double boiler that the bottom of the pan doesn't touch the simmering water; if it does, the whites will cook and the batter will "grain" (get lumpy) when you beat it. Also, you must keep the whites in motion at all times by constantly whisking them over the heat. When making an angel food cake, a little lemon juice helps to lighten the color of the egg whites and keep them nice and white when baked.

1. Set the oven rack in the middle position. Preheat the oven to 350°F. Line a baking sheet with parchment paper or a nonstick silicone baking mat; set aside.

2. Bring 1 inch of water to a boil in the bottom of a double boiler. In the top of the double boiler, whisk together the egg whites, ¾ cup of the sugar, the lemon juice, cream of tartar, salt, and vanilla seeds, if using, or add the vanilla paste or extract. Whisk over (not in) the simmering water until warm to the touch and the sugar dissolves, 3 to 5 minutes (make sure the bottom of the top of the double boiler doesn't touch the water). Transfer the mixture to the bowl of a standing mixer fitted with the whisk attachment and beat until the meringue is glossy and stiff peaks form. Be careful not to overbeat the whites; they should be stiff, but not dry. Fold in the flour and the remaining ¾ cup sugar with a large rubber spatula.

3. Scrape the batter into a 10-inch tube pan with removable bottom, preferably nonstick. Tap a couple of times on the countertop to remove air bubbles, and smooth the top. Bake on the prepared baking sheet until the cake springs back when touched and is lightly browned, 35 to 40 minutes.

4. Invert the pan onto a wire rack (the cake will still be inside the pan) and let cool for 1 hour. Set the pan back on its bottom and use your fingers to gently pull the cake away from the sides of the pan to release it. Invert the pan onto a wire rack, and remove the rim. Using your fingertips, pull the cake away from the bottom and from around the center tube, and gently remove the tube. Cut the cake with a serrated knife or angel food cake cutter.

Variation: BROWN SUGAR ANGEL FOOD CAKE

Follow the method above, using 14 egg whites, 1½ cups light brown sugar, 1 teaspoon cream of tartar, 1 teaspoon salt, 1 tablespoon pure vanilla extract, and 1¼ cups cake flour.

Chocolate Angel Food Cake

This cake is very moist and delivers a lot of good chocolate flavor with only a slight amount of cocoa. Baking soda is the secret ingredient in this cake because it activates and intensifies the rich chocolate color. Serve with fresh fruit or ice cream topped with warm chocolate sauce.

MAKES ONE 10-INCH TUBE
CAKE, SERVES 12

1 cup cake flour

2 tablespoons Dutch-processed unsweetened cocoa powder

2 ounces semisweet chocolate, grated on the large holes of a grater

½ teaspoon baking soda

12 large egg whites (1¾ to 2 cups)

1½ cups sugar

1 teaspoon lemon juice

½ teaspoon cream of tartar

½ teaspoon coarse salt

2 teaspoons pure vanilla extract

TECHNIQUE TIP: An angel food cake is one of the few recipes that call for an *un*greased pan. The tube pan must be dry so that the batter will cling and rise. Nonstick is my pan of choice for these cakes. When unmolding, be sure to use your fingers to pull the cake away from the pan; never use a knife, which will permanently damage your pan, if scratched, and give the cake a ragged appearance. And like a delicate soufflé, angel food cakes and flourless cakes should not be rotated during baking, as their flour-free, fragile structures can collapse very easily.

1. Place an oven rack in the middle position. Preheat the oven to 350°F. Line a baking sheet with parchment paper or a nonstick silicone baking mat; set aside.

2. In a medium bowl, sift the flour with the cocoa powder, grated chocolate, and baking soda; set aside.

3. Bring 1 inch of water to a boil in the bottom of a double boiler. In the top of the double boiler, whisk together the egg whites, ¾ cup of the sugar, the lemon juice, cream of tartar, and salt. Whisk over the simmering water until warm to the touch and the sugar dissolves, 3 to 5 minutes. (Make sure the bottom of the top of the double boiler doesn't touch the water.) Transfer the mixture to the bowl of a standing mixer fitted with the whisk attachment and beat until the meringue is glossy and stiff peaks form. Be careful not to overbeat the whites; they should be stiff, but not dry. Beat in the vanilla. Fold in the dry ingredients and the remaining ¾ cup sugar with a large rubber spatula.

4. Scrape the batter into a 10-inch tube pan with removable bottom, preferably nonstick. Bake on the prepared baking sheet until the cake springs back when touched, 35 to 40 minutes.

5. Invert the pan on a wire rack (the cake will still be inside the pan) and let cool for 1 hour.

6. Set the pan back on its bottom and use your fingers to gently pull the cake away from the sides of the pan to release it. Invert the pan and remove the rim. Using your fingertips, gently pull the cake away from the bottom and from around the center tube, and remove the tube. Cut the cake with a serrated knife or angel food cake cutter.

Hazelnut Cake with Praline and Milk Chocolate Buttercream Frosting

We sell this delicious and sophisticated cake at the bakery throughout the fall months. It's one of my absolute favorites. In my opinion, there simply is no other better flavor combination. Hazelnut sponge cake is layered with praline buttercream and frosted with milk chocolate buttercream. It reminds me of the Italian classic hazelnut spread Nutella. The rich chocolate frosting is a nice complement to the airiness of the cake. The praline buttercream gives it even more dimension. Hazelnut sponge cake is prepared the same way the classic Yellow Sponge Cake (page 172) is, with the addition of finely ground hazelnuts and almond extract for a more nutty flavor. Praline paste is available at gourmet specialty stores.

MAKES ONE 9-INCH THREE-LAYER CAKE, SERVES 12

Hazelnut Sponge Cake

¼ **cup whole hazelnuts**
¾ **cup sugar**
9 **tablespoons cake flour**
6 **tablespoons cornstarch**
3 **large eggs, at room temperature**
3 **large egg yolks, at room temperature**
¾ **teaspoon coarse salt**
1 **tablespoon almond extract**
¾ **cup vegetable oil**

TECHNIQUE TIP: When making buttercream frosting, use butter that's firm, but not straight out of the refrigerator. Set it out for 30 to 60 minutes (depending on the temperature of your kitchen) before using, until just slightly softened.

1. Place an oven rack in the middle position. Preheat the oven to 375°F. Spray a 9 by 2-inch (or 9 by 3-inch) round cake pan with vegetable spray. Line a baking sheet with parchment paper or a nonstick silicone baking mat; set aside.

2. To make the sponge cake: Grind the hazelnuts in a food processor with ¼ cup of the sugar. In a medium bowl, sift together the flour, cornstarch, and hazelnut mixture; set aside.

3. In the bowl of a standing mixer fitted with the whisk attachment, beat the whole eggs, the yolks, remaining ½ cup sugar, salt, and almond extract on high speed until thick and pale yellow colored, and the mixture holds a thick ribbon when the whisk is lifted from the bowl, 7 to 8 minutes.

4. Remove the bowl from the stand. Add the dry ingredients and quickly and gently fold them into the batter with a rubber spatula. Gradually drizzle in the oil, while folding.

5. Pour the batter into the prepared cake pan, set it on the prepared baking sheet, and bake until a tester comes out clean when inserted into the center of the cake, about 25 minutes. Remove from the oven and turn the cake out immediately onto a wire rack. Let cool for at least 1 hour.

6. To make the buttercream: Bring 1 inch of water to a boil in the bottom of a double boiler. In the top of the double boiler, whisk the egg whites with the sugar and the salt over (not in) the simmering water until warm to the touch, 1 to 2 minutes (make sure the

bottom of the top of the double boiler doesn't touch the water). Transfer to the bowl of a standing mixer fitted with the whisk attachment and beat until stiff peaks form. With the machine running, gradually beat in the butter, piece by piece. When all the butter is added, the mixture will break, but it will become smooth again as you continue to beat. Beat in the vanilla. Divide the buttercream in half, returning one half to the mixer bowl for the chocolate flavor, and setting aside the other half for the praline buttercream.

7. Meanwhile, melt the milk chocolate in a heatproof bowl, or in the top of a double boiler, set over 1 inch of simmering water. While it is still warm, beat the chocolate into half of the buttercream. Add the cocoa mixture and beat until the buttercream is cool.

8. Use a metal offset spatula to spread the praline paste onto a clean work surface. Smooth the paste with the spatula, working out any lumps. When smooth, add ½ cup of the plain buttercream to the praline paste, and using the spatula, incorporate the praline paste by folding it into the butter-cream. Once the paste and buttercream are fully combined and there are no lumps, add the mixture to the remaining plain buttercream and fold with a rubber spatula to combine.

9. Using a long serrated knife, trim the top of the cake if necessary to level it. Split the cake into even thirds. Place one layer on a 9-inch cake round and spread with 1/3 to ½ inch praline buttercream. Set the second layer on top and spread with the rest of the praline buttercream. Spread a thin layer of milk chocolate buttercream over the top and sides of the cake—this is called a "crumb" layer, and its purpose is to glue the crumbs to the cake so that they don't end up stuck to the frosting on the outside of the cake. Refrigerate the cake for 15 minutes, until the crumb layer is set. Then spread the cake with the rest of the milk chocolate buttercream.

Milk Chocolate Buttercream

- 5 large egg whites
- 1⅓ cups sugar
  Pinch of coarse salt
- 1 pound unsalted butter, firm but not chilled, cut into cubes
- ½ teaspoon pure vanilla extract
- 8 ounces milk chocolate, finely chopped
- 2 tablespoons Dutch-processed unsweetened cocoa powder mixed with 2 tablespoons water
- ¼ cup praline paste

Apple Spice Cake with Brown Sugar Frosting

We put this dense, moist spice cake on our menu at SoNo Baking Company in late August, when local Connecticut apples are just starting to come into season. It's an ideal choice to bring to a picnic or potluck meal, as it can easily be transported in its pan. Here the cake is frosted with a brown sugar buttercream frosting. For more intense flavor, you can use dark brown sugar, rather than light brown as written here. This cake can also be removed from the pan and then iced on the top and sides with the buttercream, and decorated with Apple Chips (page 188). If you ice the sides, increase the buttercream to a 3-egg-white buttercream (page 188).

MAKES ONE 8-INCH
SQUARE CAKE, SERVES 16

Apple Cake

- 2 cups all-purpose flour
- 1 teaspoon baking soda
- ¾ teaspoon baking powder
- ¾ teaspoon coarse salt
- ¾ teaspoon ground cinnamon
- ¼ teaspoon grated nutmeg
- 1⅓ cups light brown sugar
- 1 cup vegetable oil
- 2 large eggs, at room temperature
- 2 cups grated peeled and cored apples (from any red baking apple, such as Cortland or Rome), about 1 pound
- 2 teaspoons pure vanilla extract
- ⅔ cup toasted walnuts, chopped (optional)

Brown Sugar Buttercream

- 2 large egg whites
- ½ cup light brown sugar
  Pinch of coarse salt
- ¾ cup (1½ sticks) unsalted butter, firm but not chilled, cut into cubes
- ½ teaspoon pure vanilla extract

1. Set the oven rack in the middle position. Preheat the oven to 350°F. Spray an 8-inch square cake pan with nonstick cooking spray. Line a baking sheet with parchment paper or a nonstick silicone baking mat.

2. To make the cake: In a medium bowl, sift together the flour, baking soda, baking powder, salt, cinnamon, and nutmeg; set aside.

3. In a large bowl, whisk together the brown sugar, oil, eggs, grated apples, and vanilla. Add the dry ingredients and fold with a rubber spatula until the flour has been absorbed. Fold in the walnuts, if using.

4. Pour the batter into the prepared cake pan. Bake on the prepared baking sheet, rotating the sheet about two-thirds of the way through the baking time, until a tester inserted into the center of the cake comes out with just a few crumbs adhering to the bottom, 50 to 55 minutes. Let cool completely in the pan on a wire rack.

5. To make the buttercream: Bring 1 inch of water to a boil in the bottom of a double boiler. In the top of the double boiler, whisk the egg whites with the brown sugar and the salt over (not in) the simmering water until warm to the touch, 1 to 2 minutes. (Be careful to not let the bottom of the top of the double boiler touch the water.) Transfer to the bowl of a standing mixer fitted with the whisk attachment and beat until stiff peaks form. With the machine running, gradually beat in the butter, piece by piece. By the time all the butter is added, the mixture will break, but it will become smooth again as you continue to beat. Beat in the vanilla.

6. Spread the buttercream over the top of the cake. Cut into squares.

Apple Chips

Be sure to make these chips on a baking sheet rather than parchment, as they will stick to parchment.

1 large Granny Smith apple, stemmed but unpeeled, cut in half lengthwise
Confectioners' sugar, for sifting

1. Place the oven rack in the middle position. Preheat the oven to 200°F. Line a baking sheet with a nonstick silicone baking mat; set aside.

2. Thinly slice the apple on a mandoline, peel and core included. Place the slices in a single layer on the prepared baking sheet. Sift confectioners' sugar over the slices. Bake until lightly browned, about 1 hour. Loosen from the mat with an offset spatula and then peel off the mat.

3-Egg-White Brown Sugar Buttercream

3 large egg whites
¾ cup light brown sugar
⅛ teaspoon coarse salt
1 cup (2 sticks) plus 2 tablespoons unsalted butter, firm but not chilled, cut into cubes
¾ teaspoon pure vanilla extract

Bring about 1 inch of water to a simmer in the bottom of a double boiler. Combine the egg whites, brown sugar, and salt in the top of the double boiler. Whisk over (not in) the simmering water until the whites are warm to the touch and the sugar dissolves, 1 to 2 minutes. Transfer to the bowl of a standing mixer fitted with the whisk attachment, and beat until the meringue is glossy and stiff peaks form. With the machine running, gradually beat in the butter, piece by piece. By the time the butter is added, the mixture will break; keep beating—it will become smooth again as you continue to beat. Beat in the vanilla.

Strawberry Shortcake

If there's one dessert all of my kids can agree on, it's this beloved American classic—moist sponge cake layered with quartered strawberries and whipped cream. It's also the #1 selling dessert at SoNo Baking Company during strawberry season.

MAKES ONE 9-INCH
THREE-LAYER CAKE,
SERVES 8

⅓ cup sliced almonds

1 Yellow Sponge Cake (page 172), cooled

2 pints ripe strawberries, stemmed and quartered (about 5 cups quartered berries)

2 tablespoons good-quality strawberry jam

1 quart heavy cream

¾ cup confectioners' sugar, plus more for garnish

1 tablespoon pure vanilla extract

10 whole ripe strawberries, for garnish

1. Preheat the oven to 350°F. Spread the almonds out in a single layer on a baking sheet. Bake for 3 to 5 minutes, until lightly browned. Set aside to cool.

2. If necessary, trim the top of the sponge cake with a long serrated knife to level it. Cut the cake into three even layers.

3. In a medium bowl, use a rubber spatula to stir the strawberries into the jam.

4. In a standing mixer fitted with the whisk attachment, beat the cream, confectioners' sugar, and vanilla until firm peaks form.

5. To assemble the shortcake, place one cake layer on a 9-inch cake round and spread with a thin (¼- to ⅓-inch) layer of whipped cream. Arrange half of the strawberries on top. Spread thinly with whipped cream to cover the strawberries. Add a second cake layer. Spread with whipped cream and top with the remaining strawberries. Spread with more whipped cream. Add the third cake layer. Spread the top and sides of the cake with whipped cream.

6. Scoop the remaining whipped cream into a pastry bag fitted with a star tip, and pipe 10 evenly spaced rosettes around the edge of the cake. Place one whole strawberry on its side, stem side out, in between each pair of rosettes. Holding the cake over a plate or baking sheet to catch the excess, edge the bottom ½ inch of the cake with the toasted almonds, pressing the almonds gently into the cream to adhere. Dust with confectioners' sugar.

Coconut Cake

We serve this buttery cake filled with coconut pastry cream year-round, but we can barely keep it in stock at Easter. Lesli Flick, our very first pastry chef, came up with the idea of frosting the top and sides with coconut buttercream and then coating it with coconut. The result looks like a beautiful, giant white snowball. For the holiday, she tops it with jellybean eggs, which sit in the shredded coconut "nest."

MAKES ONE 9-INCH
THREE-LAYER CAKE,
SERVES 12

Coconut Cake

1½ cups all-purpose flour

1½ teaspoons baking powder

3 large eggs, at room temperature, separated

2 tablespoons granulated sugar

½ cup (1 stick) unsalted butter, at room temperature

2 cups confectioners' sugar

½ teaspoon coarse salt

½ cup (4 ounces) coconut milk

2 tablespoons cream of coconut

1 teaspoon coconut extract

Coconut Pastry Cream

4 large egg yolks

½ cup sugar

¼ cup cornstarch

2 cups milk

¼ teaspoon coarse salt

½ vanilla bean, split in half lengthwise and scraped, or 1½ teaspoons pure vanilla extract

3 tablespoons cold unsalted butter

1 cup shredded, sweetened coconut

1. Set an oven rack in the middle position. Preheat the oven to 375°F. Brush a 9 by 2-inch round cake pan with softened butter. Line a baking sheet with parchment paper or a nonstick silicone baking mat; set aside.

2. To make the cake: In a medium bowl, whisk together the flour and the baking powder; set aside.

3. In the bowl of a standing mixer fitted with the whisk attachment, beat the egg whites on medium speed until frothy. With the mixer running, gradually sprinkle in the granulated sugar and beat until stiff peaks form. Scrape the meringue into a bowl; set aside.

4. Exchange the whisk for the paddle attachment. Wash and dry the bowl. Add the butter, confectioners' sugar, and salt to the mixer bowl. Beat on medium-high speed until light and fluffy, about 2 minutes, scraping down the sides of the bowl halfway through. Add the egg yolks one at a time, beating after each addition. Beat in the coconut milk, cream of coconut, and coconut extract.

5. With the mixer on low speed, add the dry ingredients, beating until the flour is absorbed. Remove the bowl from the stand and fold in the meringue.

6. Scrape the batter into the prepared cake pan. Bake on the prepared baking sheet, rotating the sheet about two-thirds of the way through the baking time, until a tester inserted into the center of the cake comes out clean, 30 to 35 minutes. Let cool in the pan on a wire rack for 20 minutes. Then turn the cake out and let cool completely on the rack.

7. To make the pastry cream: In a medium bowl, whisk together the egg yolks, about half of the sugar, all the cornstarch, and ½ cup of the milk.

8. In a saucepan, combine the remaining sugar, the remaining 1½ cups milk, the vanilla extract or vanilla bean, and the salt. Bring to a

RECIPE CONTINUES . . .

Coconut Buttercream

5 large egg whites

1⅓ cups sugar

Pinch of coarse salt

1 pound unsalted butter, firm but not chilled, cut into cubes

½ teaspoon pure vanilla extract

2 tablespoons coconut extract

2½ to 3 cups shredded, sweetened coconut, for decorating

TECHNIQUE TIP: When assembling a layer cake, pastry cream, and buttercream frosting, first pipe a line of buttercream around the edge of the cake to create a "dam," which will keep the pastry cream from oozing out into the buttercream when you spread it over each layer.

simmer. Whisking constantly, pour the hot milk into the egg mixture, gradually at first to temper it, and then more quickly. Set a strainer over the saucepan. Strain the custard mixture back into the saucepan and bring to a boil over medium heat, whisking constantly. Boil for 10 seconds, whisking. (Make sure the custard boils for 10 seconds in the center of the pan, not just around the sides.) The mixture should thicken to a pudding-like consistency. Discard the vanilla bean, if using.

9. Transfer the pastry cream to the bowl of a standing mixer fitted with the paddle attachment and beat on medium speed for 2 to 3 minutes, to cool slightly. Beat in the vanilla extract, if using. With the mixer running, beat in the butter a little at a time, until incorporated. Beat in the coconut. Transfer to a bowl, press plastic wrap directly over the cream to prevent a crust from forming, and chill until firm, 1 to 2 hours.

10. To make the buttercream: Bring 1 inch of water to a boil in the bottom of a double boiler. In the top of the double boiler, whisk the egg whites with the sugar and the salt over (not in) the simmering water until warm to the touch, 1 to 2 minutes (be careful to not let the bottom of the top of the double boiler touch the water). Transfer to the bowl of a standing mixer fitted with the whisk attachment and beat until stiff peaks form. With the machine running, gradually beat in the butter, piece by piece. By the time all the butter is added, the mixture will break, but it will become smooth again as you continue to beat. Beat in the vanilla and coconut extracts.

11. To assemble the cake, use a long serrated knife to trim the top of the cake, if necessary, to level it. Cut the cake into three equal layers. Set one layer on a 9-inch cake round. Scoop some of the buttercream into a pastry bag fitted with a plain tip. Pipe a line of buttercream around the edge of the cake layer to create a dam. Spread about half of the pastry cream over the cake, inside the buttercream "dam." Set the second cake layer on top and repeat to make a buttercream dam, and spread with the remaining pastry cream. Set the third layer on top and spread the top and sides of the cake with a crumb layer (a very thin layer of buttercream used to capture any loose crumbs, preventing them from getting into the outer frosting). Refrigerate the cake for 15 minutes, until the buttercream is set. Spread the cake with the remaining buttercream. Gently press the coconut all over the cake to coat completely.

Red Velvet Cupcakes

When I was working with Martha Stewart, she would often hand me a recipe she had collected on her travels—notes scribbled on a napkin, a page ripped out of a local magazine, a letter from a recent visitor—and ask me to develop a version for the television show or the magazine. After a trip to the South, she brought back a recipe for red velvet cake that I tweaked and tested and now serve in both cake and cupcake form at SoNo Baking Company. Kids and adults can't resist the deep rich color and tender texture. As with muffins and cookies, it's best to bake cupcakes one pan at a time. Top with chocolate sprinkles or shavings, as pictured on page 194.

MAKES 18 CUPCAKES

Cupcakes

- 1 cup buttermilk
- 1 teaspoon pure vanilla extract
- ½ cup (1 stick) unsalted butter, at room temperature
- 1½ cups sugar
- 1 teaspoon coarse salt
- 2 large eggs, at room temperature
- ¼ cup (2 ounces) red food coloring
- 2 tablespoons Dutch-processed unsweetened cocoa powder
- 2¼ cups cake flour, sifted
- 1 teaspoon baking soda
- 1 tablespoon white wine vinegar

Frosting

- 3 tablespoons all-purpose flour
- 1 cup milk
- 1 cup (2 sticks) unsalted butter, at room temperature
- 1 cup sugar
- Pinch of coarse salt
- 1 teaspoon pure vanilla extract

1. Set the oven rack in the middle position. Preheat the oven to 350°F. Spray a 12-cup and a 6-cup muffin pan with nonstick cooking spray. Line a baking sheet with parchment paper or a nonstick silicone baking mat; set aside.

2. To make the cupcakes: In a medium bowl, combine the buttermilk and vanilla; set aside.

3. In the bowl of a standing mixer fitted with the paddle attachment, cream the butter, sugar, and salt on medium-high speed until light colored and creamy, scraping down the sides of the bowl halfway through, 2 to 3 minutes. Add the eggs one at a time, beating after each addition.

4. In a small bowl, stir the food coloring and the cocoa together to form a paste. Add to the butter-sugar mixer and beat to combine.

5. Starting with the flour, alternate adding the flour with the buttermilk mixture in three batches, ending with the flour. Let stand for 15 minutes.

6. In a small bowl, stir together the baking soda and vinegar, which will help boost the red coloring. Let stand until foamy; fold into the batter. Divide the batter among the cups in the 12-cup muffin pan and the 6-cup pan.

7. Bake one pan at a time on the prepared baking sheet, rotating the sheet about two-thirds of the way through the cooking, until the cupcakes spring back when gently touched, 18 to 23 minutes.

RECIPE CONTINUES . . .

8. Transfer the pans to a wire rack and let cool for 10 minutes. Use an offset spatula to gently lift and turn the cupcakes on their sides in the muffin cups. Let cool completely in the pans.

9. To make the frosting: In a saucepan, whisk the flour with ¼ cup of the milk, smoothing out any lumps with a rubber spatula. Gradually whisk in the rest of the milk. Bring to a simmer over medium heat, whisking, and cook for 1 minute. Set aside to cool.

10. In the bowl of a standing mixer fitted with the paddle attachment, beat the butter, sugar, salt, and vanilla until light and fluffy, about 2 minutes. Add the cooled milk mixture and beat until the frosting has the consistency of whipped cream, 7 to 10 minutes.

11. Frost the cooled cupcakes with the vanilla frosting.

TECHNIQUE TIP: At the bakery we frost the cupcakes using a pastry bag fitted with either a large open rosette pastry tip, swirled in a circular motion as shown at left, or we use a large plain tip to create a solid round of frosting, as on page 197. Try practicing frosting techniques on a baking sheet. Scoop the frosting back into the pastry bag when you are ready to frost the actual cupcakes. Try using a variety of tips and techniques to achieve the finish you like best.

Carrot Cake Cupcakes

*My daughter Nola made her television debut at the tender age of
12 months when she appeared with me on a Martha Stewart Living
television cupcake segment. Nola sat patiently in her high chair throughout the show while Martha and I decorated a variety of cupcakes. When
we finally put one in front of her, she went to town, getting more of the
cake and icing on herself than in her mouth! While typical carrot cakes
can be heavy and dense, this version is light and moist. The carrots lend
a warm color, sweetness, and texture to the cake and the grated ginger
adds brightness and a kick to the traditional cream cheese frosting.*

MAKES 1 DOZEN CUPCAKES

Cupcakes

1¼ cups cake flour
¾ teaspoon baking soda
¾ teaspoon baking powder
¾ teaspoon coarse salt
¼ teaspoon ground cinnamon
⅛ teaspoon grated nutmeg
⅓ cup golden raisins
8 ounces (about 3 medium) carrots, peeled and shredded on the fine holes of a grater
⅓ cup sour cream
1 cup granulated sugar
½ cup vegetable oil
2 large eggs

Cream Cheese Frosting

8 ounces cream cheese, at room temperature (taken out of the refrigerator at least 4 hours in advance)
½ cup (1 stick) unsalted butter, at room temperature
Pinch of coarse salt
3 cups confectioners' sugar
Grated zest of 1 orange
2 teaspoons finely grated fresh ginger (grated on a Microplane)
12 carrot peels, approximately 3 inches in length, for garnish

1. Set an oven rack in the middle position. Preheat the oven to 350°F. Coat a 12-cup muffin pan generously with nonstick cooking spray. Line a baking sheet with parchment paper or a nonstick silicone baking mat; set aside.

2. To make the cupcakes: In a medium bowl, sift the flour with the baking soda, baking powder, salt, cinnamon, and nutmeg. Stir in the raisins; set aside.

3. In a large bowl, whisk together the grated carrots, sour cream, sugar, oil, and eggs. Add the dry ingredients and fold with a rubber spatula until the flour has been absorbed.

4. Place the prepared muffin pan on the prepared baking sheet. Use a 2-inch (¼ cup) ice cream scoop to divide the batter evenly among the muffin cups.

5. Bake, rotating the sheet about two-thirds of the way through the baking time, until the tops of the cupcakes spring back when touched, the edges are golden brown, and a cake tester inserted in the center of a cupcake comes out clean, 18 to 22 minutes.

6. Transfer the pan to a wire rack to cool for 10 minutes. Use an offset spatula to gently lift and turn the cupcakes on their sides in the muffin cups. Let cool completely in the pan.

7. To make the frosting: In the bowl of a standing mixer fitted with the paddle attachment, beat the cream cheese, butter, and salt until light and creamy, about 2 minutes. Add the confectioners' sugar and beat for 1 minute. Beat in the grated zest and ginger.

8. Frost the cooled cupcakes with the cream cheese frosting. Roll each carrot peel tightly and place atop the cupcakes.

SoNo Cheesecake

Cheesecake was always my father Joseph's favorite dessert. I'm sure he would have loved my version of the classic New York–style favorite that sits atop a nutty pistachio-flavored crust and is topped with seasonal fresh fruit. It is one of our all-time best-selling desserts. Here, we use raspberries, but feel free to try strawberries, blueberries, or kiwi. The combination of vanilla paste (vanilla seeds suspended in glycerin, sold at culinary specialty stores) and vanilla extract makes for a strong infusion of flavor.

MAKES ONE 9-INCH CHEESECAKE, SERVES 10

Pistachio Graham Cracker Crust

- ¼ cup shelled, unsalted pistachios
- ¼ cup granulated sugar
- ¼ teaspoon coarse salt
- 1¼ cups graham cracker crumbs
- 5 tablespoons unsalted butter, melted and cooled

Filling

- 2 pounds cream cheese, at room temperature for at least 6 hours
- 1⅓ cups granulated sugar
- ½ teaspoon coarse salt
- 2 teaspoons pure vanilla extract
- 1 tablespoon vanilla paste, or seeds from 1 whole vanilla bean
- 5 large eggs, at room temperature
- ⅔ cup sour cream

- ½ cup apricot jam
- ½ cup shelled, unsalted pistachios, pulsed in a food processor until coarsely ground
- 3 (½-pint) containers raspberries
- Confectioners' sugar, for dusting (optional)

1. Preheat the oven to 300°F. Bring water to a boil for a water bath. Butter the bottom and sides of a 9 by 2-inch cake pan; set aside.

2. To make the crust: In a food processor, pulse the pistachios with the sugar and the salt until coarsely ground. Transfer to a large bowl, add the graham cracker crumbs and butter, and mix to combine. Press the graham cracker mixture over the bottom of the buttered pan. Set aside.

3. To make the filling: In the bowl of a standing mixer fitted with the paddle attachment, beat the cream cheese, sugar, salt, vanilla extract, and vanilla paste or seeds on medium-high speed, scraping down the bowl several times, until the mixture is completely smooth, about 5 minutes.

4. Turn the mixer to low and beat in the eggs one at a time, until blended, scraping down the sides of the bowl after each addition. Beat in the sour cream until blended.

5. Place the cake pan in a roasting pan. Pour the cream cheese mixture into the cake pan—it will come all of the way to the top of the pan. Place the roasting pan in the oven and pour in the boiling water to come about ½ inch up the sides of the cake pan. Bake until the filling is set but still jiggles slightly in the center, 1 hour 15 minutes to 1 hour 20 minutes. Remove from the water bath and let cool to room temperature. Chill for 4 to 6 hours, or overnight, in the pan.

6. To finish, heat the bottom of the pan over a flame or an electric element to loosen the crust. Invert the pan onto a 9-inch cake round or large plate. Remove the pan from the cake and invert once more onto a 9-inch round or large plate so the crust is on the bottom. In a

RECIPE CONTINUES . . .

Cheesecakes are traditionally made in springform pans wrapped in aluminum foil and placed in a water bath. Water often leaks into the pans, creating a soggy crust. Instead, as with this recipe, try making cheesecakes in a regular cake pan to ensure that water won't leak into the pan. To serve the cake, remove it from the refrigerator, then heat it over a flame or electric element just enough to warm the sugar and butter in the crust; invert the pan and the cake will release easily.

small saucepan, warm the strained jam over low heat until liquid. Strain through a fine strainer. Brush the top and sides of the cheesecake with the strained jam. Cover the top of the cake with a single layer of raspberries. Holding the cake with one hand under the bottom, and working over a sheet pan to catch the excess, gently press the ground pistachios all around the side of the cake. Dust with confectioners' sugar, if desired.

Pumpkin Cheesecake

Cheesecakes are wonderful make-ahead desserts when you're planning an elaborate meal. This one can be made a day or two in advance. We sell this simple-to-make pumpkin pie–like cheesecake during the autumn months, but it tastes great any time of year.

MAKES ONE 10-INCH
CHEESECAKE, SERVES 12

Graham Cracker Crust

- 1½ cups graham cracker crumbs
- 6 tablespoons (¾ stick) unsalted butter, melted and then slightly cooled
- ¼ cup granulated sugar
- ¼ teaspoon ground cinnamon

Filling

- 1 cup light brown sugar
- 1 teaspoon ground cinnamon
- ¼ teaspoon grated nutmeg
- ¼ teaspoon ground ginger
- ⅛ teaspoon ground cloves
- 1 tablespoon all-purpose flour
- 1 pound cream cheese, at room temperature for at least 6 hours
- 1 (15-ounce) can pumpkin puree
- 1 tablespoon brandy
- 1 tablespoon heavy cream
- 4 large eggs

TECHNIQUE TIP: A water bath, or bain-marie, ensures that the entire cake cooks evenly and uniformly. When preparing a water bath, always place the cake in the roasting pan, then place the roasting pan in the oven, and then pour the boiling water into the roasting pan, once it's safely in the oven.

1. Butter the bottom and sides of a 9 by 2-inch cake pan; set aside.

2. To make the crust: In a medium bowl, combine the graham cracker crumbs, melted butter, sugar, and cinnamon. Using your hands, mix thoroughly until the ingredients come together. Press the graham cracker mixture over just the bottom of the prepared pan; set aside.

3. To make the filling: In a small bowl, combine the brown sugar, cinnamon, nutmeg, ginger, cloves, and flour; set aside.

4. In the bowl of a standing mixer fitted with the paddle attachment, beat the cream cheese on medium speed until light and fluffy, about 4 minutes, scraping down the sides of the bowl halfway through. With the mixer on low, gradually add the sugar-spice mixture; mix until combined. Add the pumpkin, brandy, and heavy cream; mix until smooth. Add the eggs one at time, beating until just combined.

5. Set the oven rack in the middle position. Preheat the oven to 300°F. Bring water to a boil for a water bath.

6. Place the cake pan in a roasting pan. Pour the cream cheese mixture into the cake pan. Place the roasting pan in the oven and pour in the boiling water to come about ½ inch up the sides of the cake pan. Bake until the filling is set but still jiggles slightly in the center, about 1½ hours. Remove from the water bath and let cool to room temperature. Chill for at least 6 hours, or overnight, in the pan.

7. To finish, heat the bottom of the pan over a flame or an electric element to loosen the crust. Invert the pan onto a 9-inch cake round or large plate. Remove the pan from the cake and invert once more onto a 9-inch round or large plate so that the crust is on the bottom. Cut and serve.

Citrus Icebox Cheesecake

When I worked at Le Bernardin, I made a mini-version of this cheesecake mousse. It was the perfect way to top off a rich French meal. The cake is lighter in texture than most cheesecakes and doesn't require baking. It can be made two days in advance and kept in the refrigerator.

1 (¼-inch thick) 9-inch round of Yellow Sponge Cake (page 172)

¼ cup water

1 tablespoon powdered unflavored gelatin

2¼ cups heavy cream

1 pound cream cheese, at room temperature for at least 6 hours

⅔ cup sugar

½ teaspoon coarse salt
Grated zest of 1 lemon
Grated zest of 1 orange

2 tablespoons freshly squeezed lemon juice

¾ cup sour cream

TECHNIQUE TIP: To get the most juice out of a lemon, let it come to room temperature, if refrigerated, and roll it on the counter before cutting and squeezing or reaming.

1. Stamp out an 8-inch round of cake with an 8-inch ring mold, discarding the outside inch of cake. Leaving the cake in the ring, place it and the ring on an 8-inch cardboard cake round. Set aside.

2. Bring 1 inch of water to a simmer in the bottom of a double boiler. In a small bowl, sprinkle the water over the gelatin and let stand for 5 minutes.

3. Using a rubber spatula, scrape the softened gelatin into the top of the double boiler, set it over the simmering water, and heat until liquid. Remove from the heat; set aside.

4. In the bowl of a standing mixer fitted with the whisk attachment, beat the cream to medium peaks. Transfer to a bowl; set aside.

5. Replace the whisk with the paddle attachment. Wash and dry the bowl. Add the cream cheese, sugar, salt, lemon and orange zest, and lemon juice to the mixer bowl, and beat on medium-high speed, scraping down the bowl several times, until the mixture is completely smooth, about 5 minutes.

6. Add a dollop of the cream cheese mixture to the gelatin and fold with a rubber spatula to blend. Return the gelatin mixture to the bowl with the remaining cream cheese mixture and fold together until completely incorporated. Fold in the whipped cream.

7. Scrape the mousse into the pastry ring and smooth the top with a metal spatula. Cover with plastic wrap and freeze until set, at least 4 hours or overnight.

8. Remove the cake, still in the ring, from the freezer. The mousse will have sunk slightly so that there is just enough room to spread the sour cream over the top of the mousse, just as if you were icing the cake. Level with a metal spatula.

9. Wet a kitchen towel with hot water and wring it out. To unmold, wrap the towel around the ring and let it warm for a minute to release the cake from the ring. (You may need to rewarm the towel a few times.) Set the cake on top of a can, and ease the ring down and off. Refrigerate for at least 2 hours before serving.

White Chocolate Mousse Roulade

This moist, bittersweet chocolate mousse cake gets its structure from cocoa rather than from flour. It is an excellent choice to serve for Passover.

MAKES ONE 17-INCH
ROLLED CAKE, SERVES 10

6 **large eggs, separated**

¾ **cup sugar**

½ **teaspoon coarse salt**

1½ **teaspoons pure vanilla extract**

½ **cup good-quality Dutch-processed unsweetened cocoa powder**

½ **recipe White Chocolate Mousse (page 153), chilled about 4 hours to set**

1. Set the oven rack in the middle position. Preheat the oven to 325°F. Butter and line a 17 by 12-inch rimmed baking sheet with parchment paper. Lightly butter the top of the parchment; set aside.

2. In the bowl of a standing mixer fitted with the whisk attachment, beat the egg yolks with 1 tablespoon of the sugar, the salt, and the vanilla on high speed until thick and pale and a ribbon forms when you lift the whisk, 7 to 8 minutes. Transfer to a large bowl.

3. Bring 1 inch of water to a simmer in the bottom of a double boiler. In the top of the double boiler, whisk together the egg whites and the remaining sugar over the simmering water until the sugar dissolves and the mixture is warm to the touch, 1 to 2 minutes. Transfer to the bowl of a standing mixer fitted with the whisk attachment and beat until stiff peaks form but the mixture is still glossy, and not dry, 3 to 5 minutes.

4. Scoop a dollop of whites into the bowl with the beaten yolks and stir. Add the rest of the whites and begin folding with a rubber spatula. Sift the cocoa over the mixture and continue carefully folding the whites and cocoa until just blended. Pour the batter onto the prepared baking sheet and spread it out evenly with an offset spatula.

5. Bake, rotating the pan about two-thirds of the way through the baking time, until the cake rises and springs back when gently touched, 15 to 17 minutes. Remove from the oven. Cover with a piece of parchment, and then a wire rack. Immediately invert onto the parchment. Pull the parchment off the top of the inverted cake, then replace it. Invert the cake again: the side that was touching the pan during baking should be on the bottom again. Arrange the cake with one of the long sides facing you and roll the cake, from the bottom, into a log. Transfer to a wire rack and let cool completely, at least 1 hour.

6. Completely unroll the cake. Discard the top sheet of parchment paper. Using an offset spatula, spread the White Chocolate Mousse over the entire cake, leaving a 1-inch border along the long sides. Gently roll the cake back into a log, wrap with the remaining sheet of parchment, and refrigerate until ready to serve, at least 30 minutes. Cut into slices.

Flourless Chocolate Cake

This cake calls for only a few ingredients, so they should be the best possible quality. Light in texture, intense in flavor, the cake gets its lift from beaten eggs paired with whipped cream. The cake rises and falls in the oven. It is a good choice for those who cannot eat wheat or gluten. Be careful not to overbake it—the cake should be fudgy in the center. Serve with a dollop of whipped cream.

MAKES ONE 9-INCH CAKE, SERVES 8

½ cup (1 stick) unsalted butter, cut into pieces

6 ounces semisweet chocolate, finely chopped

5 large eggs, at room temperature

½ cup sugar

½ teaspoon coarse salt

1 tablespoon ground espresso (beans ground for an espresso machine), or 2 teaspoons instant espresso powder

¼ cup Dutch-processed unsweetened cocoa powder

1. Set an oven rack in the middle position. Preheat the oven to 375°F. Generously butter a 9 by 2-inch cake pan. Line a baking sheet with parchment paper or a nonstick silicone baking mat.

2. Bring about 1 inch of water to a simmer in the bottom of a double boiler. In a large heatproof bowl or the top of the double boiler, combine the butter and chocolate; set the bowl over (not in) the simmering water and heat until melted.

3. Meanwhile, in the bowl of a standing mixer fitted with the whisk attachment, beat the eggs, sugar, salt, and ground espresso on medium-high speed until the mixture forms a thick ribbon when the whisk is lifted from the bowl, 7 to 8 minutes. Remove the bowl from the stand. Fold in the melted chocolate with a rubber spatula. Fold in the cocoa powder.

4. Pour the batter into the prepared cake pan and bake until it is firm to the touch but crumbs still adhere to a tester inserted into the center of the cake, 20 to 25 minutes. Let cool in the pan on a wire rack. Refrigerate in the pan until completely chilled, about 2 hours.

5. To unmold, warm the bottom of the pan over a flame or electric element to loosen the cake from the bottom of the pan. Carefully invert onto a serving plate.

Breads and Focaccias

SoNo Cornmeal Bread

Multigrain Bread

Classic White Bread

Cinnamon-Swirl Bread

Italian Rustic Bread

Irish Soda Bread

Country French Bread

Potato-Rosemary Bread

Brioche

Challah

Classic Croissants

Almond Croissants

Herb Focaccia

Sausage, Peppers, and Feta Focaccia

Potato, Onion, and Rosemary
Focaccia

Sunday Brunch Dried Fruit Focaccia

Focaccia with Tomato, Mozzarella,
and Pesto

Chapter Seven

While we're known for our desserts, SoNo Baking Company also sells hundreds of loaves of fresh bread each day, including a Classic White Bread (page 212) that stands up to any sandwich filling, Cinnamon-Swirl Bread (page 215), which is delicious toasted or made into french toast the next day, Country French Bread (page 222) and Italian Rustic Bread (page 217), both wonderful additions to any meal, and Classic Croissants (page 231), delicious served anytime, not just for breakfast.

There are a few tips to follow when it comes to baking breads. First, each time you make it, bread dough requires a different amount of liquid depending on how dry the flour is, which is based on how humid your kitchen is. With the exception of Brioche (page 226), the recipes here are written with the expectation that you will add all but about 2 tablespoons of the amount of liquid called for in the ingredient list, and then add more only as needed. The dough should be damp and tacky, not so sticky that it sticks to your hands and work surface. It's best to err on the side of too much liquid, as you can always add a bit more flour.

Second, the bowl you use for rising should always be lightly oiled or buttered. The easiest way to do this is to spray it with nonstick vegetable cooking spray. Be sure to spray the plastic wrap or plastic grocery bag you use to cover it with oil as well.

Third, as with all breads, you can let dough rise only once if you're in a hurry, but the flavor will develop better if you allow for two risings. Dough has risen correctly when it has increased in size by about 1½ times and is very soft. Overrisen or overproofed dough will taste yeasty and dry.

Finally, breads, with the exception of the focaccias, should feel light and hollow when they come out of the oven. For the best flavor, be sure to let them cool completely on a wire rack before slicing.

So whether you have a few hours or a few days, I urge you to get in the kitchen and start kneading!

SoNo Cornmeal Bread

Each day at SoNo Baking Company we offer a "bread of the day." This crusty bread is always offered on Thursdays. It's so popular that it always sells out by lunchtime. Unlike American cornbread, which is more cakelike in consistency, this is a yeasted bread. With its hearty texture and deep flavor, it can stand up to thick stews, cassoulets, and chili, or can accommodate a thick slice of aged cheese. A boule is a round loaf of bread. In this case, it is about 9 inches in diameter.

MAKES 1 BOULE

2 teaspoons active dry yeast

¾ cup warm (105° to 110°F) water

¼ cup olive oil

1¾ cups plus 1 tablespoon bread flour

½ cup coarse yellow cornmeal, plus 2 tablespoons for the baking sheet

2½ teaspoons coarse salt

1. In a medium bowl, combine the yeast and half of the warm water, and let proof for about 5 minutes.

2. When the yeast has proofed, add the olive oil. Combine the flour, cornmeal, and salt in the bowl of a standing mixer fitted with the paddle attachment. Add the yeast mixture and the remaining water and beat on low speed, scraping the bowl down once, until a soft, slightly tacky dough forms, about 1 minute.

3. Turn the dough out onto a lightly floured work surface. Knead by successively scooping the dough up from underneath with the thumb and the first two fingers of each hand, then folding it over on itself. Give it a quarter-turn and repeat. As the gluten develops, the flour absorbs moisture; as you work it, the dough will pull together into a ball and become less tacky. Knead for 5 to 7 minutes, or until the dough is smooth and springy. Stretching it gently, fold in the left and right sides of the dough to the center, then the top and bottom, to make a rough ball. Place the dough, smooth side down, in a lightly oiled bowl, and then turn the dough over so that the smooth side faces up and both sides are coated with oil. Cover with oiled plastic wrap, and let rise in a warm place (at least 70°F) until increased in bulk by 1½ times and very soft, 1 to 1½ hours.

4. To deflate the dough, use a plastic pastry scraper to fold the top down, the bottom up, and the sides in. Turn the dough in the bowl so that the smooth side faces up. Cover with plastic wrap and let rise again until increased in bulk by 1½ times, about 1 hour.

5. Sprinkle a baking sheet or pizza peel with the 2 tablespoons cornmeal.

6. To shape the boule, turn the dough out onto an unfloured surface so that the top is facing down. Fold in the top and bottom and the sides, as you did before. Flip the dough so it is top side up. Then

quickly shape it between the palms of your hands into a round. Place your hands, palms up, on either side of the dough round. Then move your hands together so that they touch underneath the dough, and give dough a quarter-turn. This will tighten the dough into a nice, firm ball. Do this two more times. Place it on the prepared baking sheet or peel. Cover and let rise again in a warm place until increased in bulk by 1½ times, 30 to 45 minutes.

7. Set an oven rack in the middle position. Preheat the oven to 500°F. (If using a pizza paddle, heat the pizza stone in the oven at the same time.)

8. Using a sharp pairing knife or a straight-edged razor, cut a ¼-inch-deep slash in the top of the boule. Place the baking sheet in the oven, or slide the boule onto the stone. Immediately reduce the oven heat to 425°F. Bake, rotating the baking sheet about two-thirds of the way through the baking time (if using a pizza stone, rotate the bread, not the stone), until the crust is golden brown and the boule sounds hollow when tapped on the bottom (use an oven mitt to carefully lift it up, and gently tap on the bottom with your knuckles), 30 to 35 minutes. Cool on a wire rack.

TECHNIQUE TIP: A plastic pastry scraper or bench scraper is an invaluable tool for bakers. The rectangular-shaped tool is used for loosening and turning dough and for scraping excess dough from a work surface. It is also handy for dividing and deflating bread doughs.

Multigrain Bread

I developed this chewy sandwich bread when I ran the commissary at Martha Stewart's former Westport, Connecticut, television studio. It gets its flavor from several different kinds of grains. It calls for coarse whole wheat flour, which is whole wheat flour that is more coarsely milled than standard whole wheat flour. It can be found in gourmet specialty stores. For a more textured bread, try adding any of the "topping" seeds (such as 1½ tablespoons pumpkin seeds and 1½ tablespoons sunflower seeds) to the dough. If you can't find coarse cornmeal, use grits or polenta (regular cornmeal is too finely textured). You will need a water spray bottle to mist the bread so that topping ingredients will stick.

MAKES ONE 8½ BY 4½-INCH LOAF

2½ tablespoons cracked wheat
3 tablespoons cracked rye
3 tablespoons coarse cornmeal
2½ tablespoons millet
1½ cups water
1¾ teaspoons active dry yeast
3 cups all-purpose flour
½ cup coarse whole wheat flour
1½ tablespoons dark brown sugar
2½ teaspoons coarse salt
1½ tablespoons poppy seeds
1½ tablespoons sesame seeds

Topping

1 teaspoon anise seeds
1 teaspoon fennel seeds
1 teaspoon flax seeds
1 teaspoon sesame seeds
1 teaspoon poppy seeds
2 teaspoons pumpkin seeds
2 teaspoons sunflower seeds
1 tablespoon old-fashioned rolled oats (not instant)

1. In a medium bowl, combine the cracked wheat, cracked rye, cornmeal, millet, and ½ cup of the water; set aside to soak.

2. In a small saucepan, heat the remaining 1 cup water to 105° to 110°F. Pour about ½ cup of the warm water over the yeast in a small bowl and let proof for about 5 minutes.

3. In the bowl of a standing mixer fitted with the paddle attachment, combine the all-purpose flour, whole wheat flour, brown sugar, and salt, and beat on low speed until combined. Combine the proofed yeast mixture, the soaked grains, and the remaining ½ cup warm water, and add to the bowl with the flours. Add the poppy and sesame seeds. Beat on low speed until the flour is absorbed and a soft dough forms, 1 to 2 minutes. The dough should be tacky when you touch it, but not so sticky that it sticks to your fingers or your work surface.

4. Turn the dough out onto an unfloured work surface. Knead by successively scooping up the dough from underneath with the thumb and the first two fingers of each hand, then folding it over on itself. Give it a quarter-turn and repeat. As the gluten develops, the flour absorbs moisture; as you work it, the dough will pull together into a ball and become less tacky. Knead for 5 to 7 minutes, or until the dough is smooth and springy. Stretching it gently, fold in the left and right sides of the dough to the center, then the top and bottom, to make a rough ball. Place the dough smooth side down in a lightly oiled bowl, and then turn it over so that the smooth side faces up and both sides are coated with oil. Cover with oiled plastic wrap, and let rise in a warm place (at least 70° F) until increased in bulk by 1½ times, and very soft, 1 to 1½ hours.

5. To deflate the dough, use a plastic pastry scraper to fold the top down, the bottom up, and the sides in. Turn the dough in the bowl so that the smooth side faces up. Cover with plastic wrap, and let rise again in a warm place until increased in bulk by 1½ times, about 1 hour.

6. Butter or oil an 8½ by 4½-inch loaf pan. Mix all of the topping ingredients on a plate or in a shallow bowl.

7. To shape the loaf, turn the dough out onto an unfloured work surface so that the smooth side faces down. Pull it out into a rough oval with a long side facing you. Gently stretch each side out and fold in to meet in the center; you want to end up with a piece of dough that is about 6 inches across. Starting from the top, roll the dough tightly into a log. Seal the seam with the heel of your hand by pressing down where the dough meets the work surface.

8. Lightly spray the top of the loaf with a mister filled with water, and invert it into seed mixture to coat the top of the loaf. Place the loaf, seam side down, in the prepared loaf pan. Cover with plastic wrap, and let the loaf rise until increased in bulk by 1½ times, 30 to 45 minutes.

9. Set an oven rack in the middle position. Preheat the oven to 500°F.

10. Slash a ¼-inch-deep line down the center of the loaf with a lame or a very sharp knife. Place the loaf on a baking sheet, place in the oven, and immediately reduce the oven heat to 375°F. Bake until the bread is nicely browned and sounds hollow when tapped on the bottom (use an oven mitt to carefully lift it up, and gently tap on the bottom with your knuckles), about 40 minutes. Remove immediately from the sheet and let cool completely on a wire rack.

Classic White Bread

You'll never buy the store-bought variety again after trying this buttery, tender bread. With its fine, tight crumb, it's a great vessel for sandwiches and makes for delicious toast. At the SoNo Baking Company we serve a variety of sandwiches on this bread, including our daily panini, in which we press different fillings between two slices of this chewy white bread.

1 cup plus 2 tablespoons warm (105° to 110°F) water
1¾ teaspoons active dry yeast
3½ cups all-purpose flour
¼ cup instant nonfat dry milk
2½ tablespoons sugar
2¼ teaspoons coarse salt
6 tablespoons (¾ stick) cold unsalted butter, cubed

1. Pour ½ cup of the warm water over the yeast in a medium bowl and let proof for about 5 minutes.

2. In the bowl of a standing mixer fitted with the paddle attachment, combine the flour, nonfat dry milk, sugar, salt, and butter and beat on low speed until the butter breaks down and dissolves completely in the dry ingredients, 3 to 4 minutes. Add the yeast mixture and the remaining ½ cup plus 2 tablespoons water, and beat on low speed until the flour is absorbed and the dough is smooth, about 2 minutes.

3. Turn the dough out onto an unfloured work surface. Knead by successively scooping up the dough from underneath with the thumb and the first two fingers of each hand, then folding it over on itself. Give it a quarter-turn and repeat. As the gluten develops, the flour absorbs moisture; as you work it, the dough will pull together into a ball and become less tacky. Knead for 5 to 7 minutes, or until the dough is smooth and springy. Stretching it gently, fold in the left and right sides of the dough to the center, then the top and bottom, to make a rough ball. Place the dough smooth side down in a lightly oiled bowl, and then turn it over so that the smooth side faces up and both sides are coated with oil. Cover with oiled plastic wrap, and let rise in a warm place (at least 70°F) until increased in bulk by 1½ times and very soft, 1 to 1½ hours.

4. To deflate the dough, use a plastic pastry scraper to fold the top down, the bottom up, and the sides in. Turn the dough in the bowl so that the smooth side faces up. Cover with plastic wrap, and let rise again in a warm place until increased in bulk by 1½ times, about 1 hour.

5. Butter or oil an 8½ by 4½-inch loaf pan.

6. To shape the loaf, turn the dough out onto the unfloured work surface so that the smooth side again faces down. Pull it out into a rough rectangle or oval with a long side facing you. Gently stretch out each side and fold in to meet in the center; you want to end up with a piece of dough that is about 6 inches across. Starting from the top, roll the dough tightly into a log. Seal the seam with the heel of your hand by pressing down where the dough meets the work surface.

7. Place the dough into the prepared loaf pan, cover with oiled plastic wrap (or place inside a sealed plastic grocery bag), and let rise until increased in bulk by 1½ times, 30 to 45 minutes.

8. Set an oven rack in the middle position. Preheat the oven to 500°F.

9. Place the loaf pan on a baking sheet, place the sheet in the oven, and immediately reduce the oven temperature to 375°F. Bake, rotating the sheet about two-thirds of the way through the baking time, until the crust is evenly golden brown and the loaf sounds hollow when tapped on the bottom (use an oven mitt to carefully lift it up, and gently tap on the bottom with your knuckles), 35 to 40 minutes. Turn the loaf out immediately, on its side, onto a wire rack to cool completely.

Cinnamon-Swirl Bread

This rich raisin-filled white bread not only showcases spirals of cinnamon-sugar on the inside, it's also brushed with butter right out of the oven and coated in cinnamon-sugar on the outside. At the bakery we use a combination of black and golden raisins for more variety and color. I use this bread at home for french toast. My wife, Veronica, always pinches a few pieces before I can get it into the pan!

MAKES ONE 8½ BY 4½-INCH LOAF

Dough

- ¾ cup warm (105° to 110°F) milk
- 1¾ teaspoons active dry yeast
- 3¼ cups all-purpose flour
- ¼ cup plus 2 tablespoons whole wheat flour
- 3 tablespoons rye flour
- 3 tablespoons sugar
- 1 tablespoon coarse salt
- 6½ tablespoons cold unsalted butter, cut into pieces
- ½ cup plus 2 tablespoons water
- ⅔ cup raisins, black and yellow mixed

Filling

- ⅔ cup sugar
- 1 tablespoon ground cinnamon
- 1 large egg, beaten, for egg wash
- 1 tablespoon unsalted butter, melted

1. To make the dough: In a small bowl, pour the warm milk over the yeast and let proof for about 5 minutes.

2. Meanwhile, in the bowl of a standing mixer fitted with the paddle attachment, combine the all-purpose, whole wheat, and rye flours, sugar, salt, and butter and beat on low speed until the butter breaks down and dissolves completely in the dry ingredients, 3 to 4 minutes. Add the yeast mixture and the water and beat on low speed until the flour is absorbed and the ingredients are well combined, 1 to 2 minutes. The dough should be tacky but not sticky when you touch it. It should be damp enough that the dough still attaches a bit to the sides of the bowl. If the dough is too dry, it will collect around the paddle—add water by the tablespoon. (Err on the side of too much water; you can always add more flour as you knead.)

3. Turn the dough out onto an unfloured work surface. Knead by successively scooping the dough up from underneath with the thumb and the first two fingers of each hand, then folding it over on itself. Give it a quarter-turn and repeat. As the gluten develops, the flour absorbs moisture; as you work it, the dough will pull together into a ball and become less tacky. Knead for 5 to 7 minutes, or until the dough is smooth and springy. Pat the dough to a 9-inch round. Sprinkle with the raisins, and knead briefly to incorporate. Stretching it gently, fold in the left and right sides to the center, then the top and bottom. Place the dough, smooth side down, into a lightly oiled bowl, then turn the dough over so that both sides are coated with oil. Cover with oiled plastic wrap, and let rise in a warm place (at least 70°F) until increased in bulk by 1½ times and very soft, 1 to 1½ hours.

4. To deflate the dough, use a plastic pastry scraper to fold the top down, the bottom up, and the sides in. Turn the dough in the bowl

RECIPE CONTINUES . . .

TECHNIQUE TIP: Before coating any baked goods with cinnamon sugar, allow the butter to cool on the item until it becomes tacky. This will prevent lumps from forming in the cinnamon-sugar mixture when it is applied.

so that the smooth side faces up. Cover with plastic wrap and let rise again in a warm place until increased in bulk by 1½ times, about 1 hour.

5. Meanwhile, to make the filling: Stir together the sugar and cinnamon in a small bowl. Measure out ⅓ cup to sprinkle on the finished loaf; reserve it separately.

6. Turn the dough out onto an unfloured work surface, smooth side facing down. Gently stretch it to flatten it to a rectangle, about 6 by 14 inches, with a short side at the bottom. Make sure that the edges are not too thick, or you'll end up with a loaf that slopes down in the center. Brush with the egg wash. Sprinkle with the cinnamon-sugar filling, allowing a 1-inch border at the top and bottom. Rolling from the top, roll the loaf as tightly as you can into a log. Gently press the seams together. Place the loaf seam side down in a buttered 8½ by 4½-inch loaf pan.

7. Cover with plastic wrap and let rise until the loaf is increased in bulk by 1½ times and has risen over the top of the pan, 30 to 45 minutes.

8. Set the oven rack in the middle position. Preheat the oven to 500°F.

9. Place the loaf pan on a baking sheet, place it in the oven, and immediately reduce the oven heat to 375°F. Bake, rotating the sheet about two-thirds of the way through the baking time, until the crust is evenly golden brown and the loaf sounds hollow when tapped on the bottom (use an oven mitt to carefully lift it up, and gently tap on the bottom with your knuckles), 40 to 45 minutes. Turn the loaf out immediately, on its side, onto a wire rack to cool.

10. Brush the cooled loaf all over with the melted butter, and sprinkle with the reserved ⅓ cup cinnamon-sugar mixture. Transfer to a wire rack and let stand until the sugar dries, about 30 minutes.

Italian Rustic Bread

I learned how to make this chewy, airy ciabatta bread while studying bread making in Bologna, Italy, with the Simili sisters, Margherita and Valeria, who are renowned for their bread-baking mastery. Italian Rustic Bread is so versatile. It can be served for any meal, and is perfect for accompanying an omelet or a salad, or as a nice bed for ripe tomatoes.

MAKES TWO 16 BY 6-INCH LOAVES

7¾ cups all-purpose flour, plus more for dusting the loaves

1 tablespoon instant yeast

3 tablespoons coarse salt

¼ cup olive oil

3 cups warm (105° to 110°F) water

Cornmeal, for the sheet pan

1. In the bowl of a standing mixer fitted with the dough hook attachment, combine the flour, yeast, salt, oil, and warm water. Mix on low speed for 5 to 6 minutes, scraping down the sides of the bowl halfway through. Raise the speed to medium and mix for 30 seconds. The dough will be very loose and sticky.

2. Cover the bowl with oiled plastic wrap and let rise in a warm place (at least 70°F) until increased in bulk by 1½ times the size, 1½ to 2 hours.

3. Using a bowl scraper, turn the dough out onto a well-floured work surface. (The dough will be very difficult to handle; add a bit of flour, but try not to add too much.) Fold the bottom edge of the dough up toward the center. Pat down lightly to deflate the dough. Fold the top edge of the dough down toward the center. The folds should overlap slightly. Repeat this step with the left and right sides, pulling the dough slightly as you fold, again making sure the ends overlap. Tap off any excess flour as you go along. Gently scoop up the dough and flip it over onto its seam. Place it in a lightly floured bowl, cover with oiled plastic wrap, and let rise in a warm place until increased in bulk by 1½ times, about 1 hour.

4. Return the dough to a well-floured surface and repeat the folding process. When finished, return it to a lightly floured bowl, cover with plastic wrap, and let rise in a warm place until increased in bulk by 1½ times, 45 minutes to 1 hour.

5. Turn the dough out onto a well-floured surface and lightly pull and lift the dough to gently stretch it into a 16 by 12-inch rectangle. Using a sharp knife or a pastry cutter, cut the dough in half to make

RECIPE CONTINUES . . .

two loaves, 6 by 16 inches each. Sprinkle a rimless cookie sheet or the back of a rimmed sheet pan with cornmeal. Transfer the dough to a rimless baking sheet or sheet pan, lightly dust the top of the loaves with flour, cover with plastic wrap, and let rest until puffed, about 20 minutes.

6. Set the oven rack in the middle position. Preheat the oven to 500°F.

7. Place the baking sheet in the oven and lower the temperature to 450°F. Bake until the crust is golden brown and the bread sounds hollow when tapped on the bottom (use an oven mitt to carefully lift a loaf, and gently tap on the bottom with your knuckles), 40 to 45 minutes. Transfer to a wire rack and cool completely.

ABOVE: Breads ready for delivery.

Irish Soda Bread

I first made this bread at a bakery called Encore that I owned in downtown Manhattan. The French couple who owned the bakery before me passed along the recipe. The buttermilk acts as a tenderizer to help lighten the dough, resulting in more of a yeast bread with less of a scone-type consistency. This bread is best eaten fresh the day it is baked, or toasted the next day.

MAKES TWO 7-INCH ROUND
LOAVES

6 **cups bread flour, plus more for dusting the loaves**

2 **tablespoons plus 2 teaspoons sugar**

1 **teaspoon baking soda**

1½ **teaspoons coarse salt**

4 **tablespoons plus 2 teaspoons instant yeast**

4 **tablespoons (½ stick) cold unsalted butter, cut into cubes**

2 **cups buttermilk**

1½ **cups raisins**

1. In a medium bowl, whisk together the flour, sugar, baking soda, salt, and yeast. Using a pastry blender, cut in the butter until the mixture resembles coarse crumbs. Add the buttermilk, and using your hands, mix until the dough just comes together. Mix in the raisins. Using a plastic bowl scraper, turn the dough out onto a lightly floured surface and knead until it is smooth and supple, 3 to 4 minutes. Shape into a round loaf.

2. Place the dough into a lightly oiled bowl, cover with oiled plastic wrap, and let rest in a warm location (at least 70°F) until doubled in bulk, about 1 hour.

3. Punch the dough down to deflate it, reshape it into a round loaf, and let it rest again until doubled in bulk, about 1 hour. With a bench scraper, divide it into two pieces, and shape them into two round loaves.

4. Preheat the oven to 400°F. Dust the top of each loaf with flour, and with a bench scraper, form an *X* through the center of the bread, pressing down deeply in both directions with the scraper, almost cutting through the loaf. Place the loaves on a lightly floured baking sheet.

5. Bake, rotating the sheet halfway through, until the crust is deep golden brown and a cake tester inserted into the center of the bread comes out clean, about 1 hour. Transfer the bread to a wire rack and let cool completely.

Country French Bread

My son Peter loves this bread. While he's too young to have teeth yet, he enjoys mouthing a crusty piece of this classic favorite. This multipurpose bread can be made into any number of shapes, including dinner rolls.

MAKES 1 BOULE

2 teaspoons active dry yeast

1¼ cups warm (105° to 110°F) water

2 tablespoons olive oil

3⅓ cups bread flour

1 tablespoon coarse salt

Cornmeal, for the baking sheet

TECHNIQUE TIP: When shaping a boule, your work surface should always remain unfloured so that the dough will "catch" on the surface and hold its shape, rather than spinning on top of a slippery floured surface. If you've got the right proportion of flour to water, the dough should not stick at all.

1. In a medium bowl, combine the yeast and 1 cup of the warm water, and let proof for 5 minutes.

2. When the yeast has proofed, add the olive oil and the remaining ¼ cup water. Combine the flour and salt in the bowl of a standing mixer fitted with the paddle attachment. Add the wet ingredients and beat on medium speed for 1 to 2 minutes, until the ingredients are well combined. The dough should be tacky but not sticky when you touch it, and damp enough that the dough attaches to the sides of the bowl with strings. If the dough is too dry, it will just collect around the paddle—add water by the tablespoon. (Err on the side of too much water; you can always add more flour as you knead.)

3. Turn the dough out onto an unfloured work surface. Knead by successively scooping the dough up from underneath with the thumb and the first two fingers of each hand, then folding it over on itself. Give it a quarter-turn and repeat. As the gluten develops, the flour absorbs moisture; as you work it, the dough will pull together into a ball and become less tacky. Knead for 5 to 7 minutes, or until the dough is smooth and springy. Stretching it gently, fold in the left and right sides of the dough to the center, then the top and bottom, to make a rough ball. Place the dough smooth side down in a lightly oiled bowl, and then turn the dough over so that the smooth side faces up and both sides are coated with oil. Cover with oiled plastic wrap, and let rise in a warm place (at least 70°F) until increased in bulk by 1½ times and very soft, 1 to 1½ hours.

4. To deflate the dough, use a plastic pastry scraper to fold the top down, the bottom up, and the sides in. Turn the dough in the bowl so that the smooth side faces up. Cover with plastic wrap and let rise again until increased in bulk by 1½ times.

5. Sprinkle a baking sheet or pizza peel with cornmeal.

6. To shape the boule, turn the dough out onto an unfloured work surface so that the top is facing down. Fold in the top and bottom

and the sides, as you did before. Turn the dough top side up. Then quickly shape it between the palms of your hands into a round. Place your hands, palms up, on either side of the dough round. Then move your hands together so that they touch underneath the dough, and give the dough a quarter-turn. This will tighten the dough into a nice, firm ball. Do this two more times. Place it on the prepared baking sheet or peel. Cover and let rise again in a warm place until the dough has increased in bulk by 1½ times and remains indented when you press gently with a finger, 30 to 45 minutes.

7. Set an oven rack in the middle position. Preheat the oven to 500°F (if using a pizza paddle, heat the pizza stone in the oven at the same time).

8. When the dough has risen, using a lame or a straight-edged razor, cut a slash in the top of the boule. Sift flour lightly over the top. Place the baking sheet in the oven, or slide the boule onto the stone. Reduce the oven heat to 450°F. Bake, rotating the baking sheet about two-thirds of the way through the baking time (if using a pizza stone, rotate the bread, not the stone), until the bread feels light and sounds hollow when tapped on the bottom (use an oven mitt to carefully lift it up, and gently tap on the bottom with your knuckles), about 25 minutes. Cool on a wire rack.

TECHNIQUE TIP: To make uniform size rolls, use a scale and weigh out 2 ounces of dough for each roll. Roll into various shapes—either rounds or oblongs.

Potato-Rosemary Bread

This crusty, rosemary-scented loaf was inspired by my time at the King Arthur Flour Baking Education Center in Norwich, Vermont. It was there that baker Jeffrey Hammelman taught me how to make a similar bread. The potato in the bread helps keep it moist.

MAKES 1 BOULE

¾ cup plus 2 tablespoons warm (105° to 110°F) water

2¼ teaspoons active dry yeast

2 cups plus 2 tablespoons bread flour

½ cup whole wheat flour

2¼ teaspoons coarse salt

4 ounces (about 1 half) baked potato, cut up (skin included)

1 tablespoon chopped fresh rosemary

1. Pour about half of the warm water over the yeast in a small bowl and let proof for 5 minutes.

2. Meanwhile, in the bowl of a standing mixer fitted with the paddle attachment, beat the bread and whole wheat flours, salt, potato, and rosemary on low speed to break up the potato into bits, 2 to 3 minutes. Add the yeast mixture and the remaining water and beat until the flour is absorbed and a firm, slightly tacky dough forms.

3. Turn the dough out onto an unfloured work surface. Knead by successively scooping up the dough from underneath with the thumb and the first two fingers of each hand, then folding it over on itself. Give it a quarter-turn and repeat. As the gluten develops, the flour absorbs moisture; as you work it, the dough will pull together into a ball and become less tacky. Knead for 5 to 7 minutes, or until the dough is smooth and springy. Stretching it gently, fold in the left and right sides of the dough to the center, then the top and bottom, to make a rough ball. Place the dough smooth side down in a lightly oiled bowl, and then turn the dough over so that the smooth side faces up and both sides are coated with oil. Cover with oiled plastic wrap, and let rise in a warm place (at least 70°F) until increased in bulk by 1½ times, 1 to 1½ hours.

4. To deflate the dough, use a plastic pastry scraper to fold the top down, the bottom up, and the sides in. Turn the dough in the bowl so that the smooth side faces up. Cover with plastic wrap and let rise again until increased in bulk by 1½ times, about 1 hour.

5. To shape the dough into a boule, turn the dough out onto an unfloured work surface so that the top is again facing down. Fold in the top, bottom, and sides as you did before. Turn the dough top side up. Then quickly shape it between the palms of your hands into a neat ball. Place your hands, palms facing up, on either side of the ball. Move your hands together so that they touch underneath the

dough, and give the dough a quarter-turn. Do this two more times. This will tighten the dough into a nice, firm ball. Place the boule on a lightly floured rimless baking sheet or pizza peel. Cover with plastic wrap and let rise again in a warm place until increased in bulk by 1½ times, 30 to 45 minutes.

TECHNIQUE TIP: For extra texture and flavor, we use unpeeled potatoes.

6. Set the oven rack in the middle position. Preheat the oven to 500°F (if using a pizza peel, heat the pizza stone in the oven at the same time).

7. Slash a ¼-inch-deep *X* in the top of the boule with a lame or a very sharp knife. Gently slide the boule onto the pizza stone, or place the baking sheet in the oven. Immediately reduce the oven heat to 425°F. Bake the bread until it's well browned and crusty, and sounds hollow when tapped on the bottom (use an oven mitt to carefully lift it up, and gently tap on the bottom with your knuckles), 30 to 35 minutes. Cool on a wire rack.

Brioche

This tender, buttery bread must be started a day in advance, but is well worth the extra time and effort. Brioche is wonderful toasted and served for breakfast or to use in bread puddings and french toast. Note that the dough for this bread is very tacky and sticky when you start kneading. Persevere—as the gluten develops, it will pull way from the work surface and your fingers. This dough can also be used to make a pastry cream and strawberry-filled Tart Tropezienne (page 37) or for Monkey Bread (page 45).

MAKES ONE 8½ BY 4-INCH
LOAF OR 12 BUNS

2 teaspoons active dry yeast
¼ cup warm (105° to 110°F) milk
3 large eggs
1 large egg yolk
1¾ cups all-purpose flour, plus extra for kneading
⅔ cup bread flour
2 tablespoons sugar
1¾ teaspoons coarse salt
14 tablespoons (1¾ sticks) cold unsalted butter, cubed
1 egg, beaten, for egg wash

1. In a medium bowl, combine the yeast and the warm milk, and let proof for 5 minutes.

2. When the yeast has proofed, add the eggs and egg yolk and whisk to blend. Combine the all-purpose flour, bread flour, sugar, and salt in the bowl of a standing mixer fitted with the paddle attachment. Add the wet ingredients and beat on low speed until the flour is absorbed and a stiff dough comes together, scraping down the sides of the bowl at least once. With the mixer on low, add the butter, 1 tablespoon at a time, and beat until the butter has been absorbed. The dough will be very sticky.

3. To knead by machine, replace the paddle with the dough hook and beat on medium-low to medium speed until the dough is smooth, shiny, and elastic, and completely cleans the sides of the bowl, 10 to 15 minutes. Add 1 to 2 tablespoons all-purpose flour as needed. (Or, to knead by hand, turn the dough out onto a lightly floured work surface. Knead by successively scooping the dough up from underneath with the thumb and the first two fingers of each hand, then slapping it down on the board as you pull your hands away. At first, the dough will stick to both board and hands, but as the gluten develops and the flour absorbs moisture, the dough will pull together into a ball and become less tacky. Knead for a good 15 minutes, adding flour as needed, or until the dough no longer sticks to the work surface.)

4. Turn the dough into a buttered bowl, cover with oiled plastic wrap, and refrigerate overnight.

5. Butter an 8½ by 4½-inch loaf pan. Turn the dough out onto a lightly floured work surface and let it soften for a few minutes. Pat or roll the dough to a rectangle (or oval) about 12 inches by 8 inches, with one of the long sides facing you. Fold in the sides so that they meet in the center and the dough is about 6 inches wide. Starting from the top, roll tightly into a log. Place the loaf seam side down in the prepared pan. Cover with oiled plastic wrap or enclose in an oiled plastic bag, and let rise until increased in bulk by about 1½ times and very soft, 2½ to 3 hours.

6. Set an oven rack in the middle position. Preheat the oven to 500°F.

7. Brush the top of the loaf with the egg wash. Place the loaf pan on a baking sheet and put it into the oven. Immediately reduce the oven temperature to 375°F and bake, rotating the sheet about two-thirds of the way through the baking time, until the brioche is golden brown and the loaf sounds hollow when tapped on the bottom (use an oven mitt to carefully lift it up, and gently tap on the bottom with your knuckles), 30 to 35 minutes. Turn the loaf out immediately on its side onto a wire rack to cool completely.

Challah

We sell this bread every Friday at the bakery, but it is not just for those observing the Jewish Sabbath. Everyone loves this soft, rich, eggy bread that gets its moistness and tight texture and density from a bit of vegetable oil.

MAKES ONE 18-INCH
BRAIDED LOAF

1 tablespoon active dry yeast

1 cup warm (105° to 110°F) water

¼ cup vegetable oil

6 large egg yolks

4 cups plus 2 tablespoons bread flour

6 tablespoons sugar

1 tablespoon coarse salt

1 egg beaten with 1 egg yolk, for egg wash

1. In a medium bowl, combine the yeast and ½ cup of the warm water, and let proof for 5 minutes.

2. When the yeast has proofed, add the oil and the egg yolks and whisk to blend. Combine the flour, sugar, and salt in the bowl of a standing mixer fitted with the paddle attachment. Add the wet ingredients and the remaining ½ cup water and beat on low speed until the flour is absorbed and a stiff, slightly tacky dough comes together, 1 to 2 minutes, scraping down the sides of the bowl at least once.

3. Turn the dough out onto a lightly floured work surface. Knead by successively scooping the dough up from underneath with the thumb and the first two fingers of each hand, then folding it over on itself. Give it a quarter-turn and repeat. As the gluten develops, the flour absorbs moisture; as you work it, the dough will pull together into a ball and become less tacky. Add a little flour as needed. Knead for 5 to 7 minutes, or until the dough is shiny, smooth, and springy.

4. Stretching it gently, fold in the left and right sides of the dough to the center, then the top and bottom, to make a rough ball. Place the dough smooth side down in a buttered bowl, and then turn the dough over so that the smooth side faces up and both sides are coated with butter. Cover with buttered plastic wrap, and let rise in a warm place (at least 70°F) until doubled in bulk, 1 to 1½ hours.

5. To deflate the dough, use a plastic pastry scraper to fold the top down, the bottom up, and the sides in. Turn the dough in the bowl so that the smooth side faces up. Cover with plastic wrap and let rise again until increased in bulk by 1½ times, about 1 hour.

6. Line a baking sheet with parchment paper, or spray it with nonstick vegetable spray.

7. Turn the dough out onto an unfloured work surface and cut it into three equal pieces. Roll each piece into an 18-inch log and arrange

RECIPE CONTINUES . . .

TECHNIQUE TIP: Use a scale to ensure equal pieces of dough for braiding.

them, side by side, on the prepared baking sheet. Press the tops of the logs together. Braid the loaf by passing the right log over the center, and then the left log over that log, pulling each strand gently to stretch it so that you have a tight braid. Continue until you've woven the three logs together into a braid. Press the bottom ends together. Enclose the baking sheet in a plastic bag and let the challah rise in a warm place until increased in bulk by 1½ times, about 1 hour.

8. Set the oven rack in the middle position. Preheat the oven to 500°F.

9. Brush the bread with the egg wash and place in the oven. Immediately reduce the oven temperature to 350°F. Bake until the challah is well browned and sounds hollow when tapped on the bottom (use an oven mitt to carefully lift it up, and gently tap on the bottom with your knuckles), 50 to 60 minutes. Slide the loaf off onto a wire rack and let cool completely.

Classic Croissants

Croissants can be a challenge, but the reward of a delicate and flaky bread pastry created by hand is unlike any other. At the bakery, we make our croissants over the course of three days, allowing the dough to sit and proof multiple times. The results are sublime. In fact, people tell us our croissants are as authentic and as good as, if not better than, the ones in Paris. The key to making good croissants is to be prepared to let the dough rest, or chill, whenever it gets difficult to work with. As you roll, it will get elastic—just put it on a baking sheet and let it rest for 30 minutes in the refrigerator if it gets too stretchy. Or, if it gets too warm at any time when you're working it, and the butter begins to melt out of it, return it to the refrigerator for 30 minutes. Additionally, it is particularly critical that the temperature for rising be around 75°F. Any warmer and the butter will melt out of the dough. Use any leftover dough for Monkey Bread (page 45).

**MAKES ABOUT
24 CROISSANTS**

1 **cup milk**

1 **tablespoon plus 1 teaspoon active dry yeast**

5 **cups all-purpose flour, plus extra for pounding the butter and rolling the dough**

½ **cup sugar**

3 **tablespoons coarse salt**

¾ **cup plus 2 tablespoons water**

1¼ **pounds (5 sticks) cold unsalted butter**

1 **large egg, lightly beaten, for egg wash**

1. In a small saucepan, heat the milk to 105° to 110°F. Pour over the yeast in a small bowl and let proof for about 5 minutes.

2. In the bowl of an electric mixer fitted with the paddle attachment, mix the flour, sugar, and salt. Add the yeast mixture and the water and mix on low speed, scraping the bowl down with a rubber spatula once or twice, until the dough just comes together, about 2 minutes.

3. Turn the dough out onto a lightly floured surface and knead to form a smooth ball, about 1 minute. Wrap in plastic wrap and refrigerate for 4 to 5 hours or overnight.

4. On a lightly floured work surface, lay the sticks of butter side by side. Sprinkle with flour. Using a rolling pin, pound the butter until flattened into a mass. Fold the mass of butter in half, and continue pounding and rolling, sprinkling often with flour as needed to keep the butter from sticking to the pin and the surface. When the butter is malleable enough (but not soft) to roll it like pastry, shape it into an 8-inch square; set aside.

5. Lightly flour the work surface. Roll out the dough to a 17 by 10-inch rectangle, about ½ inch thick, short side facing you. Place the butter package on the bottom half of the dough. Fold the top half over the butter. Seal the edges by pressing or pinching the dough together.

6. Give the dough a quarter-turn so that the seam is on the left. Roll it again to a 16 by 10-inch rectangle, keeping the corners as square as

RECIPE CONTINUES . . .

possible. Fold the rectangle into thirds, like a letter: first fold one end into the middle, then the other end overlapping the first (this is called a "turn"). Wrap in plastic wrap and refrigerate for 1 hour.

7. Repeat the rolling and folding two more times, always rolling with the seam on the left and letting the dough rest in the refrigerator for 1 hour in between turns. After completing all three turns, wrap the dough in plastic wrap and refrigerate for at least 6 hours or overnight.

8. Place the chilled dough on a lightly floured work surface. Roll out the dough to a 29 by 17-inch rectangle. (The dough will fight you on this, particularly if your kitchen is warm. As often as needed, transfer the dough to a baking sheet—you'll need to fold the dough in half—and refrigerate it for about 30 minutes, or until the dough is well chilled. Then continue.) Once the dough is rolled, place it on the baking sheet and chill for another 30 minutes.

9. Line two baking sheets with parchment paper; set aside. Return the dough to a lightly floured surface. Using a ruler and a pastry cutter, trim the dough to 28 by 16 inches; reserve the scraps for Monkey Bread (page 45). Cut the dough in half lengthwise, making two 28 by 8-inch rectangles. Brush off any excess flour with a pastry brush. Lay one rectangle on top of the other, lining up all edges, with the long side facing you.

10. Now arrange the ruler along the top edge of the dough rectangle. Starting from the left-hand side, nick the dough to mark off a 2-inch section. Then mark off a 4-inch section. Continue marking off 4-inch sections until you get all the way to the end of the dough. Now, working along the bottom edge and starting from the left-hand side, mark off 4-inch sections. Using the ruler as a guide, cut the dough into triangles, 8 inches high with a 4-inch base. You should have 12 doubled triangles, plus scraps. Add the scraps to the pile for Monkey Bread; wrap well in plastic and freeze or refrigerate. Lay the triangles out individually on the work surface. Cut a 1-inch vertical slit in the center of each base.

RECIPE CONTINUES . . .

11. To shape each croissant, stretch the two inner points of the slit to widen it; fold each point toward the outside and press to adhere. Then, stretching the dough slightly outward and using your thumbs and fingertips, roll the base of the dough up and out toward the outer edges until the triangle is completely rolled, tucking the tip under the croissant. Bend the two end tips toward you, forming a crescent. Repeat this for each triangle.

12. Line two baking sheets with parchment paper or nonstick silicone baking mats, and arrange the crescents on them at a slight diagonal. You should be able to fit 12 to a sheet. Cover with plastic wrap and let them rise in a warm (70° to 75°F) place until increased about 1½ times in bulk.

13. Set an oven rack in the middle position. Preheat the oven to 500°F.

14. Lightly brush each croissant with egg wash. Place one baking sheet in the oven and immediately reduce the oven temperature to 400°F. Bake, rotating the sheet about two-thirds of the way through the baking time, until the croissants are golden brown, 18 to 20 minutes. Transfer to a wire rack to cool slightly. Raise the oven temperature to 500°F. Place the second sheet in the oven and reduce temperature to 400°F. Serve warm or at room temperature.

Almond Croissants

An easy and simple variation on the classic croissant. Make these almond cream–filled pastries with half a batch of homemade Classic Croissants (page 231), or save time and use a dozen high-quality store-bought croissants.

MAKES 12 CROISSANTS

Sugar Syrup

- 1 cup water
- 1 cup granulated sugar

Almond Cream

- ½ cup blanched whole almonds
- 6 tablespoons granulated sugar
- 1 teaspoon coarse salt
- 6 tablespoons (¾ stick) unsalted butter, at room temperature
- 2 large eggs, at room temperature
- 1½ teaspoons almond extract
- 3 tablespoons all-purpose flour

- 12 Classic Croissants (page 231) or store-bought croissants
- 1 cup sliced almonds
  Confectioners' sugar

1. To make the syrup: Combine the sugar and the water in a small saucepan, and bring to a boil over medium-high heat. Cook, stirring occasionally, until the sugar has dissolved. Let cool to room temperature. Transfer to a shallow bowl; set aside.

2. To make the Almond Cream: In a food processor, pulse the almonds with the sugar and salt for about 10 seconds, until finely ground. Add the butter and process to blend. Add the eggs, blending after each addition and scraping the bowl between eggs. Add the almond extract. Add the flour and process until combined; set aside.

3. Set an oven rack in the middle position. Preheat the oven to 400°F. Line a baking sheet with parchment paper or a nonstick silicone baking mat; set aside.

4. Cut the croissants in half horizontally with a serrated knife. Spread about 1 tablespoon Almond Cream over the bottom half of each croissant. Set the top halves on top and spread with about 1 more tablespoon Almond Cream. Sprinkle with the sliced almonds, pressing the almonds gently into the cream to adhere. Dip the top of each croissant into the sugar syrup, so that the top is completely saturated.

5. Place the croissants on the prepared baking sheet. Bake, rotating the sheet about two-thirds of the way through the baking time, until the almonds are golden brown and the croissants are crisp, 10 to 12 minutes. Transfer the baking sheet to a wire rack. Place confectioners' sugar in a fine sieve, and sprinkle lightly over the warm croissants. Serve warm.

Herb Focaccia

The following is my basic recipe for focaccia. At the bakery we sell different varieties of these pizzas, altering the toppings based on what we have in stock. We make our focaccia in 8-inch round deep-dish pizza pans (I still use my grandfather's tin pans), but this recipe will also make enough for two 9 by 12-inch pans, or one 17 by 12-inch pan. Focaccia is a very wet dough, too wet to knead on a work surface, so we do it in a large mixing bowl. For a little variation, try making it with dried herbes de Provence instead of fresh herbs. For best results, always use the best possible olive oil when making focaccia, for the both the dough and the topping.

MAKES FOUR 8-INCH ROUNDS

Dough

3½ cups warm (105° to 110°F) water
 1 tablespoon active dry yeast
7¼ cups all-purpose flour
 3 tablespoons coarse salt
 ½ cup olive oil

Topping

¼ cup olive oil
 2 tablespoons chopped fresh woody herb, such as rosemary, thyme, or oregano, or a combination of herbs
 4 teaspoons flaky coarse salt, such as Maldon

1. To make the dough: In a small bowl, combine ¼ cup of the warm water and the yeast and let proof for about 5 minutes.

2. In a very large bowl, stir together the flour and salt and make a well in the center. When the yeast has proofed, pour it into the well along with the remaining 3¼ cups water and ¼ cup of the oil. Using a plastic pastry scraper, gradually pull the flour into the wet ingredients, folding to mix, until a very wet dough forms. Then knead the dough in the bowl for 5 minutes, by folding the dough over on itself with the plastic pastry scraper while you turn the bowl. Scrape the dough out onto a clean work surface; wash and dry the bowl. Smear the bottom of the bowl with olive oil. Scrape up the dough with the plastic scraper, return it to the bowl, and turn to coat with oil. Cover with an oiled sheet of plastic wrap. Let stand in a warm place (at least 70°F) for about 1½ hours, or until the volume increases by 1½ times.

3. Use the plastic scraper to turn the dough out onto a lightly floured surface, and to cut it into equal quarters.

4. Coat each of four 8-inch cake pans with 1 tablespoon of the remaining olive oil. Gently shape each piece of dough into a round. Put one piece of dough in each pan, smoothest side down, and coat with the oil. Turn the dough over so that the smooth side faces up. With your fingertips, push the dough out toward the edges of the cake pan, creating dimples and bubbles, until the dough fills the pan and is dimpled all over. If the dough contracts, just set it aside for 10 minutes to allow it to rest, and try again. Cover with oiled plastic wrap and let rise until puffy and increased about 1½ times in bulk, 30 to 45 minutes.

5. Set an oven rack in the bottom third of the oven. Preheat the oven to 425°F.

TECHNIQUE TIP: Focaccia should always come out of the pan immediately after baking so that it doesn't steam and get doughy.

6. To make the topping: Drizzle each focaccia with 1 tablespoon olive oil, using your fingers to spread the oil over the top. Sprinkle each round with ½ tablespoon of the chopped herbs and 1 teaspoon of the salt.

7. Set two of the pans on a parchment-lined baking sheet. Bake, rotating the sheet about two-thirds of the way through the baking, until the focaccias are evenly golden on top and bottom, 30 to 35 minutes. Remove the focaccias from the pans with a knife or offset spatula and let cool on a wire rack.

8. Repeat to bake the remaining two focaccias.

Sausage, Peppers, and Feta Focaccia

This is like a deep-dish pizza. It reminds me of the sausage and pepper heroes I used to eat as a kid. Here, I substituted the sharper taste of feta cheese for the milder mozzarella. I like to slice garlic cloves on the mandoline so that they're very thin and cook evenly, like garlic chips.

MAKES APPROXIMATELY
1 DOZEN SQUARES

1 recipe Herb Focaccia (page 236), without the herb topping

¼ cup olive oil

Topping

3 tablespoons olive oil

12 ounces sweet Italian sausage (casings removed), crumbled

4 garlic cloves, thinly sliced

3 bell peppers (one each orange, yellow, and red), stemmed, seeded, and cored, cut into ¼-inch-wide strips

1 tablespoon chopped fresh oregano

1 teaspoon salt

¼ teaspoon freshly ground black pepper

4 ounces feta cheese, crumbled

1. Make the focaccia dough through the first rise (step 2).

2. To make the topping: In a large skillet, heat 1 tablespoon of the oil over medium heat. Add the sausage and cook until the fat is rendered and the sausage is no longer pink, about 5 minutes. Remove from the pan with a slotted spoon.

3. Add 2 tablespoons oil to the pan. Add the garlic and cook over medium-low heat until softened, about 2 minutes. Add the peppers, oregano, salt, and pepper; raise the heat to medium, and cook until the peppers are tender, 10 to 12 minutes. Return the sausage to the pan and give the mixture a stir. Remove from the heat and set aside.

4. Coat a 17 by 12-inch rimmed baking sheet with the ¼ cup olive oil. Turn the dough out onto the oiled baking sheet and coat thoroughly with oil. Turn the dough so that the oiled side is up. Press the dough out to the edges of the pan with your fingertips until the dough fills the baking sheet and is dimpled all over. If the dough contracts, set it aside for 10 minutes to relax, and try again. Cover with oiled plastic wrap and let rise until puffy and increased about 1½ times in bulk, 30 to 45 minutes.

5. Scatter the sausage-and-pepper mixture over the dough. Sprinkle with the cheese. The dough will have deflated some—set it aside to rise again for 20 minutes.

6. Set the oven rack in the middle position. Preheat the oven to 425°F.

7. Bake, rotating the sheet about two-thirds of the way through the baking time, until the focaccia is evenly golden on top and bottom, 50 to 60 minutes. Immediately slide the focaccia onto a wire rack. Cut into squares and serve warm or at room temperature.

Potato, Onion, and Rosemary Focaccia

Inspired by my walks through New York's SoHo neighborhood, eating a piece of Sullivan Street Bakery's delicious flatbread, this classic combination pairs caramelized onions with thinly sliced potatoes on top of the chewy spongelike bread. A perfect accompaniment to a hearty bowl of soup or some mixed greens.

MAKES APPROXIMATELY
1 DOZEN SQUARES

1 recipe Herb Focaccia (page 236), without the herb topping

Topping

¾ **cup olive oil**

1 **medium onion, thinly sliced**
Salt and freshly ground black pepper to taste

1 **russet potato, thinly sliced (on a mandoline), ⅛ inch thick**

1 **tablespoon fresh rosemary, finely chopped**

¼ **cup grated Parmesan cheese**

1 **tablespoon coarse sea salt (optional)**

1. Make the focaccia dough through the first rise (step 2).

2. To make the topping: Heat 3 tablespoons of the olive oil in a medium skillet over medium heat. Add the onion, salt, and pepper and sauté until soft, 3 to 4 minutes; set aside.

3. Coat a 17 by 12-inch rimmed baking sheet with ¼ cup of the oil. Turn the dough out onto the oiled baking sheet and coat thoroughly with oil. Turn the dough so that the oiled side is up. Press the dough out to the edges of the pan with your fingertips until the dough fills the sheet pan and is dimpled all over. If the dough contracts, set it aside for 10 minutes to relax, and try again. Cover with plastic wrap and let rise until puffy and increased about 1½ times in bulk, 30 to 45 minutes.

4. Drizzle the remaining 5 tablespoons oil on top of the dough. Shingle the potatoes on top of the focaccia in overlapping concentric circles. Sprinkle with the onion, rosemary, Parmesan, and sea salt, if desired. The dough will have deflated some—set it aside to rise again for 20 minutes.

5. Set the oven rack in the middle position. Preheat the oven to 425°F.

6. Bake, rotating the sheet about two-thirds of the way through the baking time, until the focaccia is evenly golden on top and bottom, 50 to 60 minutes. Immediately slide the focaccia onto a wire rack. Cut into squares and serve warm or at room temperature.

Variation: ONION, PEPERONOTA, AND FETA

Prepare the recipe up to the topping step. After drizzling ¼ cup of olive oil on top of the focaccia, scatter the onion, 1½ cups peperonota cut into strips, and 1 cup crumbled feta cheese over the top. Finish with the sea salt and bake according to the recipe.

Sunday Brunch Dried Fruit Focaccia

Most focaccias offer a savory combination of herbs, vegetables, and cheeses. Here, macerated dried fruit is worked into the body of the dough, where it remains moist and chewy, rather than baked on top, where it can get dried out. This focaccia is wonderful served for breakfast or brunch.

MAKES APPROXIMATELY
2 DOZEN SQUARES

¾ **cup dried cherries**
¾ **cup golden raisins**
¾ **cup dried currants**
¾ **cup dried cranberries**
4 **cups boiling water**
5 **cups all-purpose flour**
½ **cup granulated sugar**
1½ **tablespoons instant yeast**
1½ **tablespoons coarse salt**
½ **teaspoon ground cinnamon**
1½ **cups extra-virgin olive oil**
Coarse sanding sugar

1. In a large bowl, combine the cherries, raisins, currants, cranberries, and boiling water and let soak until plump, about 10 minutes. Drain the fruit, reserving 2½ cups of the soaking liquid; set aside.

2. In the bowl of an electric mixer fitted with the dough hook, combine the flour, sugar, yeast, salt, and cinnamon; mix to combine. With the mixer on low, add the reserved fruit, reserved soaking liquid, and ½ cup of the olive oil. Mix until the dough is completely combined but remains tacky, 2 to 3 minutes.

3. Pour ½ cup of the olive oil onto a 17 by 12-inch rimmed baking sheet, completely coating the bottom. Place the dough on top of the oil, and with your fingers, spread the dough out as much as possible without ripping it. It may not fill the whole baking sheet at this point. Cover loosely with plastic wrap and set in a warm place (at least 70°F) to rest and let rise. Continue to press out the dough every 10 to 15 minutes until it fills the pan. Let the dough sit until doubled in bulk, about 1 hour.

4. Preheat the oven to 400°F. When the dough has doubled, drizzle the top with the last ½ cup olive oil and sprinkle generously with sanding sugar. Bake, rotating the baking sheet halfway through, until the focaccia is golden brown on top and bottom, 30 to 40 minutes.

5. Immediately remove from the oven and slide the focaccia onto a wire rack to cool slightly. Cut the bread into 3-inch squares and serve warm or at room temperature.

Focaccia with Tomato, Mozzarella, and Pesto

Add some mixed greens and you have yourself a hearty and satisfying lunch with this layered focaccia. This recipe will also make enough for two 9 by 12-inch pans, or one 17 by 12-inch pan. At the farmers' markets where we sell our goods people eat this pizza right out of hand while walking through the stands. It's great for breakfast or lunch.

MAKES FOUR 8-INCH ROUNDS

1 recipe Herb Focaccia (page 236), without the herb topping

Topping

6 tablespoons prepared pesto

4 ounces fresh mozzarella cheese

4 to 6 canned peeled tomatoes, preferably San Marzano

¼ cup grated Parmigiano, Romano, or Grana Padano

1. Make the focaccia dough through the second rise (step 4).

2. To make the topping: Place 1 to 1½ tablespoons pesto on each of the four breads, and using your fingers, dab the pesto over the top of each dough round. Tear about one-quarter of the cheese over the top of each, and then shred the tomatoes over the tops in large pieces. Sprinkle each round with 1 tablespoon of the grated cheese.

3. The focaccias will have deflated somewhat; set them aside to rise again for 20 minutes.

4. Set an oven rack in the bottom third of the oven. Preheat the oven to 425°F.

5. Line a baking sheet with parchment paper or a nonstick silicone baking mat. Set two of the pans on the baking sheet and bake, rotating the sheet about two-thirds of the way through the baking, until the focaccias are evenly golden on top and bottom, 30 to 35 minutes. Transfer the focaccias immediately from the pans to a wire rack.

6. Repeat to bake the remaining two focaccias.

Savories: Tarts, Quiches, Pies, and Bites

I n addition to our retail shop, SoNo Baking Company also has a large catering division. We provide menus for all types of affairs, ranging from corporate luncheons to intimate dinner parties to baby showers to weddings. Many of the savory recipes in this chapter are favorites that we serve regularly at these events.

Quiches are incredibly versatile, can be served for any meal, and are a good choice for large gatherings. They are a wonderful way to use up what's in your refrigerator—peppers, onions, potatoes, asparagus, broccoli, cheeses, leftover roast beef or pork, good-quality smoked ham or cold cuts, fresh herbs. You name it—the combinations are endless when it comes to filling these baked custards.

These quiches can be made a few hours in advance of your event and reheated just before serving. Try making them in a mini tart pan for an instant hors d'oeuvre. Crispy Grissini breadsticks (page 262) and warm, cheesy Gougères (page 259) are also good options for a little nibble to accompany cocktails. All of these items (except for Gougères) can be served at room temperature. They are excellent first-course options and can be served in smaller quantities for hors d'oeuvres.

Finally, I've added some of my favorite comfort foods to this chapter—rich Tomato Cobbler (page 253), Pulled Pork Empanadas (page 254), with their golden cornmeal crust, and hearty Individual Chicken Pot Pies (page 256)—all hard to resist, all welcome anytime.

Tomato Tartlets

I developed this delicious summer tart for Martha Stewart Television. It quickly became a part of Martha's Baking Handbook. *The version here offers individual servings. They make a wonderful first course, and can be paired with a salad for a light lunch. This tomato tart is always a big seller at all of the farmers' markets we participate in.*

MAKES SIX 4½-INCH
TARTLETS

3 garlic cloves

¼ cup extra-virgin olive oil

½ recipe Pâte Brisée (page 98), chilled

½ cup grated fontina cheese

1 large ripe tomato, cored and sliced ¼ inch thick

Salt and freshly ground black pepper to taste

1. Place the oven rack in the middle position. Preheat the oven to 350°F.

2. Place the garlic in a piece of aluminum foil, drizzle with 1 tablespoon of the olive oil, and season with salt. Close up the foil and roast in the oven until the garlic is soft and golden brown, about 45 minutes; set aside to cool.

3. While the garlic cooks, on a lightly floured work surface, roll out the dough to about ⅛ inch thick. Cut out six 5½-inch rounds of dough, re-rolling scraps as necessary. Fit the dough into six 4½-inch tart pans with removable bottoms, pressing the dough into the edges. Press the excess dough against the sharp edge of the rim of the pan with the heel of your hand to cut it level with the pan. Chill until firm, about 30 minutes.

4. Using your fingers, squeeze the garlic out of their skins into a bowl, and mash with a fork; set aside.

5. Raise the oven temperature to 425°F. Line a baking sheet with parchment paper or a nonstick silicone baking mat; set aside.

6. Divide the garlic evenly among the tartlets, spreading it over the bottom of each shell. Sprinkle half of the cheese evenly among the tartlets. Arrange 2 overlapping tomato slices on each tartlet. Season with salt and pepper. Sprinkle each tartlet with the remaining cheese. Drizzle with the remaining olive oil.

7. Bake the tartlets on the prepared baking sheet until the crusts are golden brown and the tomatoes are soft but still retaining their shape, 30 to 40 minutes. Let cool for 15 minutes on a wire rack; then serve warm or at room temperature.

Corn, Crab, and Chive Tart

Late summer corn is the star of this savory brunch or luncheon tart. The subtle addition of crab and chives to the sautéed corn lends a mellow flavor to the filling and makes this a more substantial dish.

½ recipe **Pâte Brisée (page 98),** **chilled**

1 large egg

1 large egg yolk

1 cup heavy cream

1 cup milk

2 tablespoons sour cream

⅛ teaspoon grated nutmeg

½ teaspoon coarse salt
Freshly ground black pepper

¾ **cup lump crabmeat, picked** **over for any shells**

1 cup fresh corn kernels

2 **tablespoons chopped fresh** **chives**

1. On a lightly floured work surface, roll the dough to a 13-inch round, about ⅛ inch thick. Fit the dough into a 10-inch round tart pan that is 1½ inches deep, and trim the dough so that it comes slightly above the rim of the pan. The dough will just fit, with no excess. Chill in the refrigerator until firm, about 30 minutes.

2. Set the oven rack in the lower third of the oven. Preheat the oven to 425°F.

3. In a medium bowl, whisk together the egg, yolk, cream, milk, sour cream, nutmeg, salt, and pepper to taste; set aside. In a separate bowl, combine the crab, corn, and chives; set aside.

4. Place the chilled tart pan on a baking sheet. Spread the crab mixture over the bottom. Place the baking sheet in the oven, and carefully pour the custard mixture into the tart shell. Bake until the crust is golden brown and the custard is just set (a knife inserted into the center of the pie will come out clean), 20 to 25 minutes. Let cool on a wire rack for at least 10 minutes. Cut the tart into wedges.

Leek, Asparagus, and Corn Tart

Rich, with a quiche-like consistency, the custard in this tart is made with both eggs and egg yolks. You'll need a 1½-inch-deep ceramic tart pan or aluminum pie plate to accommodate the filling. You can also cut the dough into small rounds and make mini quiches in a mini-muffin tin to serve for tea or as an hors d'oeuvre, or bake in 3½-inch tartlet pans and serve individually with mixed greens as a first course or light lunch.

MAKES ONE 10-INCH TART, SERVES 8

½ recipe Pâte Brisée (page 98), chilled

½ bunch medium asparagus, top third only, cut into 1-inch pieces (reserve remaining stalks for another use)

3 medium leeks, cleaned, root ends trimmed, dark green parts discarded

1 tablespoon unsalted butter

1 tablespoon extra-virgin olive oil

Coarse salt and freshly ground black pepper

1 cup fresh or frozen thawed corn kernels

4 large eggs

2 large egg yolks

1 cup milk

1 cup heavy cream

⅓ cup chopped chives

Grated nutmeg

⅔ cup grated Gruyère cheese (2½ to 3 ounces)

TECHNIQUE TIP: When making quiches or other custard-filled savory tarts, I prefer to use a ceramic tart pan, as opposed to a metal tart pan with a removable bottom. The ceramic pan conducts heat better, causing the bottom crust to cook through more easily.

1. On a lightly floured work surface, roll the dough to a 13-inch round, about ⅛ inch thick. Fit the dough into a 10-inch tart pan that is 1½ inches deep, and trim the dough so that it comes slightly above the rim of the pan. The dough will just fit, with no excess. Chill in the refrigerator until firm, about 30 minutes.

2. Meanwhile, bring a saucepan of salted water to a boil. Add the asparagus pieces and cook until just tender, 1 to 2 minutes. Drain and cool under cold running water; set aside.

3. Cut the leeks in half lengthwise; slice into ¼-inch-thick rounds (you should have about 3 cups). In a large sauté pan, melt the butter with the olive oil over medium-low heat. Add the leeks, season with salt and pepper, cover, and cook, stirring often, until tender, 10 to 12 minutes. Add the corn during the final 2 to 3 minutes. Let cool.

4. Set the oven rack in the lower third of the oven. Preheat the oven to 425°F.

5. In a large bowl, whisk the eggs and egg yolks to combine. Add the milk, cream, and chives, and whisk to blend. Season with ½ teaspoon salt, ¼ teaspoon pepper, and the nutmeg.

6. Place the chilled tart shell on a baking sheet. Sprinkle about half of the cheese over the bottom. Add the leeks and corn in an even layer, then add the asparagus. Place the baking sheet in the oven, and carefully pour the custard mixture into the tart shell. Sprinkle with the remaining cheese. Bake until the crust is golden brown and the custard is just set (a knife inserted into the center of the pie will come out clean), 35 to 40 minutes.

7. Let cool on a wire rack for at least 10 minutes. Cut the tart into wedges.

Kalamata Olive and Red Onion Tart

This rectangular tart is almost like a thin-crust pizza. The olives are baked into the dough and the tart is scattered with caramelized red onions and then sprinkled with goat cheese. Serve this tart with lightly dressed mixed greens.

SERVES 4 TO 6

Kalamata Olive Dough

- ¾ cup warm water
- ½ teaspoon sugar
- 1 teaspoon active dry yeast
- 1¾ cups all-purpose flour, plus extra for kneading
- 1 teaspoon coarse salt
- 1 cup pitted Kalamata olives, coarsely chopped
- 1 tablespoon extra-virgin olive oil

Topping

- 3 tablespoons extra-virgin olive oil
- 2 pounds red onions, sliced thin (8 firmly packed cups)
- 1 garlic clove, thinly sliced
- 1 tablespoon chopped fresh thyme, plus thyme branches
- 1½ teaspoons coarse salt
- ½ teaspoon freshly ground black pepper
- 6 ounces fresh goat cheese, crumbled

TECHNIQUE TIP: When working with yeast, don't add cold ingredients or it will slow down the process. Always use warm water to proof (105° to 110°F), and make sure the rest of the water and ingredients that you're adding to the dough are at room temperature or warmer.

1. To make the dough: In a small bowl, combine ¼ cup of the warm water, the sugar, and the yeast and let stand until frothy, about 5 minutes. In a large bowl, stir together the flour, salt, and olives. When the yeast has proofed, add it to the flour mixture along with the remaining ½ cup warm water and the oil, and stir together.

2. Turn the dough out onto a lightly floured surface and knead by successively scooping the dough up from underneath with the thumb and the first two fingers of each hand, then slapping it down on the board as you pull your hands away. As the gluten develops, the flour absorbs moisture; as you work it, the dough will pull together into a ball and become less tacky. Knead for 5 to 7 minutes, or until the dough is smooth and springy. The dough will be a little tacky—try not to add too much flour.

3. Place the dough into a lightly oiled bowl. Turn the dough to coat with the oil, cover with oiled plastic wrap, and let stand for about 1½ hours, or until the volume increases by 1½ to 2 times.

4. Lightly oil a baking sheet. Turn the dough out onto the sheet and press it out to cover the surface. Cover with plastic wrap and set aside in a warm place (at least 70°F) to rise until puffy, 30 to 40 minutes.

5. Meanwhile, make the topping: Heat the oil in a large sauté pan over medium-high heat. Add the onions, garlic, chopped thyme, salt, and pepper, and sauté, stirring, until the onions are soft and sweet, about 20 minutes. Reduce the heat if the onions begin to stick.

6. Set the oven rack in the lower third of the oven. Preheat the oven to 425°F.

7. Spread the onions over the tart dough. Dot with the goat cheese and strew with thyme. The dough will deflate, so cover it with plastic wrap and let it rise again until puffy, 15 to 20 minutes.

8. Bake for 15 minutes. Rotate the baking sheet and continue baking until the crust is crisp and golden brown, 12 to 15 more minutes. Remove from the oven, and immediately slide the tart off the pan onto a wire rack. Cut into pieces and serve.

Quiche Lorraine

Many versions of quiche Lorraine are made with Gruyère, but I prefer fontina for its subtler taste. At the bakery we make a variety of quiche fillings, using everything from sautéed mushrooms to roast turkey. This basic recipe is very flexible and can accommodate most roasted or sautéed vegetables, cheeses, and/or meats. Try using any of the following or a combination of lardons, thick-cut slab bacon, and good-quality smoked ham. Quiche Lorraine is also a great way to use up leftover shredded pork from Pulled Pork Empanadas (page 254). Experiment with different combinations until you find your favorite.

MAKES ONE 9½- OR
10-INCH QUICHE,
SERVES 8 TO 10

½ recipe Pâte Brisee (page 98), chilled

8 ounces thick-cut slab bacon, cut into ⅓- to ½-inch dice (about 1¼ cups)

1 large onion, thinly sliced (about 2 cups)

4 large eggs

2 large egg yolks

1 cup milk

1 cup heavy cream

½ teaspoon coarse salt

¼ teaspoon freshly ground black pepper

Pinch of grated nutmeg

⅔ cup grated fontina cheese (about 3 ounces)

TECHNIQUE TIP: When making savory quiches and tarts, I often skip blind-baking the crust because it will inevitably shrink, causing problems for the liquid filling. Instead I place the prepared ceramic pan directly on a baking sheet, without parchment or nonstick silicone baking mats so the heat goes directly from the sheet pan to the tart pan to help bake the crust through. Finally, pour in the custard mixture when the tart shell is in the oven, to keep from spilling.

1. On a lightly floured work surface, roll the dough to a 12½- to 13-inch round, about ⅛ inch thick. Fit the dough into a 9½- to 10-inch ceramic tart pan that is 1½ inches deep, and trim the dough so that it comes slightly above the rim of the tart pan. The dough will just fit, with little or no excess. Chill in the refrigerator until firm, about 30 minutes.

2. Meanwhile, cook the bacon in a sauté pan over medium heat until the fat is rendered and the bacon is lightly browned, about 15 minutes. Remove the bacon with a slotted spoon. Discard all but about 2 tablespoons of the bacon fat. Add the onion, and cook until softened and lightly browned, 12 to 15 minutes. Let cool.

3. Set the oven rack in the lower third of the oven. Preheat the oven to 425°F.

4. In a large bowl, whisk the eggs and egg yolks to combine. Add the milk and cream and whisk to blend. Season with the salt, pepper, and nutmeg.

5. Place the chilled tart shell on a baking sheet. Sprinkle about half of the cheese over the bottom. Add the cooked onion and bacon in an even layer. Place the baking sheet in the oven, and carefully pour the custard mixture into the tart shell. Sprinkle the remaining cheese over the top. Bake until the crust is golden brown, the quiche puffs, and the custard is just set (a knife inserted into the center of the pie will come out clean), 35 to 40 minutes.

6. Let cool on a wire rack for at least 10 minutes. Cut the tart into wedges.

Three-Pepper and Feta Quiche

This quiche is a perfect and delicious way to use up a bounty of peppers in your garden. You can use crumbled goat cheese instead of feta, or try using 2 teaspoons fresh chopped thyme (or 1 teaspoon dried) instead of basil. Serve with a loaf of good crusty bread.

MAKES ONE 9½- TO
10-INCH QUICHE,
SERVES 8

½ recipe Pâte Brisée (page 98), chilled

2 tablespoons extra-virgin olive oil

3 bell peppers (1 red, 1 yellow, 1 orange), stemmed, cored, seeded, and thinly sliced

½ onion, thinly sliced
Coarse salt and freshly ground black pepper

4 large eggs

2 large egg yolks

1 cup milk

1 cup heavy cream

½ cup thinly sliced basil leaves (about ½ small bunch)

½ cup crumbled feta cheese
Pinch of grated nutmeg

1. On a lightly floured work surface, roll the dough to a 12½- to 13-inch round. Fit the dough into a 9½- to 10-inch ceramic tart pan that is 1½ inches deep and trim the dough so that it comes slightly above the rim of the pan. The dough will just fit, with no excess. Chill in the refrigerator until firm, about 30 minutes.

2. In a large sauté pan, heat the olive oil over medium-low heat. Add the pepper strips and onion, season with 1 teaspoon salt and ¼ teaspoon pepper, and cook until tender, 15 to 20 minutes. Reduce the heat to low if the peppers begin to brown.

3. Set the oven rack in the middle position. Preheat the oven to 425°F.

4. In a large bowl, whisk the eggs and egg yolks to combine. Add the milk, cream, and half of the basil, and whisk to blend. Whisk in ¼ cup of the feta, breaking it up with the whisk to blend. Season with ½ teaspoon salt, ¼ teaspoon pepper, and the nutmeg.

5. Place the chilled tart shell on a baking sheet. Spread the pepper-onion mixture over the bottom. Place the baking sheet in the oven, and carefully pour in the custard mixture. Sprinkle with the remaining ¼ cup feta. Bake until the crust is golden brown and the custard is just set, 35 to 40 minutes.

6. Let cool on a wire rack for at least 10 minutes. Garnish with the remaining basil. Cut the tart into wedges.

Tomato Cobbler

This savory side dish is a favorite at the end of summer, when tomatoes are at their peak of flavor. The Pâte Brisée crust used here offers the rich flavors of Jarlsberg and fresh thyme. Using an assortment of multicolored cherry tomatoes provides a burst of color in every bite.

MAKES ONE 10-INCH COBBLER, SERVES 12

Crust

- 1 cup plus 2 tablespoons all-purpose flour
- 1 teaspoon sugar
- ½ teaspoon coarse salt
- ½ cup (1 stick) cold unsalted butter, cut into small pieces
- ½ cup grated Jarlsberg cheese
- 1 tablespoon fresh thyme
- 2 tablespoons ice water

Filling

- 2 tablespoons olive oil
- 1 small onion, diced
- 2 large shallots, diced
- 2 garlic cloves, minced
- 2 pounds cherry tomatoes (yellow, red, and orange if possible)
- 6 tablespoons all-purpose flour
- 1½ teaspoons sugar
- 2 teaspoons coarse salt
- 1 teaspoon freshly ground black pepper

- 1 large egg, beaten, for egg wash
- ¼ cup grated Jarlsberg cheese

1. To make the crust: In the bowl of a food processor, combine the flour, sugar, and salt. Add the butter and pulse the mixture until it resembles coarse crumbs, about 10 seconds. Add the Jarlsberg cheese and thyme, and pulse until just combined. With the machine running, add the ice water through the feed tube in a slow and steady stream, a little bit at a time until the dough just comes together. The dough should not be wet or sticky. If the dough is too dry and does not hold together, add a little more water.

2. Turn the dough out onto a clean work surface. Wrap in plastic wrap, shaping it into a flattened disk. Chill for at least 1 hour.

3. Place an oven rack in the middle position. Preheat the oven to 375°F. Line a baking sheet with parchment paper or a nonstick silicone baking mat; set aside.

4. To make the filling: Heat the olive oil in a medium skillet over medium heat. Add the onion, shallots, and garlic and sauté until tender, 5 to 6 minutes. Remove from the heat and set aside to cool.

5. In a large bowl, toss the tomatoes with the flour, sugar, salt, and pepper until well coated. Add the onion mixture and toss until well combined. Pour the tomato mixture into a 10-inch pie plate; set aside.

6. On a lightly floured work surface, roll out the chilled dough to a 12-inch round. Place it on top of the tomato mixture and tuck any overhanging dough underneath. Brush the top with the egg wash and sprinkle with the Jarlsberg cheese. Use a knife or scissors to cut a vent in the crust. Set the pie plate on the prepared baking sheet and bake, rotating the sheet about two-thirds of the way through the baking time, until the crust is golden brown and the juices are bubbling, 45 to 55 minutes. Let cool completely before serving.

Pulled Pork Empanadas

These authentic Latin flavored empanadas use a version of Pâte Brisée, with cornmeal added, so that the texture is somewhat hardier. At the bakery we cut the empanadas into triangles to save time and cut down on wasted dough, but you can also cut the dough into rounds and fold them over to make half-moon shapes; then gather up any scraps, chill, and re-roll them to get roughly the same amount. It's hard to find a pork shoulder that weighs less than 4 pounds, so plan on using only half of the cooked pork for the empanadas. Slice and eat the remaining half for dinner with some of the deglazed pan juices as a sauce, or shred for sandwiches or use as a quiche filling (see page 249). Finally, be sure to start this recipe in advance, as the meat should sit in the spice rub overnight before cooking, and the actual cooking time is then 8 to 9 hours at low heat for the extra-tender texture needed for shredding.

MAKES 14 TO 16 EMPANADAS

Spice Rub

- 2 tablespoons coarse salt
- 2 tablespoons light brown sugar
- 2 tablespoons paprika
- 1 tablespoon coarsely ground black pepper
- ½ teaspoon cayenne pepper
- ½ teaspoon ground allspice

- 3½ to 4 pounds pork butt or picnic shoulder roast, preferably with bone

Pastry Dough

- 2 cups all-purpose flour
- ½ cup coarse-ground cornmeal
- 2 teaspoons granulated sugar
- 1 teaspoon coarse salt
- 1 teaspoon coarsely ground black pepper
- ¼ teaspoon paprika
- 1 cup (2 sticks) cold unsalted butter, cut into pieces
- 5 to 6 tablespoons ice water

1. To make the rub: In a small bowl, mix all of the ingredients for the spice rub. Rub all over the pork, cover, and refrigerate overnight.

2. The next day, preheat the oven to 200°F. Place the pork in a small roasting pan and roast until the meat registers 165° to 170°F on an instant-read thermometer, 8 to 9 hours. Transfer the pork to a platter and set aside to cool.

3. Add ½ cup water to the roasting pan, set over medium heat, and bring to a simmer. Cook, scraping the bottom of the pan with a wooden spoon to pick up the caramelized sugars, until the liquid has reduced slightly and has a good, strong flavor; set aside 3 to 4 tablespoons for the filling.

4. To make the pastry: In the bowl of a food processor, combine the flour, cornmeal, sugar, salt, pepper, and paprika. Add the butter and pulse until the mixture resembles coarse crumbs, about 10 seconds. With the machine running, add the ice water through the feed tube in a slow and steady stream, a little bit at a time until the dough just comes together. The dough should not be wet or sticky. If the dough is too dry and does not hold together, add a little more water. Turn the dough onto a clean work surface. Divide in half and shape each into a square or rectangle for ease of rolling. Wrap in plastic wrap, and chill for at least 1 hour.

5. To make the filling: Remove the pork from the bone. Remove any skin; discard skin and bone. Using two forks or your fingers, shred 3 cups of the pork. Wrap the rest of the pork for another use. Put the shredded pork in a medium bowl. Add the reserved pan deglaze, the

vinegar, Worcestershire sauce, sugar, paprika, corn, chopped jalapeño, cilantro, and salt to taste, and mix.

6. Set the oven rack in the bottom third of the oven. Preheat the oven to 375°F. Line a baking sheet with parchment paper or a nonstick silicone baking mat; set aside.

7. On a lightly floured work surface, roll one piece of the dough into a rectangle about 1/8 inch thick, 9 inches wide, and however long you can comfortably roll. With a large knife, trim the rectangle to 8 inches wide. Cut six dough squares. Gather the scraps, and re-roll to make one or two more squares.

8. To fill the empanadas, brush two sides of a dough square with egg wash. Scoop out a scant 1/4 cup filling, and place it in the center of the square. Starting with the half that has not been egg-washed, fold half of the dough over the filling on the diagonal to enclose it and make a triangular package. Press the edges together with your fingers and press all the way along the folded edge with the tines of a fork to make a decorative edging. Place on the prepared baking sheet. Continue to fill the remaining empanadas and place them all on the baking sheet. Brush all over with egg wash. Sprinkle the tops with fennel seeds, and cut vents to allow the steam to escape.

9. Bake, rotating the sheet about two-thirds of the way through, until the crust is golden brown and crisp, and the filling is bubbling, 25 to 30 minutes. Remove to a wire rack to cool for 10 minutes before serving.

10. Repeat to fill and bake seven to eight more empanadas.

Variation: ROASTED VEGETABLE EMPANADAS

Make and roll the dough exactly the same as above. Make a filling by cutting the following vegetables into 1/2-inch dice: 1 peeled sweet potato, 1 red onion, 2 shallots, 1 carrot, 1 red potato, 1 peeled turnip, and 1 peeled beet (you can also replace sweet potato and carrot with butternut squash).

Toss with: 3 tablespoons olive oil, 1 1/2 tablespoons chopped fresh thyme or rosemary, 1 1/2 teaspoons salt, and 1/2 teaspoon pepper.

Roast at 425°F, rotating halfway through for about 30 minutes. Using a fork, mash about one-quarter of the vegetables and fold in the remaining roasted vegetables. Let cool, proceed as above.

Filling

- 3 tablespoons apple cider vinegar
- 2 teaspoons Worcestershire sauce
- 1 teaspoon granulated sugar
- 1/4 teaspoon paprika
- 3/4 cup fresh or frozen (unthawed) corn kernels
- 1 to 2 jalapeño peppers, finely chopped
- 1/2 cup chopped cilantro
  Salt

- 1 egg, beaten, for egg wash
- 1 tablespoon fennel seeds, for sprinkling

Individual Chicken Pot Pies

The ultimate comfort food—creamy chicken and vegetable filling sitting beneath a thyme-infused Pâte Brisée crust. This dish is very popular with kids at the bakery throughout the winter months. Poaching the chicken and using the poaching liquid for the required stock gives an extra dimension of flavor. If you are short on time, buy a roast chicken and shred 3 firmly packed cups, and use 2½ cups canned stock. You will need four ovenproof bowls or ramekins that each hold about 1½ cups of filling.

Herbed Pâte Brisée

2¼ cups all-purpose flour

2 teaspoons sugar

1 teaspoon coarse salt

2 tablespoons chopped fresh thyme

1 cup (2 sticks) cold unsalted butter, cut into small pieces

¼ cup ice water

Filling

1 whole chicken, 3 to 3½ pounds
Coarse salt and freshly ground black pepper

6 tablespoons (¾ stick) unsalted butter

½ large red onion, chopped fine (about 1 cup)

3½ ounces shiitake mushrooms, stemmed and quartered (about 2 cups)

3 carrots, cut into ½-inch dice (about 1⅓ cups)

1 parsnip, cut into ½-inch dice (about 1 cup)

2 tablespoons brandy

½ cup all-purpose flour

1½ cups milk

¾ cup frozen peas

¾ cup frozen pearl onions

2 teaspoons chopped fresh thyme

1 tablespoon chopped parsley

1 egg, lightly beaten, for egg wash

1. To make the pastry: Follow the directions for making a standard Pâte Brisée (page 98), but pulse the thyme into the flour, sugar, and salt mixture, then add the butter and ice water. Chill for 30 minutes.

2. To make the filling: Rinse the chicken. Put it into a large saucepan or small pot, just large enough to hold the chicken comfortably, and add water to cover. Bring to a simmer over high heat. Reduce the heat and skim the foam that is floating on the top of the water. Add 1 tablespoon salt and ½ teaspoon pepper. Simmer until the chicken is cooked through, 40 to 45 minutes. Remove the chicken from the pot with a large slotted spoon and let cool. Pull the meat from the bones; discard skin and bones.

3. Strain the stock through a fine strainer. Measure 2½ cups, and set aside separately. Refrigerate or freeze the remaining stock for another use.

4. In a large saucepan, heat the butter over medium-low heat. Add the red onion, mushrooms, carrots, and parsnip; season with salt and pepper, and cook for 5 minutes to soften. Add the brandy and simmer to evaporate. Add the flour, stir to blend with the butter, and cook for 30 seconds. Add the reserved chicken stock, bring to a simmer, and cook for 2 to 3 minutes. Add the milk, bring to a simmer, and cook until the vegetables are tender and the sauce has reduced to the consistency of a thick white sauce, 7 to 10 minutes. Add the peas, pearl onions, thyme, parsley, nutmeg, and shredded chicken. Season with salt and pepper.

5. Preheat the oven to 375°F. Arrange a rack in the center of the oven. Line a baking sheet with parchment paper or a nonstick silicone baking mat.

6. Roll the dough ⅛ inch thick. Cut rounds slightly larger than the diameter of your ovenproof bowls or ramekins. Place the rounds on another baking sheet and set aside in the refrigerator.

7. Ladle the chicken mixture into the ramekins. The mixture should come all the way up to the top of the bowl so that the crust doesn't sink into the filling and soak. Top each with a round of dough, tucking the excess around the edges of the ramekins. Brush with the egg wash. Use a knife or scissors to cut a vent in the crust. Set the dishes on the prepared baking sheet and bake, rotating the sheet about two-thirds of the way through the cooking, until the crust is golden brown and the juices are bubbling, 30 to 40 minutes.

Easter Pie

I make this pie every year during Easter, both at the bakery and for friends and family at home. It reminds me of my grandmother Julia, who used to make it all the time, not just for the holiday. She used a pizza dough for the crust, but my version uses Pâte Brisée, a buttery pastry that holds up nicely to bitter greens. This recipe calls for escarole, mozzarella, and pecorino Romano, but you can try a variety of vegetables, cheeses, and meats, including roasted peppers, spinach, Parmesan and ricotta, cured meats such as salami, soppresatta, and capricola, and more. This dish is also good eaten the next day (reheat for 30 minutes in a 250°F oven).

MAKES ONE 9½-INCH PIE

2 **pounds escarole, trimmed, cut into 1-inch pieces, washed, and drained**
¼ **cup extra-virgin olive oil**
3 **garlic cloves, sliced**
¼ **teaspoon red pepper flakes**
¼ **cup raisins**
1¼ **cups ricotta cheese**
⅔ **cup grated low-moisture mozzarella cheese**
3 **large eggs, at room temperature**
⅔ **cup grated pecorino Romano Coarse salt and freshly ground black pepper**
1 **recipe Pâte Brisée (page 98), chilled**
1 **egg, lightly beaten, for egg wash**

1. Bring a large pot of water to a boil. Add half of the escarole and cook until wilted, 3 to 5 minutes. Remove to a bowl with a slotted spoon; drain, and refresh under cold running water. Return the water to a boil; add the rest of the escarole and repeat to cook until wilted; drain. Squeeze the escarole to remove as much water as possible; set aside.

2. Heat the oil with the garlic in a large skillet over medium heat until the garlic turns a light golden color, 2 to 3 minutes. Add the red pepper flakes and give it a stir. Add the escarole and stir to coat with the oil. Cook for 2 to 3 minutes to evaporate any water. Stir in the raisins. Remove from the heat and let cool.

3. In a large bowl, stir together the ricotta, mozzarella, eggs, and pecorino. Add the cooled escarole and stir. Season to taste with salt and black pepper.

4. Set the oven rack in the bottom third of the oven. Preheat the oven to 375°F. Line a baking sheet with parchment paper or a nonstick silicone baking mat.

5. Roll one pastry disk to a 13-inch round and fit it into a 9½-inch glass pie pan; trim the edges to about ½ inch above the rim. Roll the remaining pastry disk to about ⅛ inch thick and cut into 1-inch-wide strips. Fill the pastry shell with the escarole mixture and smooth the top. Arrange the pastry strips on top in a lattice design, about ½ inch apart. Fold the edges of the bottom crust toward the center and crimp.

6. Brush the pastry with the egg wash. Bake on the prepared baking sheet, rotating the sheet about two-thirds of the way through the baking time, until the pastry is cooked through and golden brown, 1 hour to 1 hour and 10 minutes. Let stand for 15 minutes before cutting, or let cool completely and serve at room temperature.

Gougères

Serve these savory cheese puffs as an hors d'oeuvre for cocktail hour. Their light texture and complex taste pair nicely with wine or mixed drinks. They are made from pâte à choux dough, which is one of the easiest and fastest pastry doughs to make. Gougères classically call for Gruyère, but try substituting other favorite cheeses, such as fontina or blue cheese. Serve these bites as soon as they come out of the oven.

MAKES 55 TO 60 PUFFS

1 cup water

½ cup (1 stick) unsalted butter, cubed

¼ teaspoon coarse salt, plus extra for seasoning

1 cup plus 2 tablespoons all-purpose flour

1½ cups coarsely grated Gruyère cheese (about 5 ounces)
Pinch of cayenne pepper

5 large eggs

¼ cup grated Parmesan cheese, for sprinkling

1. In a medium, heavy-bottomed saucepan, combine the water, butter, and salt, and bring to a rolling boil over medium heat. Remove from the heat. Add the flour all at once and stir with a wooden spoon to incorporate. Return the pan to low heat and cook, stirring, until the dough comes together into a mass and pulls away from the sides of the pan, 2 to 3 minutes. Stir in the Gruyère cheese until melted. Season with salt and cayenne pepper.

2. Transfer the dough to a standing mixer fitted with the paddle attachment. Add 4 of the eggs, one at a time, beating until incorporated after each addition. (The batter will not be completely smooth.) Whisk the remaining egg in a bowl, and add a little at a time, beating after each addition, until the dough is smooth and shiny, loose enough that it falls easily from a spoon but tight enough that it makes a peak when you pull the spoon away.

3. Preheat the oven to 425°F. Line three baking sheets with parchment paper or nonstick silicone baking mats.

4. With a rubber spatula, scoop the dough into a pastry bag fitted with a round (⅝-inch) tip. Pipe balls, each a little smaller than a golf ball, about 2 inches apart onto the prepared baking sheets. (If you don't have a pastry bag, you can use two spoons.) Sprinkle with the Parmesan cheese. Bake one sheet at a time, rotating the sheet two-thirds of the way through, until the Gougères are puffed and golden, 16 to 20 minutes. Remove to a wire rack. Serve warm.

Cheese Straws

These cheese straws are really simple to make, requiring very few ingredients. They should, however, be made with the best quality ingredients you can find—especially the puff pastry, which should be flaky and full of real butter. Dufour is a good brand that can be found at many gourmet specialty stores. You can vary the amount of cayenne pepper for more or less kick. If you have any straws left over, reheat in a 350°F oven for a few minutes to crisp them up.

MAKES ABOUT 40 CHEESE STRAWS

1⅓ cups grated good-quality Parmesan cheese (about 5 ounces)

⅔ teaspoon paprika

⅛ teaspoon cayenne pepper

½ teaspoon coarse salt

1 sheet (14 ounces) good-quality frozen puff pastry, thawed in the refrigerator for 2 to 3 hours

1 large egg, beaten, for egg wash

TECHNIQUE TIP: The key to using puff pastry is to chill, chill, chill. Keep putting the pastry back in the refrigerator, as required, in order to shape it properly and keep it from having too much elasticity when you're twisting or rolling it.

1. In a small bowl, toss together the cheese, paprika, cayenne pepper, and salt.

2. On a lightly floured work surface, roll the pastry to a rectangle about 11 by 14 inches, and about ⅛ inch thick. With a pastry cutter and a ruler, trim to a rectangle 10 by 13 inches, with one long side facing you. Brush with the egg wash, and sprinkle with the cheese mixture. Gently roll the mixture just slightly into the dough with the rolling pin.

3. Line two baking sheets with parchment paper or nonstick silicone baking mats.

4. Cut the pastry rectangle in half vertically, so that you have two sheets, 6½ by 10 inches each. Working with one half at a time, use the ruler to mark off ½-inch sections along the two long (10-inch) sides. Use the ruler and pastry cutter to cut 6½ by ½-inch strips. Place each strip on a prepared baking sheet, twisting to give the strips a spiral shape. Cover and refrigerate for at least 15 minutes.

5. Preheat the oven to 425°F and arrange a rack in the center of the oven. Bake one sheet at a time until crisp and lightly browned, 12 to 15 minutes. Let cool on the baking sheets on a wire rack for a few minutes. Serve warm.

Grissini

These long, skinny, crisp breadsticks are easy to make and are a great addition to any buffet table or cheese and cracker plate. The Grissini are shaped on top of a layer of semolina flour, which sticks to the breadsticks and adds crunch and texture.

MAKES ABOUT
35 BREADSTICKS

1½ **cups warm (110°F) water**
1¾ **teaspoons active dry yeast**
3¾ **cups all-purpose flour**
2½ **teaspoons coarse salt**
   1 **teaspoon honey**
1½ **tablespoons olive oil**
   Semolina flour

Variations: For a slightly different flavor, try any of the options below.

TOMATO GRISSINI: Stir and dissolve 1½ tablespoons of tomato paste into the cup of water in step 2 before adding to the flour combination.

HERB GRISSINI: Add 1½ tablespoons of any favorite freshly chopped herbs to the flour and salt in step 2 before adding the wet ingredients.

BLACK PEPPER GRISSINI: Add 1½ teaspoons freshly ground black pepper to the flour and salt in step 2 before adding the wet ingredients.

1. In a small bowl, combine ¼ cup of the water and the yeast and let stand until frothy, 5 minutes.

2. In a large bowl, stir together the flour and salt, and make a well in the center. When the yeast has proofed, pour it into the well along with the remaining 1¼ cups water, the honey, and the oil. Using a plastic scraper, gradually pull the flour into the wet ingredients, folding to mix, until a soft dough forms. Then knead the dough in the bowl for 5 minutes, by folding the dough over itself while you turn the bowl. Scrape the dough out onto a board. Wash and dry the bowl. Smear the bottom of the bowl with olive oil. Scrape up the dough with the plastic scraper and return it to the bowl. Turn the dough in the bowl to coat with the oil. Cover with an oiled sheet of plastic wrap. Let stand in a warm place (at least 70°F) about 1½ hours, or until the volume increases by 1½ to 2 times.

3. Line two baking sheets with parchment paper or nonstick silicone baking mats; set aside. Sprinkle a work surface generously with semolina flour so that it covers an area about 4 inches by 25 inches.

4. Place the dough on top of the semolina and stretch it out to about 4 inches wide and ½ inch thick, to cover the semolina. If the dough gives you trouble stretching, let it relax for 20 minutes and try again. Sprinkle the top of the dough with more semolina flour. Using a ruler and a pastry cutter, cut the dough into pieces 4 inches long by ½ inch wide.

5. Holding one end of a piece of dough in each hand, stretch it out to the length of the baking sheet by twirling it gently. Place on the prepared baking sheet. Repeat to form all of the breadsticks. Cover with plastic wrap and let rise in a warm place until soft and puffy, about 20 minutes.

6. Set an oven rack in the middle position. Preheat the oven to 325°F.

7. Bake one sheet at a time, rotating the sheet two-thirds of the way through, until the breadsticks are dry and crisp—around 12 to 15 minutes. Transfer to a wire rack to cool.

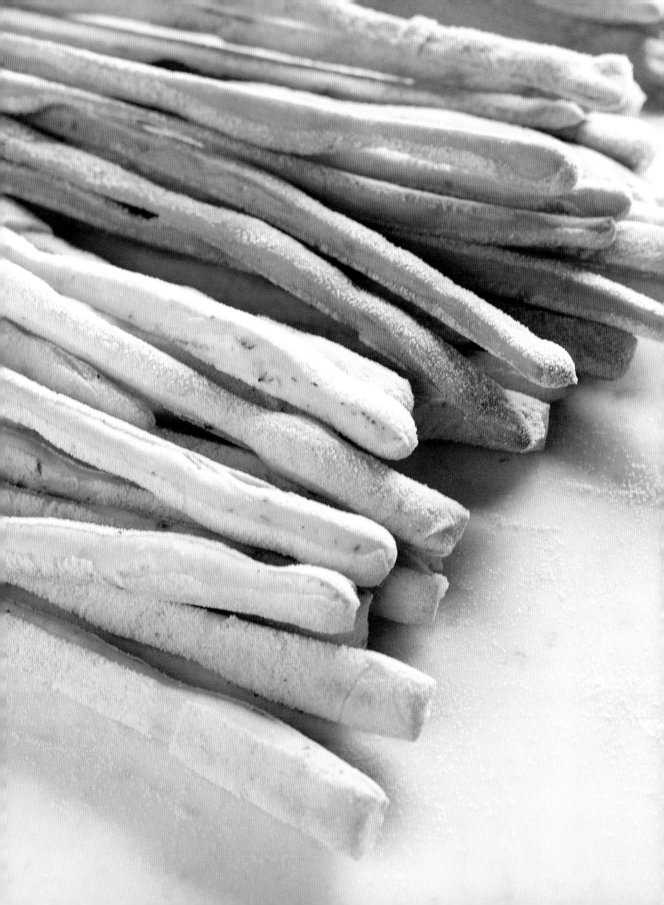

Ingredients Glossary

BAKING POWDER

Baking powder is a leavening agent that reacts by releasing carbon dioxide when it first comes into contact with liquids, and then again during baking. It is important to check the expiration date on the can, as baking powder loses its leavening power over time. It's best to buy small quantities of it and replace it at least every six months.

BAKING SODA

Baking soda is a leavening agent that is activated by an acidic element such as sour cream, buttermilk, yogurt, or lemon juice. Once the baking soda comes into contact with one of these ingredients in a batter, carbon dioxide bubbles are produced, causing the batter to rise. It's best to bake the item as soon as possible after the baking soda is added in order to get the most rise out of it. Buy new baking soda every few months, as its potency can weaken.

BUTTER

This essential fat helps create flaky layered pastries, tender piecrusts, and a golden color in baked cookies. Butter by U.S. standard definition is 80 percent milkfat, with the remaining 20 percent consisting of water and milk solids. Always use unsalted butter for baking. Margarine is not a suitable replacement, as its chemical compound is different, causing it to not melt, cook, or combine the same way butter does. Unsalted butter can be refrigerated for up to three weeks and frozen for up to six months.

BUTTERMILK

This tangy acidic liquid (the thicker cultured version is created by adding special bacteria to nonfat and low-fat milk for a thickened texture) lends moistness and flavor to a range of baked goods, including muffins, cakes, and panna cottas. Its acidic qualities also help activate the leavening agents in baking soda.

CHOCOLATE

When it comes to chocolate, the better the quality you use, the better your dessert will be. At the bakery we like to use Callebaut chocolate, as it is both affordable and of good quality. Experiment with a few different high-quality brands to find a favorite. While there is a wide range of chocolates and percentage chocolates (referring to the amount of chocolate liquor present) available, all of the recipes in this book call for either bittersweet chocolate, semisweet chocolate, white chocolate, or unsweetened cocoa powder. They are defined as follows:

Bittersweet and semisweet chocolates are often used interchangeably, though bittersweet generally has more chocolate liquor, a paste formed from ground roasted cocoa beans. Semisweet chocolate contains at least 35 percent chocolate liquor, while finer bittersweet chocolates contain 50 percent or more chocolate liquor.

White chocolate does not contain any chocolate. It is derived from cocoa butter, which produces a slight chocolate flavor. The cocoa butter is combined with milk and sugar to form the white confection, which is used for both eating and baking.

Cocoa powder is the dry powder that remains after cocoa butter is extracted from the chocolate liquor. Dutch-processed cocoa is treated with an alkali to achieve a deep, rich color and is commonly used in baking recipes.

COCONUT

Most of the recipes in this book call for either sweetened or unsweetened shredded or flaked coconut. The sweetened version is commonly available at grocery stores, while the unsweetened version is more likely available at specialty stores. Store for up to 6 months unopened. Refrigerate after opening and store for up to 2 months.

CORNMEAL

This grain, also known as polenta, consists of dried corn kernels that have been ground into a fine, medium, or coarse texture. It is similar to semolina in texture. Cornmeal is a versatile ingredient that can be used in both sweet and savory dishes. In this book we use it to enhance crusts for empanadas and to make a textured cornmeal bread. Store in an airtight container in the refrigerator for up to four months.

CREAM

The recipes in this book call for heavy cream, also known as heavy whipping cream, with a milkfat content of between 36 and 40 percent. Cream is called for in a range of recipes and can be used for anything from a wash for pastries to whipped cream.

CRÈME FRAÎCHE

A thickened cream with a smooth, rich texture and tangy sour taste. It is a wonderful accompaniment to any sweet dessert, adding a dimension to each bite. Crème fraîche is available at specialty markets, or you can make your own by combining 1 cup whipping cream and 2 tablespoons buttermilk in a small bowl. Cover and let stand at room temperature for 8 to 24 hours, until thickened.

EGGS

Nature's "perfect food" is indispensable for performing a variety of baking functions, including leavening, binding, thickening, emulsifying, and glazing baked goods. At the bakery we use local natural large brown eggs. Never use anything smaller than size large eggs. The key to good eggs is freshness. Never buy them in bulk, as eggs are porous and can take on odors and bacteria. Instead, buy only as many as you might use in a week (regardless of the expiration date) and then replenish.

FLOUR

There is a wide range of specialty flours available, but this book calls mostly for all-purpose flour and occasionally cake flour, bread flour, and whole wheat flour. They are defined below:

All-purpose flour is used in a wide variety of baked goods, including cookies, quick breads, and some yeast breads. It is milled from a combination of high-gluten (a protein found in wheat, rye, barley, and oats) hard wheat and low-gluten soft wheat. Its fine texture comes from the inner part of the wheat kernel and contains none of the germ or bran of the wheat. This flour may be bleached (a process that speeds up the natural lightening of and maturing of flour) or unbleached (my preference). Both may be enriched with vitamins and iron.

Cake flour is used for making cakes, cookies, pastries, and some breads. Its texture is fine and it is made from soft wheat with a low protein content.

Bread flour is unbleached wheat flour that is higher in protein (gluten), allowing for better yeast bread dough development and flavor.

Whole wheat flour is made by grinding the entire wheat kernel, including the bran and germ.

HONEY

A thick, sweet liquid made by bees from the nectar of flowers. For baking, use a neutral-flavored honey—nothing with herb infusions or additional flavoring agents.

MAPLE SYRUP

Although extremely expensive, there is no substitute for real, pure maple syrup. Never use maple-flavored syrups, which are artificially flavored and contain little to no real maple syrup. At the bakery we use the Grade B Dark Amber variety for our Maple Pecan Tart (page 127) and to flavor a range of other desserts.

MILK

We always use whole milk, which contains 3 to 3½ percent milkfat, for all of our desserts, never skim or low-fat.

MOLASSES

This thick sweetener is a by-product of processed sugar. It is available in light, dark, unsulfured (my preference), and blackstrap variations that range from weak to strong in flavor. It is also added to granulated sugar in varying amounts to make light or dark brown sugar.

NUTS

The recipes in this book call for a wide range of nuts, including almonds, hazelnuts, macadamia nuts, pecans, pistachios, and walnuts. If you are allergic to any of these nuts, feel free to omit them from most any recipe. Most nuts are available already shelled, halved, chopped, and roasted. Nuts should be stored in an airtight container in a cool place. Shelled nuts can be refrigerated for up to four months and frozen for up to six months.

OATS

Old-fashioned whole, rolled oats are preferable for baking, rather than instant oats. The old-fashioned oats are larger and provide a heartier texture in each bite and won't absorb too much liquid.

SOUR CREAM COFFEE CAKE, SEE PAGE 54

SALT

All of the recipes in this book call for coarse salt (kosher salt), which is additive-free. A few recipes call for the more flavorful Maldon Sea Salt (available at gourmet specialty stores) as a finishing touch.

SOUR CREAM

We use whole-milk sour cream in our recipes. It contains 18 to 20 percent fat and has been treated with lactic acid culture to provide tanginess.

SUGARS

A number of different sugars are called for in this book. They are defined as follows:

Granulated sugar is a highly refined cane or beet sugar. In addition to the sweet flavor it imparts to baked goods, it also provides tenderness to doughs, stability to mixtures such as beaten egg whites for meringue, and a golden brown finish to many baked items.

Brown sugar comes in two forms: the more intensely flavored dark brown sugar and the lighter light brown sugar. Dark brown sugar contains more molasses than light brown sugar. To avoid hardening of either sugar, store it in an airtight container. Brown sugar must be packed tightly into a dry measure for accuracy.

Confectioners' sugar, also know as powdered sugar, is sucrose that is ground to a fine powder and mixed with a little cornstarch. It is commonly used for baking and to make frostings and glazes.

Sanding sugar is a refined sugar product that has a larger crystal size than normal granulated sugar. It comes in both a regular and a coarse texture. The sugar does not melt when baked in the oven; instead, it keeps its unique texture when sprinkled on top of cookies, muffins, and other baked items.

VANILLA

Vanilla is an essential flavoring agent. Three types of vanilla products are called for in this book. They are defined as follows:

The vanilla bean, a long, thin, wiry pod, is the fruit of an orchid. The three most common vanilla beans are Bourbon-Madagascar from the southeast coast of Africa, Mexican, and Tahitian.

Vanilla extract is the most common form of vanilla used today. It's made by macerating chopped vanilla beans in an alcohol-water solution and then aging it for several months. There is simply no substitute for pure vanilla extract. Never use imitation vanilla extract, as the taste is much weaker and artificial.

Vanilla paste is a sweet, concentrated vanilla extract that has vanilla bean seeds in the mix. It delivers pure vanilla flavor in a convenient form and is available at gourmet specialty stores.

VEGETABLE COOKING SPRAY

This inexpensive ingredient is essential for helping to release baked goods from pans. Flavorless and odorless, it can be used instead of butter to grease pans and to spray plastic wrap to allow breads to rise without sticking.

YEAST

Active dry yeast is a leavening agent used in doughs and batters. It's most commonly available in a dry, granulated form (which can also be compressed into cakes, which is what we use at the bakery). It is best activated at a temperature of about 110°F. Water that is too cold or too hot will fail to activate the yeast, so always check the water with a thermometer before adding it to the yeast. Always check the date on the package to make sure the yeast is fresh and active. Proofing active dry yeast is another way to make sure it is fresh: Let it sit in a bowl of warm (110°F) water for 5 minutes before adding additional ingredients. If bubbles form, the yeast is still active.

Instant yeast, or quick rising yeast, which is occasionally called for in this book, doesn't require proofing and can be added directly to the mixture with warm water.

ZEST

The outer skin of citrus fruit that, when grated or peeled, is used to flavor foods and liquids. The rind of citrus fruits such as orange, grapefruit, lime, and lemon contains essential oils that lend an extra dimension of flavor to baked goods. When zesting, be careful not to include the white pith of the fruit, as it can add bitterness. For optimal zesting, use a Microplane grater (page 275).

Equipment Glossary

BAKING DISH

A shallow container made of glass, metal, or ceramic that can be used for both baking and serving. Perfect for everything from baking cobblers to roasting fish.

BAKING SHEETS

A rimmed or rimless flat sheet of rigid aluminum used for baking a wide range of items including cookies, breads, scones, and more. Rimmed sheets are ideal for anything that might run while baking. Rimless sheets, or cookie sheets, are good for sliding things like baked bread directly onto a cooling rack. Baking sheets come in a variety of sizes. A 17 by 12-inch size is most often called for in this book.

BOX GRATER

A standing grater with sharp grooves of different sizes that create different textures of grated/shredded foods. A requirement for grating chocolate, cheese, potatoes, and more.

BUNDT PAN

Classic Bundt pans have curved, fluted sides and hold 12 to 15 cups of batter. Perfect for pound cakes and tea cakes, they are sold in cast aluminum (which requires thorough greasing) and nonstick (for easy release and cleanup) versions.

CAKE PANS

As the name suggests, these pans are used for baking multitiered cakes and come in a range of shapes and sizes including round, square, and rectangular. Stock your kitchen with a minimum of one pair of 8-inch round pans and one 8-inch square pan. I prefer to use aluminum cake pans, rather than nonstick, as they reflect heat and produce cakes with tender crusts that aren't overly browned (as may sometimes be the case with nonstick varieties).

CITRUS REAMER

This rigid teardrop-shaped handheld tool comes in metal, wood, or plastic and is used to create small amounts of fresh-squeezed citrus juices quickly and efficiently.

COOLING RACK

A raised wire or metal rack used to cool baked goods such as cookies, cakes, pies, tarts, and breads. It is raised to allow air circulation around the baked goods, which hastens cooling and prevents the items from steaming in their pan.

CULINARY TORCH

Sold in most cookware stores, a culinary blowtorch is a must for caramelizing sugar on the tops of desserts such as crème brûlée. It's also helpful for heating up the exterior of pastry rings to help release a cold or frozen dessert for serving. The butane cartridge is refillable and should last for approximately 1 hour.

CUTTERS

Made of metal or plastic, these molds allow you to cut round, square, or decorative shapes from cookie dough. Biscuit cutters are metal rings with a handle that come in graduated sizes and are helpful when cutting out small rounds of dough, in addition to biscuits.

DOUBLE BOILER

A double-pan arrangement whereby two pots fit together, one partly inside the other. A single lid fits both pots. The lower pot is used to hold simmering water, which heats or melts the contents of the upper pot. The indirect heat is optimal for gently heating egg whites with sugar for buttercream frosting and for melting chocolate.

ICE CREAM SCOOP

In addition to getting ice cream out of a container, ice cream scoops are invaluable for portioning out everything from cookie dough to muffin batter. The scoop gives you control over portion size as well uniform rounded shapes. I prefer spring-loaded stainless steel scoops. The ¼ cup and ½ cup capacities are most commonly used for portioning out cookies and muffins.

KNIVES

Most of the recipes in this book call for the use of the following knives: 3½-inch paring knife for preparing fruit and cutting vents in doughs and breads; 8-inch offset serrated knife for slicing biscotti and chopping chocolate; 8-inch chef's knife for everything from chopping or crushing nuts to dicing onions; 12-inch serrated bread knife for cutting breads and even horizontal cake layers.

LOAF PANS

These rectangular pans are used for baking yeast breads, quick breads, and loaf-shaped cakes. They come in glass, ceramic, and metal and in a variety of sizes. The most commonly used size is 9 by 5 inches.

MEASURING CUPS

A graduated set of metal, straight-sided cups is essential for precisely measuring dry ingredients such as flour, sugar, or cornmeal. Dry ingredients should be scooped into the cup and leveled off with the back of a knife for precise measuring. Every kitchen should also have at least one glass or plastic measuring cup that holds liquid volume, which is different from dry ingredient volume.

MEASURING SPOONS

Another must for all kitchens is a graduated set of metal measuring spoons in the following basic sizes: 1 tablespoon, 1 teaspoon, ½ teaspoon, ¼ teaspoon, ⅛ teaspoon.

METAL TONGS

This handheld tool is invaluable in any kitchen. Whether turning a steak or removing a pan from a hot water bath, tongs will help grab the required item, and they make for safer and easier handling of foods and equipment.

MICROPLANE GRATER

With its razor-sharp edges and micro-size grooves, this grater has reinvented grating and zesting. It makes easy work of creating delicate flakes of hard cheese, chocolate, and citrus zest.

MIXING BOWLS

Every kitchen needs a set of mixing bowls for a variety of tasks. Buy a few in varying sizes in glass, metal, plastic, or ceramic.

MUFFIN PANS

Standard muffin pans have 6 or 12 muffin cups to a pan, and each cup is roughly 2½ inches in diameter. These pans are invaluable for making muffins, cupcakes, and individual quiches. Mini muffin pans are also available for making smaller mini-size versions or hors d'oeuvres.

NONSTICK SILICONE BAKING MATS

Heat-resistant silicone sheets fitted to a standard-size baking sheet. They are nonstick, reusable, and easy to clean, no matter what spills on them. Perfect for baking cookies or scones, or to bake pies on to avoid a major sticky cleanup.

OVEN THERMOMETER

An accurate temperature reading in your oven is essential for successful baking. Buy an inexpensive oven thermometer and keep it housed in your oven for accurate temperature readings.

PARCHMENT PAPER

A silicone-based paper that can withstand high heat. It is often used to prepare confections because they do not stick to the paper. Parchment paper may be reused several times and is essential for easy cleanup.

PASTRY BAG AND FITTED TIPS

A cone-shaped bag made of canvas, plastic, or plastic-lined cloth used to pipe foods, such as frosting or whipped cream, into a decorative pattern. Fitted tips come in a variety of shapes and sizes and are inserted at the small end of the bag, where they help deliver the contents in any number of decorative ways.

PASTRY BLENDER

This handheld tool consists of several *U*-shaped wires or metal blades attached to a handle. It is used to cut butter or shortening into flour, which is an essential step in pastry making.

PASTRY BRUSH

Made of natural bristles or nylon, pastry brushes are used to apply glazes, jams, egg washes, or melted butter, and to brush away excess flour.

PASTRY CUTTER

Similar to a pizza cutter, this smaller version helps cut clean edges through dough of virtually any thickness. This tool is essential for creating pastries and lattice-style piecrusts. It also comes with a fluted wheel for more decorative edges.

PASTRY RINGS

These metal ring molds, which come in a variety of sizes, can be used for a number of things. The smooth, rigid sides offer support for packing, pouring, and pressing desserts such as mousses and other molded desserts.

PASTRY SCRAPER

A rectangular-shaped tool with a metal or plastic blade used for loosening and turning dough and for scraping excess dough from a work surface. It is also handy for dividing and deflating bread doughs.

PIE PLATE

Available in glass (my preference for easy monitoring of color during baking), metal, and ceramic. They are usually 9 or 10 inches in diameter and should be either regular depth or "deep dish" to accommodate a larger quantity of filling.

PIE WEIGHTS

Although dried beans can hold down a tart or piecrust, pie weights are more effective at keeping pastry from shrinking or forming bubbles while it bakes. Ceramic or metal reusable pie weights help bake the top of the pastry during blind baking, and help hold the pastry shell in place during baking and cooling.

PIZZA STONE

A flat, porous stone or piece of ceramic or earthenware used to evenly distribute oven heat to pizzas or other baked goods while absorbing moisture, thus helping to create crisp crusts.

PIZZA WHEEL

Similar to a pastry cutter (see above), a pizza wheel can be used to efficiently cut pizza, dough, and pastry without damaging your work surface.

ROLLING PIN

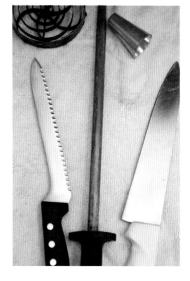

A must for rolling out piecrusts, tart doughs, puff pastry, and more, these cylinder-shaped tools are a required item for any kitchen. For maximum hand control, I prefer a traditional "French" wooden rolling pin that is shaped like one long baton, without handles.

RULER

A metal ruler is an essential item, used to measure dimensions for doughs, pan sizes, and more. Metal will stand up to knives and pastry cutters better than a plastic one.

SHEARS

Kitchen shears are useful for an endless variety of tasks including snipping herbs, cutting poultry, sizing children's food, and more. Invest in a good pair and they will last for years.

SIEVE (OR STRAINER)

A tool with a mesh bottom used to strain liquids or semi-liquids, removing impurities or solids. It may also be used to sift or "dust" dry ingredients such as flour and confectioners' sugar. A *tamis,* which is a fine strainer shaped like a snare drum with a cylindrical edge made of metal or wood that supports a fine metal or nylon mesh, may also be used for straining mixtures.

SPATULAS

Every kitchen should have a variety of spatulas, including a flexible metal spatula (ideal for transferring cookies from a baking sheet to a cooling rack), offset spatula (a long, narrow flat spatula that comes in a variety of lengths and widths and is a necessity for frosting cakes), rubber spatula (its flexibility allows for easy and thorough removal of batters and doughs from mixing bowls), and flexible silicone heatproof spatula (able to withstand heat from a skillet when making an omelet or when mixing an ingredient in a double boiler).

STANDING MIXER

This multifunction small appliance is more powerful than a hand mixer and has the additional benefit of being hands-free. Standing mixers offer a variety of attachments, including beaters for mixing all types of batters, dough hooks for kneading heavy dough, and whisks for whipping lighter batters.

TART PAN/TARTLET PAN

Used to bake everything from tarts to tartlets to quiches, fluted tart pans come in a range of sizes and shapes. Metal tart pans often have removable bottoms, whereas ceramic or porcelain tart pans are one piece.

TIMER

A kitchen timer is a must for any home cook and baker. Many ranges, ovens, and microwave ovens have built-in timers. Free-standing timers are also available at cookware stores.

TUBE PAN

A ring-shaped baking pan with deep sides and a hollow center tube that ensures even baking throughout. It is used for baking cakes such as angel food cake.

WHISK

Layers of stainless steel wires contained in a handle and joined together to form a teardrop shape. Whisks are used to incorporate air into ingredients such as cream, egg whites, and more. They are also used to keep mixtures in motion when they are being heated, when tempering egg mixtures, and to break down any lumps in batters. They come in a variety of shapes and sizes.

ICING A BLUEBERRY TEA CAKE, SEE PAGE 57

[*Sources*]

THE BAKER'S CATALOGUE/KING ARTHUR
FLOUR
135 Route 5 South
P.O. Box 1010
Norwich, VT 05055
800-827-6836
www.kingarthurflour.com
Baking and pastry equipment, tools, specialty
flours, praline paste, vanilla beans, and other
specialty ingredients.

BRIDGE KITCHENWARE
563-C Eagle Rock Avenue
Roseland, NJ 07068
973-240-7364
www.bridgekitchenware.com
Kitchen tools, bakeware, pastry rings, and
decorating equipment.

J.B. PRINCE
36 East 31st Street
New York, NY 10016
800-473-0577
www.jbprince.com
Baking and pastry equipment, tools, and
cookbooks.

NIELSEN-MASSEY VANILLAS, INC.
1550 Shields Drive
Waukegan, IL 60085-8307
Telephone: 800-525-PURE (7873)
www.nielsenmassey.com
Extracts, orange blossom water, rose water,
vanilla paste.

SUR LA TABLE
800-243-0852
www.surlatable.com
Bakeware, molds, nonstick silicone baking
mats, and specialty tools, appliances, and
books.

WILLIAMS-SONOMA
877-812-6235
www.williams-sonoma.com
Bakeware, molds, nonstick silicone baking
mats, specialty tools, appliances, and books.

[Index]

TART TROPEZIENNE, SEE PAGE 37

A VARIATION ON FRENCH BLUEBERRY TARTLET, SEE PAGE 115